VICTORIAN HONEYMOONS

While Victorian tourism and Victorian sexuality have been the subject of much recent critical interest, there has been little research on a characteristically nineteenth-century phenomenon relating to both sex and travel: the honeymoon, or wedding journey. Although the term "honeymoon" was coined in the eighteenth century, the ritual increased in popularity throughout the Victorian period, until by the end of the century it became a familiar accompaniment to the wedding for all but the poorest classes. Using letters and diaries of sixty-one real-life honeymooning couples, as well as novels from *Frankenstein* to *Middlemarch* that feature honeymoon scenarios, Michie explores the cultural meanings of the honeymoon, arguing that, with its emphasis on privacy and displacement, the honeymoon was central to emerging ideals of conjugality and to ideas of the couple as a primary social unit.

HELENA MICHIE is Agnes C. Arnold Professor in Humanities and Professor of English at Rice University. She is the author of *The Flesh Made Word: Women's Figures, Women's Bodies* (1987) and of *Sororophobia: Differences Among Women in Literature and Culture* (1991).

CAMBRIDGE STUDIES IN NINETEENTH-CENTURY
LITERATURE AND CULTURE

General editor
Gillian Beer, *University of Cambridge*

Editorial Board
Isobel Armstrong, *Birkbeck College, London*
Kate Flint, *Rutgers University*
Catherine Gallagher, *University of California, Berkeley*
D. A. Miller, *Columbia University*
J. Hillis Miller, *University of California, Irvine*
Daniel Pick, *Queen Mary University of London*
Mary Poovey, *New York University*
Sally Shuttleworth, *University of Sheffield*
Herbert Tucker, *University of Virginia*

Nineteenth-century British literature and culture have been rich fields for interdisciplinary studies. Since the turn of the twentieth century, scholars and critics have tracked the intersections and tensions between Victorian literature and the visual arts, politics, social organization, economic life, technical innovations, scientific thought – in short, culture in its broadest sense. In recent years, theoretical challenges and historiographical shifts have unsettled the assumptions of previous scholarly synthesis and called into question the terms of older debates. Whereas the tendency in much past literary critical interpretation was to use the metaphor of culture as "background," feminist, Foucauldian, and other analyses have employed more dynamic models that raise questions of power and of circulation. Such developments have reanimated the field. This series aims to accommodate and promote the most interesting work being undertaken on the frontiers of the field of nineteenth-century literary studies: work which intersects fruitfully with other fields of study such as history, or literary theory, or the history of science. Comparative as well as interdisciplinary approaches are welcomed.

A complete list of titles published will be found at the end of the book.

VICTORIAN HONEYMOONS

Journeys to the Conjugal

HELENA MICHIE

CAMBRIDGE
UNIVERSITY PRESS

CAMBRIDGE UNIVERSITY PRESS
Cambridge, New York, Melbourne, Madrid, Cape Town, Singapore, São Paulo

Cambridge University Press
The Edinburgh Building, Cambridge CB2 2RU, UK

Published in the United States of America by Cambridge University Press, New York

www.cambridge.org
Information on this title: www.cambridge.org/9780521868747

First published 2006

Printed in the United Kingdom at the University Press, Cambridge

A catalogue record for this publication is available from the British Library

ISBN-13 978-0-521-86874-7 hardback
ISBN-10 0-521-86874-2 hardback

To Scott

Contents

Illustrations

TABLES

Preface

I have been working on *Victorian Honeymoons* long enough to have had conversations about the project with many different kinds of people in many different kinds of places: on airplanes, from facedown on a massage table, in grocery stores, at museums and record offices, and at academic conferences. It is the academics who joke that there can be nothing to say on the topic. What they mean, of course, is that they think "nothing happened" on the typical Victorian honeymoon, and what they mean by "nothing" is that there was probably no sex, or somehow that there was no sex that counted (it was not good enough, expert enough, fun enough, talked or written about enough). This book, as it turns out, does involve a certain amount of counting – of how many people in my sample of sixty-one couples who took their honeymoon in the period from 1830 to 1898 went to Europe, for example, or, more bewilderingly, of how many women likely got pregnant – but the project is in many ways an attempt to get beyond what I think of as honeymoon accounting, especially the binary kind that positions sex against no sex, consummation against the failure to consummate, successful against unsuccessful honeymoons.

But I am beginning with the endpoint of my project's own honeymoon journey. Although my project ended up questioning the calculus of honeymoon accounting and its constitutive binaries of success and failure, it began – as does Chapter 1 – with a honeymoon infamous for having failed (and one for whose failure one person was held publicly accountable). I came to the topic of honeymoons through the story of Victorian art critic, political philosopher, and Victorian sage John Ruskin and his bride, Effie, and through the many stories of their wedding night told and retold by the Ruskins themselves, by their families, friends, and legal representatives, and by twentieth-century scholars of John Ruskin and of the Victorian period more generally. Although, for many reasons that I discuss in Chapter 1, John Ruskin was not, perhaps, representative of many Victorian husbands, the stories piqued my curiosity in ways that extended beyond what has become the Ruskin "case" to consider how the wedding night might have been experienced by other Victorian couples. Imagining the "typical" wedding night for the period requires, I think, an almost Victorian investment both in the work of the imagination and in realist detail. I tried – as I try throughout this project – to "realize," as Victorian actors might say, the pressures that might have been experienced by many, perhaps by most, middle- or upper-middle-class Victorian couples thrust suddenly together, in many cases at some geographical distance from their families of origin and the familiar landmarks of daily life. I thought first – and this was borne out by future research – of how *tired* many of them might have been. For those going to Europe, it was common to take a train to Dover and to stay for at least one night at one of the large and anonymous hotels that overlooked the English Channel and – on a fine day – the dim outlines of a future destination. For those traveling domestically, the journey was often completed in one day, following a morning wedding. The logistics of travel might have been complicated by a sense of geographical and bodily disorientation as couples would be expected to move in the course of a long day from the requirements of public spectacle at the wedding to the very different exigencies of withdrawal into the contradictory "alone together" of life as a couple.

There would, of course, have been sexual pressures, both anticipatory and in the moment. While some honeymooners would be relatively ignorant of the mechanics or even the existence of sex, and while some would be more experienced and/or more knowledgeable, most of them would have felt that the wedding night was a crucial and potentially transformative moment, perhaps with implications for the rest of the marriage and for their gendered sense of themselves. Apart from – although perhaps intricately connected to – issues of sexuality would be issues of space, body, and privacy: how were these men and women to negotiate dressing for dinner, dining à deux, sharing a hotel room or rooms, bathing, praying, or resting with someone at newly close proximity?

Finally, there might have been the pressures of expectation, of negotiating personal desires – whether for sex, rest, or food, say – with a sense of obligation derived from the culture at large. In other words, the wedding night – and again I do not mean only the metonymic act of sex – would be influenced by the participants' expectations of what such a night should be like; it would also be influenced by what they knew or imagined about sex, marriage, religion, and the proper relations between men and women. In this sense, as well as perhaps in the more typical one, the wedding night and its ritual of firsts would be performative: the new husbands and wives would be measuring themselves and each other against standards from books, images, and conversations.

And, of course, these standards and expectations would be different for women and for men. The lived experiences of Victorian honeymoons unfolded in the context of a sexual double standard that was far more tolerant of men's premarital sexual experimentation than it was of women's. For men and women of some sexual experience – and particularly for women – this might have added the burden of guilt and perhaps deception to a ritual defined by novelty and transformation. The vast majority of reports from my sample, however, do not comment upon previous sexual experience, even for men. With the exception of a brief mention of one wedding night in which the bride discovered that her husband had syphilis, all my accounts either ignore the possibility of male sexual experience or address the question in the idiom of ignorance, confusion, and surprise. But honeymoons could also be gendered in more subtle ways: I argue, for example, in Chapter 2, that the experience of landscape, particularly the natural and historical "sights" of Europe, might, for reasons of education, access, and power, have been very different for the men and women of my sample. Women were expected to negotiate landscape differently: in the Swiss Alps, for example, most women rode mules while their husbands – and often also their guides – walked beside them. Women were far more likely than men to spend parts of the honeymoon alone indoors: several of my longer honeymoon accounts by women detail the process of waiting for their husband's return from a walk, a sightseeing experience, or an errand. In some ways, of course, these different roles suggest a rehearsal of marriage, but some dynamics of excursion and return were specific to the honeymoon context. Women on the honeymoon also tended – with some exceptions – to be more closely in touch with friends and relatives; since women were typically responsible for correspondence with those left behind, we see more acutely, perhaps, their struggles with separation from previous lives.

Many notable elements of the Victorian wedding night might still be in play today. I want to argue, however, that, despite recent revisionary accounts of Victorian gender relations suggesting that engaged couples spent more time together and that Victorians in general might have had more sexual knowledge than was previously thought, Victorian women and men experienced the physical and psychic intimacies of the honeymoon in a way that stressed the novelty of the experience.

Relatively new as well, but on a larger scale, were the historical expectations of marriage as the privileged form of emotional intimacy; Victorian couples would be caught up in a variety of ways in a discourse of newness, even if, for example, they had to one degree or another been physically intimate before the wedding.

My second interest arising out of the Ruskin example has to do not with Victorians but with the scholars who study them, with the persistent interest of Victorianists in the hows, whys, and wherefores of (for example) John Ruskin's behavior on the wedding night. How do scholars of the Victorian period manage the information they are able to obtain and that which is inevitably unavailable? What claims are they able to make about the representativeness or even the importance of this "failed" wedding night? What kinds of assumptions allow Ruskin scholar Mary Luytens, for example, to compare John and Effie's wedding night to the contemporaneous failed political revolutions of 1848? What is the relation of the most indicatively private of moments to public discourses of history?

My double interest in the wedding night as a historical phenomenon and as a way of thinking about the possibilities and limits of historical scholarship led me to what historicist literary scholars have learned to call, in the somewhat mystifying singular, "the archive": to repositories of Victorian family papers, to the letters, diaries, and other domestic documents written by people living in the period. All too quickly I came to the limits of that archive: there were very few detailed accounts of wedding nights. Whether that scarcity was due to the disappearance over time of intimate letters and diaries or to infamous Victorian propriety, I do not and cannot know. Since wedding nights in Victorian fiction are also infrequently represented in detail, often occurring between chapters or books, I suspect that the relative silence about wedding nights also had something to do with the genre limitations for both fictional and nonfictional texts.

My way into the wedding night was, again, a way out. It helped, I found, to consider the wedding night in context, not as a single dramatic event, but as one night among many nights and days that constituted that most Victorian of institutions – the honeymoon. While there is very little primary material on the wedding night, I found much more on honeymoon journeys, some explicitly and attentively marked as such, some treated in letters and diaries like any other journey for health, business, or pleasure. The move from wedding night to honeymoon as my object of inquiry opened up the scope of my project in a number of ways: it gave me access to a wealth of new material, both visual and textual; it allowed me to write against climactic and binary narratives and to see sexual consummation as only one of the potentially transformative elements of the honeymoon; it allowed me to take advantage of some of the rich theoretical and ethnographic work on travel published in the last twenty years; and, most importantly, it encouraged me to think of the history and conduct of the honeymoon in terms of both time and place. As I began to take the honeymoon seriously as a ritual and as an institution, I became more fully and richly aware of how it placed bodies in relation to each other, to culture, and to landscape.

The goal of this book has been precisely to elaborate a variety of contexts for the definitional sexual work of the honeymoon and to identify the honeymoon's larger cultural work of transformation. Honeymoons were, of course, supposed to include sex and were, to some extent, defined by this expectation; they also, however, required a more comprehensive adjustment of self to what I came to call, after thinking about a number of roughly equivalent terms, "conjugality": the expectation not only that Victorian husbands and wives depended primarily on each other for support, affection, and interaction but that they defined themselves away from the birth family and the community and in terms of the conjugal couple. The honeymoon, as I discuss in Chapter 2, became an important vehicle for the transition or "reorientation" from one identity to the other.

The new directions of my work put me in conversation both with scholars of sex and with scholars of marriage (not often the same people and rarely, to my surprise, in direct conversation with each other). In thinking about the sexual experiences of nineteenth-century honey-mooners, I found myself working out my relationship with the new revisionary history of Victorian sexuality that, for the last twenty years, has begun to challenge assumptions about Victorian ignorance and prudery. My analysis of this debate appears in Chapter 3, as I take up the specifically sexual experiences of the men and women of my sample. Because of the honeymoon's central position in histories of marriage that depend, like Lawrence Stone's, on a shift toward more affective marriages in the late eighteenth century, I have also had to confront the historical novelty of conjugality and its implications for larger histories of marriage. I offer some comments on this issue in Chapter 1.

A word about the methodology of this project. Although *Victorian Honeymoons* depends to some extent on archival sources and to a larger extent on a historical case study to which those archival materials contribute, my training as a literary critic makes my treatment of historical material – published and unpublished – different from what it might have been had I trained as a historian. I see this potential difference working in at least two different areas. The first, where I think the difference is perhaps less significant, has to do with the relationship between the historical materials on honeymooning and fictional representations on which I also rely. While Chapter 1 focuses on historical material and Chapter 4 exclusively on fiction, the middle chapters consider the two together. Like a historian, I try not to use fictional representations as evidence of the way things really were; like a historian, I try to see novels as expressions of attitudes and ideals not only of the particular author but of the culture in which the author is, however uncomfortably, situated. I am, however, unlike most historians, also profoundly interested in questions of genre and writerly convention: in how choices about what kind of text to write influence what one says or thinks one can or should say. While the genre of the marriage-plot novel in which most of my fictional examples of honeymoons are embedded produces specific readerly expectations, so too, I argue, do diaries or letters. I try at all times to be attentive to the requirements of genre, even and especially in the rare cases where I see people trying to flout or to change them.

The second difference I see between this project and a hypothetical treatment of the subject by a historian is my willingness to look for – and to find – latent as well as manifest content in my sources. In other words, I am as attentive to how people say things as I am to what they say – through figurative language or favorite words, for example. My method also involves paying attention to what people do not say, or do not say clearly: to euphemisms, blanks, awkward syntax, even mistakes in spelling or chronology. When the prose of a letter or even a conduct book becomes suddenly complex, garbled, or purple, I see this as signifying, at the very least, an uneasiness with the topic. While this method of reading is associated with the methods of psychoanalysis, I never – well, except in Chapter 2 with Minnie Thackeray's horror at the specter of a mountain poking its head through the window and in Chapter 1 with a conduct book's reference to the horror of stray curls – refer to a standard psychoanalytic model. I rarely suggest a one-to-one "translation" of a euphemism, and I resist, when I can, the triumphant identification of phallic imagery or double entendres. Throughout the writing of this project I have been very grateful to historian colleagues who have occasionally (and very gently) rebuked me for "over-reading." For example, one colleague objected to my suggesting a psychosomatic explanation for the frequency of honeymoon illness in my case study, suggesting instead that travel of all kinds would involve, especially in the Victorian era, exposure to different water, foods, and germs. In this case I not only listened but withdrew my speculations. There have been times, however, when I have used a passage from a letter or a diary previously quoted in a work by a historian and have ended up treating it quite differently. A passage in Chapter 3, in which Margaret Gladstone receives a letter of sexual advice from her sister is one example. In her wonderful book, *Women, Marriage, and Politics*, Patricia Jalland quotes the passage, as far as I can tell, for the first time. Although, to my mind the passage, which has to do with how to manage the hymeneal blood, is filled with images of disease and foreboding, Jalland does not comment on the passage, moving immediately after she quotes it to a declaration that Margaret's marriage was a happy one. Although I have no argument with Jalland's conclusion about the success of Margaret's marriage, I found that I could not ignore the tone of the passage or stop myself from reading with and against its syntactical intricacies. Such a reading complicates, although it by no means negates, the journey to marital happiness as it is recorded by Jalland. I suspect that many other literary scholars would also have succumbed to the temptation to read strongly, and to linger in the uneasy verbal constructions of Bella's advice.

Symptomatic readings of the sort I practice here constitute, I think, disciplinary flashpoints for historians and literary critics; they need to be taken seriously as indicating real methodological differences. I think of my literary training as supplying me with a distinct set of skills that allow me to see all kinds of texts as productions of unconscious as well as conscious desires, as efforts, in other words, to exercise control over and, in the case of my honeymooners, as ways of rendering palatable by social standards elements that might be difficult, painful, or taboo.

The book is divided into five chapters. The first lays out a variety of contexts for the institutionalization of the honeymoon, including historical developments in ideas about marriage and Victorian ideas about and ideals for the honeymoon as expressed in popular materials like conduct books. It is also the chapter where I introduce and begin to analyze my sample. The raw data for the sample can be found in the Appendix in the form of a table. The second chapter introduces the concept of "reorientation," outlining what I take to be the primary cultural work of the honeymoon: the movement away from the birth family to an affective, legal, and social identification with the conjugal couple. This is the chapter most overtly concerned with tourism and the consumption of landscape. In it I suggest that one goal of the honeymoon is the production of a unified "conjugal gaze" in which men and women – and the visual burden is mostly on women – learn to align their views of landscape and the historical and natural "sights" of the wedding journey.

While Chapter 2 places sexuality in the context of other – always eroticized – forms of reorientation, the third chapter explicitly takes up the issue of honeymoon sex. It is in this chapter that I think through the relation of my findings to traditional and revisionist notions of Victorian sexuality. I find it helpful, here and in the following chapter, to think of the work of the honeymoon in terms of what I call "carnal knowledge," or "carnal knowledges," – those new ideas, feelings, and pieces of information brought together under the rubric of the sexual. I find myself relying on the plural form "knowledges" – its awkwardness echoing George Eliot's resonant term "privacies" to describe relations between public and private knowledge – to embody one of the central arguments of the book: that knowledge is not singular but made up of ideas and attitudes that are always partial and often in conflict with each other. Chapters 3 and 4, then, in their different ways, attempt to construct an epistemology of the honeymoon. The fourth chapter turns from historical to literary materials and specifically to five fictional texts that are part of a genre I call the "honeymoon gothic," in which honeymoons are the (often violent) sites for the exploration of sexual or financial secrets. I argue that honeymoons, with their link to ideas of carnal knowledge, are ways of representing competing and usually gendered epistemologies.

While I ask questions throughout the book about the limits of what we can know about the private lives of Victorians and about the limitations and expectations of the archive, the final chapter reflects most acutely on the impossibility of perfect historical reconstruction. It uses an exemplary case – the honeymoon diary of Martha Rolls Macready – to dramatize the problem of what we can and cannot know. The diary, written in 1840, is the most detailed and sustained I came across – but it is by no means self-explanatory. Filled with secrets, coded references, and tantalizing blanks, it defies any notion of completeness. The first part of the chapter is an annotated edition of Martha's diary; the second part, the last section of the book, is a frankly fictional reconstruction of some moments from the five-month honeymoon. The fictional ending is both a sign of my frustration with the historical record and a way of positing and thinking through different kinds of truth.

Because the structure of the book is topical, texts or people tend not to be confined to one chapter. I think of the book as structured in part by revisitation: in particular, three "visitors" appear in several different chapters and contexts. George Eliot's *Middlemarch* – to me the primal scene of fictional honeymoons – appears in Chapters 1 and 2, reflecting Eliot's own commitment to thinking about honeymoons and, indeed, marriage from different literal as well as figurative points of view. Eliza Dickinson, a honeymooner who articulates the case histories' most melancholy account of sexual initiation, appears also in several contexts; her brief words about her wedding night haunt this book, appearing in Chapters 1, 2, and 3. Finally, and even more hauntingly, Martha Rolls Macready appears in four out of the five chapters, and her experiences, as I come to understand them, constitute Chapter 5. The book records through its structure as well as through explicit commentary the pull of Martha's story as I struggled with the epistemological and generic issues raised by the honeymoon. Other real-life honeymooners make brief appearances in multiple contexts; for the convenience of the reader I have included in the Appendix a list of chapters in which various honeymooning couples appear. This column of the Appendix hints at a sort of counterstructure to the book, which, I hope, can be read across chapters as a series of short narratives about real-life couples.

My final words on methodology have to do with a term I use, perhaps too easily, as a shorthand for the time frame in which these honeymoons took place. As many scholars of the period have noted, the term "Victorian" covers a long period of years brought together somewhat arbitrarily by the figure of one woman – in many ways a figure*head* – who happened to outlive, or at least to out-reign – her fellow English monarchs. My examples from the beginning and the end of the period feel quite different to me. This is partly due to crucial developments in the technologies of travel; when my chronologically last honeymooner, Maud Sambourne, appeared on a bicycle in her letters to her mother, I felt very much as I did when reading a late novel by Mrs. Humphrey Ward in which a telephone suddenly went off, breaking and reshaping a textual silence that I had long seen as definitional of the Victorian novel. Improvements in travel certainly led to more honeymoons – and to the possibility of shorter and cheaper honeymoons. But the difference is more than a matter of statistics or even of the sound of bicycle or telephone bells; there are other new sounds as well: new slang, new euphemisms, new ways of thinking and speaking, and an explosion of books on sex and sexuality. While I end Chapter 3 with two honeymoons from late in the century, I return to the relative quiet of 1840 and of the peaceful seaside resort of Littlehampton to revisit – for the final time – Edward and Martha Macready. Participants neither in the "Regency spirit," as one commentator puts it, of some earlier honeymooners nor in the emerging standards of new womanhood at the end of the century, the Rolls-Macready honeymoon has the last quiet word.

Over the years, I have inflicted *Honeymoons* on so many audiences, and have shown or talked through parts of the project with so many colleagues that I am filled with fear as I write this that I will forget someone who needs to be thanked.

I am in no danger of forgetting what I owe to my colleagues at Rice in the faculty workshops that have been the center of my intellectual life for fifteen years: Nineteenth-Century Enquiry (NICE) and the Feminist Reading Group (FRG), both of which were supported for much of that time by Rice's interdisciplinary Center for the Study of Cultures. I am deeply grateful to Logan Browning, Karen Fang, Alan Grob, Deborah Harter, Janice Hewitt, Natalie Houston, Thad Logan, Robert Patten, and Lynn Voskuil from NICE and Lynne Huffer, Elizabeth Long, Susan Lurie, Carol Quillen, and Paula Sanders of FRG for the challenge and support they so consistently offered. I am especially grateful to Martin Wiener of NICE for the help he gave me as I took on my first sustained archival project. When negotiating what we at NICE have come to call "disciplinary flashpoints," I often find it helpful to imagine an interlocutor from history: I am extremely fortunate that my imagination of such an interlocutor has been shaped by Marty's generosity, his wide knowledge, and his respect for disciplinary difference.

This project would not have taken the shape it did had it not been for my friends and colleagues at the Dickens Project, who pulled me back into the nineteenth century and persuaded me that I was, if not a Dickensian, at least (once again) a Victorianist. I was fortunate to be sitting next to Joseph Childers when I conceived the idea for the book. Although skeptical of originary moments, I have returned many times fondly to this one and to our excited and exhausted listing of novels with bad honeymoons. Thanks to all in the orbit of the Dickens Universe who provided the intellectual and personal context for many other moments of inspiration, including Murray Baumgarten, Rosemarie Bodenheimer, Allison Booth, John Bowen, Janice Carlisle, Jay Clayton, Eileen Cleere, Carolyn Dever, Ed Eisner, John Glavin, Johnathan Grossman, John Jordan, Gerhard Joseph, James Kincaid, Joseph Litvak, Teresa

Mangum, Paul Morrison, Robert Newsom, Rob Polhemus, Hilary Schor, Rebecca Stern, Ronald Thomas, and Robyn Warhol. I think it is appropriate to thank someone twice (especially when he appears in such different clothes according to context). Thank you, Bob Patten, the Dickensian.

Over the ten years I have worked on this project, I have been the beneficiary of the research, computer, and textual talents of three wonderful research assistants: Basak Demirhan, Duncan Hasell, and Louise Penner. I thank them for all their many contributions. As usual, Theresa Munisteri has been invaluable in the editing of the book. I have also had wonderful experiences in libraries and archival collections across the UK and the US. Special recognition must go to Tony Hopkins of the Gwent Record Office and Rolf Zeegers of the Littlehampton Museum, both of whom went far beyond the call of duty to help me with images and permissions. I am also grateful to the helpers with the living archive, Pamela Baker, Colin Cowles, and Barbara Shelton of the Rolls Golf Course and Hotel. They will find themselves acknowledged in a different way in Chapter 5.

Closer to home, I can only admire the flexibility and patience of my family. Many academics with children know the pleasures and frustrations of the vacation that is also a research trip (finances kept, of course, scrupulously discrete). Paul and Ross Michie-Derrick have followed me to vacation sites probable and improbable. (Fortunately the Victorians had excellent taste in honeymoon destinations, although seemingly less canonical preferences in terms of where they deposited their records.) I thank Ross and Paul for patiently dropping me off and picking me up at archives in the UK, for killing time by playing soccer and miniature golf in the drizzle of English and continental summers, and for displaying (somewhat quizzical) good cheer in the face of their mother's professional commitments.

The presiding genius of those trips was my husband, Scott Derrick. From our early holidays in graduate school, to our own honeymoon (resolutely archival), to the many journeys literal and metaphoric of the recent past, he has been for twenty-five years my ideal traveling companion. I have finally written the book that can be dedicated only to him.

CHAPTER I

Reading honeymoons

If, as Leo Tolstoy famously suggested, narrative interest inheres only in unhappy marriages, this might help to explain why the most famous honeymoon stories are stories about failure. One could come up with a canon of honeymoon narratives, real and fictional, all of which end in disaster. In the realm of fiction, perhaps the place to begin is with the shortest honeymoon: Victor Frankenstein's abortive trip to Évian, where his bride, Elizabeth Lavenza, is murdered and probably raped by the monster as Victor ponders the Alpine scenery that was to become so central to Victorian ideals of the wedding journey. The richly realistic honeymoon in George Eliot's *Middlemarch* is also, in conventional terms, a failure, as the newly married Dorothea Casaubon is found weeping in her hotel room by the young man who will later become her second husband. The honeymoons in *Tess of the D'Urbervilles* and *Daniel Deronda* share elements of what I will be calling the honeymoon gothic: apparitions, spectral and otherwise, of other women and illegitimate sexual pasts; haunted jewels and symbolic caskets that in *Tess* become literal coffins; sleepwalking and female hysteria. The record of real-life stories is hardly more inspiring. The most famous story, with which we will have much to do, is the 1848 honeymoon of John and Effie Gray Ruskin, the subject of a variety of books, scholarly articles, and, most recently, a play. The Ruskin honeymoon is in the most obvious sense a story of what did *not* happen, as the marriage remained unconsummated until it was annulled at Effie's instigation. Also probably unconsummated, although not without incident, George Eliot's own honeymoon featured a dramatic leap from the hotel room into the canal on the part of the young groom.

One project of this book is to take us not so much *beyond* as *through* these spectacular honeymoon failures to provide a more nuanced and fuller account of a ritual that became, by the mid-nineteenth century, an important part of the landscape of British marriage. Part of the task here will be to redefine failure and success, or rather to open up the question of what constitutes the success of a honeymoon. Put another way, this book tries to identify and to describe *what the honeymoon was supposed to do*. I argue in Chapter 2 that, for all of its enforced leisure, the honeymoon was expected to accomplish some very difficult cultural work: fusing two people with limited experience of the opposite sex, who often deeply identified with their families of origin and with communities of same-sex friends, into a conjugal unit that was to become their primary source of social and emotional identification. If the wedding ceremony served as a moment of legal transformation, the more extended rituals of the honeymoon were imagined to consummate and – in the language of the Victorian stage – to realize those changes, producing, if successful, a couple newly aligned with one another and with Victorian ideals of intimacy and sexuality. It is perhaps not surprising that this undertaking so often, for those who could afford it, involved a journey away from familiar landscapes to a place that thematized otherness in its very terrain: honeymoons, replete with their consuming rituals of tourism, sex, and shopping, produced, if successful, different subjects in different bodies and different clothes and with different kinds of knowledge.

I begin this project of tracing the imperatives of this work by juxtaposing two "real-life" Victorian honeymoons: one infamous, the other obscure. The first – the 1848 wedding journey to Scotland of John and Effie Gray Ruskin [1] – comes to us straining under the weight of its own perpetual retelling and the consensual sense of its failure. The other – the 1838 honeymoon trip of Eliza Dickinson Wemyss and Francis Wemyss from Bombay to Malabar Point – challenges notions of success and failure as it tantalizes with the incompleteness of its record.

The Ruskin affair is so well known that I risk telling a story with which people are all too familiar. Its ubiquity derives from several sources. First, of course, is the fame of John Ruskin, whose place as a Victorian art critic, social philosopher, and – more diffusely – cultural sage ensured attention to all aspects of his private life before and after his death. The

---

[1] It was a challenge throughout the writing of this book to choose what surnames to use for the women in my case study. Since I tend to catch them at a moment of transition – and since this is precisely the point of the project – it was often hard to know whether to identify them by the surname of their birth family or by their married name. This problem was further complicated by the differences in archival organizations: Martha Rolls Macready's diaries, for example, are listed in the Rolls Family Papers, while Margaret Gladstone MacDonald's are catalogued under her married name. I have attempted to resolve this problem by using both surnames in my initial reference to the women of my sample.

Ruskin honeymoon, and in particular the wedding night, became, through the legal procedures surrounding the annulment, a matter of public record. The story is also compelling because of its climactic narrative structure, exemplifying by its very failure the Victorian expectation that the honeymoon accomplish a specific and difficult task.

The story of the Ruskins also compels because it is at its core a mystery story, inviting speculation about the honeymoon's central (non-)act. We do not know for certain what did or did not happen on the Ruskin wedding night, although, as we shall see below, there is no shortage of theories about and rehearsals of what did or did not take place as the Ruskins retired to bed. Like all good mystery stories, the Ruskin honeymoon deals in character as well as plot: the mystery of John Ruskin's motivation for not consummating his marriage is as endlessly canvassed as the mystery of his actions that night. (Effie's own motivations are usually treated as secondary; it is John who is imagined as the primary actor.) John and Effie's activities on a particular April night of 1848 also have been made to stand in for the larger unresolved mysteries of Victorian sexuality. Despite its unique features, the Ruskin honeymoon would seem to offer a window onto a rarely glimpsed moment – the wedding night – and a rarely glimpsed act of middle-class Victorian sex.

The Wemyss honeymoon, by contrast, involves actors by no means as prominent as John Ruskin. While Francis Wemyss was part of a relatively distinguished military family – Francis was a major in the Bombay Engineers – the young couple made no claims on the historical imagination, Francis's early death preventing him from making any particular mark. All we know about the honeymoon comes to us from a few pages in the meticulous diaries of each of the two protagonists: private, sometimes illegible documents about day-to-day life unstructured by a motivating event like the Ruskin annulment. Unlike accounts of the Ruskin honeymoon, many of which were written long after the wedding night to justify a choice or an opinion, the accounts of the Wemyss honeymoon are contemporaneous with each other and with the event. The sources for the Wemyss honeymoon are, however, unusual in their own way: in my sample of sixty-three honeymooning couples, the Wemysses are the only couple for whom I found parallel honeymoon diary entries.

Neither the Ruskin nor the Wemyss honeymoon went exactly as the couples had imagined. John Ruskin had planned an extensive trip to what became over the course of the century consecrated honeymoon ground: France, Switzerland, and the sights of the European continent. They were to have been accompanied by John's parents and to have stayed for three months. The couple's honeymoon plans, however, were scuttled by the revolutions of 1848 that made travel to the Continent dangerous, so they went instead to Blair Atholl, in Scotland, for two weeks. The Wemyss honeymoon from Bombay to nearby Malabar Point, where they borrowed the home of wealthy friends, was one day longer than the bride wanted it to be: Eliza wanted to shorten the honeymoon and to return to her mother's house after three days but was apparently prevented from doing so by her mother's social obligations.

The two journeys are helpful in thinking through what makes a successful honeymoon. Certainly, in terms of the presence of the definitive sexual act, it would seem that the Wemyss honeymoon was a success, the Ruskin honeymoon a failure. Although the limits (and temptations) of this kind of binary thinking about the honeymoon will be explored in detail in Chapter 3, I stress that the issues for these particular honeymoons are more complex than the legal and narrative binaries of annulment might suggest. Certainly the Ruskin honeymoon read like a success to John's parents when the couple returned. John's parents remarked approvingly on John's weight gain, claiming they had never seen him look so healthy in his life.[2] While I will argue in Chapter 2 that signs of positive change, readable upon the body, were expected outcomes of the honeymoon and thus might affect how friends and relatives saw and reported on couples as they returned from their wedding journeys, clearly the older Ruskins, who were not on the whole overjoyed about the marriage, saw the honeymoon as having done productive work. That they couched their satisfaction in terms of what seems like an improbable weight gain for a two-week period, suggests that they already had in mind a positive model of honeymoon transformation in terms of which they were willing to read their son's newly healthy body.

As far as we know, the Wemyss honeymoon was indeed consummated. The only indication of this is an oblique and negative one – Eliza's diary entry in which she vowed never to return to Malabar Point:

Though everything was arranged for our comfort and it was the place I would rather have been at the last few days than anywhere else, yet it is associated with a period altogether I should think the most unpleasant in a girl's life ... I don't know what would have become of me with anyone other than David [her name for Francis], he has been very kind and good and considerate.[3]

[2] Mary Luytens, *The Ruskins and the Grays* (London: Murray, 1973), p. 111.
[3] Eliza Dickinson [Mrs. Francis Wemyss], entry for 27 January 1838, Ms. diary, vol. 111, 1838, Colchester-Wemyss Family Papers, D36 F35.

Eliza's discomfort – perhaps this is too weak a word – ironically suggests the honeymoon's success in conventional terms. It also brings the experience on Malabar Point into line with climactic narratives as Eliza rhetorically marks off the honeymoon period, suggesting that whatever happened during those three days is now over. Her diary entry relegates the honeymoon experience to a specific time and place in which she does not want to linger and to which she most emphatically does not want to return.

We might, of course, think of the success or failure of a honeymoon in different terms – for example, as leading to a happy or unhappy marriage. Again, these issues get complicated. While in novels bad honeymoons lead inevitably and metonymically to bad marriages, testimony from real-life honeymooners suggests that wedding journeys and marriages were made up of a series of acts – from shopping to sex, from sightseeing to reading, talking, quarreling, sulking, or swimming – that may not have all tended the same way. Despite having bad memories of Malabar Point, Eliza Dickinson was careful to record Francis's kindness; the diary, which was begun during their courtship and continued after marriage, seems to place the honeymoon in the context of a long and loving, if not always perfectly harmonious, relationship. (Francis and Eliza's courtship was a somewhat problematic one, Eliza arguing for a delay in their marriage until Francis's relatives in England could be informed and Francis arguing for an early day.) The Ruskin annulment and surrounding scandal have tended to force a teleological reading of the wedding journey; Effie's letter to her father officially beginning the annulment procedure cites the honeymoon as the first and germinal moment of the problems that were to plague the marriage for its duration. But even Effie's letters and diaries make her seem – perhaps only seem – happy with John and with her marriage on many different occasions.

The success or failure of honeymoons brings us inevitably to the charged question of Victorian sexual knowledge and the related but by no means identical issue of sexual pleasure. Recent studies of Victorian sexuality have suggested that the Victorians might have been far less ignorant than was for a long time popularly assumed.[4] The two honeymoons in question, although by no means representative, raise a number of questions about the sexual knowledge of the participants. Effie's letter

---

[4] For a discussion of these "sex-positive" accounts of Victorian culture, see Chapter 3. Many of these studies argue for a Victorian knowledge about and emphasis on female orgasm as well as for a surprisingly widespread attitude that marital sex could and should be separated from reproduction.

to her father describing the sexual history of her relationship to John claims almost complete ignorance about the "duties" of marriage: "To go back to the day of my marriage the 10th of April 1848. I went as you know away to the Highlands – I had never been told the duties of married persons to each other and knew little or nothing about their relations in the closest union on earth."[5] Effie's ignorance might well be attributed to the special status of middle-class girls. But what of their male counterparts? Certainly it seems as though John knew something about what was expected of him on the wedding night – if only because he offered a series of explanations about why he had failed to fulfill them – but the record suggests that he too might have suffered from lack of sexual knowledge in a slightly different sense. This becomes clear when, in the same letter, Effie lists for her father the reasons John gave over time for what apparently became an active refusal to consummate the marriage:

For days John talked about this relation to me but avowed no intention of making me his Wife – He alleged various reasons, hatred to children, religious reasons, a desire to preserve my beauty, and finally this last year told me the true reason (and this to me is as villainous as all the rest) *that he had imagined women were quite different to what he saw I was*, and that the reason he did not make me his Wife was because he was disgusted with my person this the first evening 10th April.[6]

Like Effie, contemporary scholars have tended to take Ruskin's final reason as the "true" one. Mary Luytens, whose many books on the Ruskin marriage make her an authoritative voice here, speculates that John's "disgust" might have stemmed from lack of exposure to the female body:

John must have been familiar with the female nude from his study of pictures. It is probable, though, that Effie was the only naked woman he ever saw. In what way could her body have been different from what he imagined? In only one particular, it seems: the female nudes that he saw in galleries – statues as well as pictures – were either discreetly veiled or depicted as children. For a man as sensitive as he it may well have been a lasting shock to discover the adult reality. Had he seen other women he would have realised that the unattractive circumstances in Effie's person were common to them all; in his ignorance he believed her to be uniquely disfigured.[7]

If we go with Luytens – and Effie – here, two different kinds of ignorance were being played out on the wedding night: Effie's lack of basic knowledge about "the" sexual act and John's ignorance of the

---

[5] Sir William James, *John Ruskin and Effie Gray* (New York: Scribner's, 1947), p. 220.
[6] *Ibid.* (italics mine).   [7] Mary Luytens, *Effie in Venice* (London: Murray, 1965), p. 21.

female body, derived, ironically enough, in part from his cultural expertise.[8]

The issues of sexual knowledge raised by the passage are not limited to the Victorian context. At crucial moments the passage seems to be not so much reporting what John or Effie said about the wedding night as identifying with John's putative gaze. When Luytens explains that if John had "seen other women he would have realised that the unattractive circumstances in Effie's person were common to them all," the word "unattractive" as applied to all women's bodies signals a slippage between author and biographical subject. It also moves the passage out of the immediate context of John's assumed degree of sexual knowledge to another domain to which the term "sexual knowledge" might refer. We might ask not only "What did the Victorians know (and when did they know it)?" but "What do we as contemporary scholars of the Victorian period know about how much they knew (and how)?"

Sexual knowledge *about* the Ruskins has often taken the form of the identification of the offending body part. Scholars since Luytens have been less restrained in naming what they imagine to be the anatomical solution to the dilemma of the Ruskin failure. Phyllis Rose's blithe summary of Luytens's argument gives us a different tone:

> According to Mary Luytens ... what disgusted John about Effie's body was probably her pubic hair. She reasons that John had never seen a naked woman in his life and that even the representations of the female nude he had seen in art were either censored or highly idealized, like classical statues. He expected therefore a smooth, hairless, small-breasted body, and the signs of sexual maturity on Effie's body (it may have been no more than her breasts – the gown may never have slipped below her shoulders) disconcerted and dismayed him.[9]

Like Luytens's solution on which this is based, Rose's speculations focus on uncovering the body part in question. The investment in the body-part-as-solution may be hinted at in the "it" of "it may have been no more than her breasts"; the "it," with its problematic grammatical referent, suggests a singular solution in the act of nominating another part of Effie's body. (Other critics, also focusing on parts above the waist, for reasons we shall see later, have weighed in on behalf of armpit hair.)

What interests me most about the debate over Ruskin's reasons, however, is not the solution to the mystery but the investment of scholars

---

[8] In *The Ruskins and the Grays*, Luytens implies that the real reason for Ruskin's refusal is the horror of children.

[9] Phyllis Rose, *Parallel Lives: Five Victorian Marriages* (New York: Knopf, 1983), p. 52.

in a singular solution that takes the form of privileging one of John's explanations over others and, indeed, one bodily part over the rest of the body. This attempt to locate on the body of Effie and in the mind of John Ruskin one element among others that produced a complicated honeymoon and marriage says as much about our desire to know the Victorians as it does about John's desire – or lack thereof – for more conventional forms of carnal knowledge.

This singular critical focus is all the stranger given that John's own accounts are characterized by repetition, revision, and contradiction. Effie's long list of reasons for John's refusal to consummate the marriage in her letter to Mr. Gray is, in fact, incomplete. In his own defense at the annulment proceedings, Ruskin also alleged, first, that he was trying to spare Effie anxiety by not forcing sex upon her and, second, that he knew even then that she was "mad." John also was not perfectly consistent about whether he would ever change his mind and try again to consummate the marriage. While at times he seemed to cast his decision as final, at others he seemed to entertain the possibility of a fully sexualized marriage. Fairly early in the marriage, in a letter to Effie, he seemed to hint at another attempt at a wedding night. Writing to Effie from Paris, having finally realized his desire to travel to the Continent with his parents (Effie was unwell and at her mother's house), he says, "Do you know, pet, it seems almost a dream to me that we have been married. I look forward to meeting you; and to your *next* bridal night; and to the time when I shall again draw your dress from your snowy shoulders: and lean my cheek upon them." [10] This passage – incidentally the evidence for John not having seen much below Effie's shoulders – gestures to several reiterations: writing from the site of his first fantasy of his honeymoon about the failures of the honeymoon that proved such a pale shadow of that fantasy, he stages in writing a repetition of the wedding night. In repeating the act of drawing the "dress from [her] snowy shoulders," however, Ruskin in effect not only repeats his actions of the first wedding night but also reiterates the point at which those actions stopped. While it is unclear what Ruskin imagines (or wants Effie to imagine) will happen on the "next bridal night" after he leans his cheek on her shoulder, the narrative, at any rate, comes to a resting place that echoes the end of the original wedding night in Blair Atholl. Once again we have the problem of too much information, too many explanations, too many honeymoons, real and imagined. To represent this record of repetition, fantasy,

---

[10] James, *John Ruskin and Effie Gray*, p. 138.

and contradiction as a matter of simple ignorance is to do an injustice to competing forms of ignorance, knowledge, and information at work in the Ruskin marriage. In the struggle to identify a single "problem," a single moment or body part, we may lose sight of the complexities raised by the infamous acts and non-acts of John and Effie's wedding night.

Eliza Wemyss's diary registers in an immediate sense not so much ignorance but fear. I make this distinction despite the fact that much contemporary scholarship on sexuality conflates these two categories as if knowledge and pleasure were synonymous terms. Her identification of the honeymoon as "a period altogether I should think the most unpleasant in a girl's life" suggests a trauma as deep as Effie's or John's to which we have no verbal access. By focusing on the general ("a girl's life"), Eliza's words suggest a degree of assumed knowledge, a sense, perhaps shared with other "girls" or women, of unpleasant routine. We cannot know, of course, whether Eliza's "knowledge" came to her before or after the wedding night; all we can know is that by the day after the wedding the unpleasantness of the wedding night had achieved almost proverbial status.

If we move, as we did with the Ruskins, from the sexual knowledge of the participants to the sexual knowledge of the contemporary commentators, the Wemyss honeymoon in many ways presents an opposite epistemological problem. If there is too much conflicting material on the Ruskin honeymoon, there is too little on the Wemysses'. Eliza's three-sentence commentary on the sexual aspects of the wedding night is as brief as it is cryptic: right after she mentions the unpleasantness of the honeymoon, she continues, "I am happy now it is one's . . . " The rest of the sentence is frustratingly illegible. The closest I could come was "duty to be reconciled."

Nothing thematizes the problem of scholarly ignorance more efficiently than the illegible letter or diary entry. If the published record of the Ruskin honeymoon forces me to question the investments of Luytens and Rose, my own experience with the unpublished archive brings questions of knowledge and desire squarely home to me. How can I know what Eliza wrote when her handwriting is unclear, much less what she meant or felt about what she wrote? While I pursue the problems raised by what I call the erotics of the archive at greater length in Chapter 3, I want to focus for a moment on the specific act of reading and interpreting Eliza's (almost) illegible sentence. The desire to know can distort reality: how can I know for certain that it was not my own wishes – for closure, for Eliza's happiness, for complete knowledge – that led me to construe Eliza's words so they read "duty to be reconciled"? Are the words illegible because Eliza herself does not quite believe in the possibility of that reconciliation and thus blurs the words as she writes them? Are they illegible to me because I do not believe in her reconciliation or because I want to believe in it too much? These questions illuminate for me my own desires for this project, from the personal and identificatory (I want Eliza to have been happy), to the ideological (I want, or wanted before I began this project, to be part of the movement in Victorian scholarship toward a revisionist, more actively erotic account of Victorian women's lives), to the epistemological (I want to know as much as I can about Eliza Dickinson, even and especially what she might not have wanted anyone to know).

If the honeymoon by definition revolves around the presence or absence of indicatively private acts, it also rewrites relations to family and community. Both honeymoons also took on the work of what in Chapter 2 I call the "reorientation" from the birth family to the new conjugal unit. In the case of the Ruskins it was the original, idealized honeymoon that included John's parents; Effie seems to have been somewhat resistant to this idea. John responds to Effie's uneasiness with a letter that exposes the tension between his roles as son and husband:

You say we can't expect to be always taken care of – I know we can't – and that's why I want to be while we *can*. It is so nice, Effie, not to have to take care of oneself. And yet, I must confess to you, that I have had more misgivings since I came home this last time, than before, about your being *quite* so happy as I had hoped – until we are indeed alone – There are little things that often sadden me now, in my father and mother – Still – I am always happiest when I am most dutiful – and although you may be sure, Effie love, that I will not sacrifice my wife's comfort in any degree to an exaggerated idea of filial duty – still, I think you will find you can give so much pleasure on this journey by very little self-denial, that you will not in the end have reason to wish it had been otherwise planned.[11]

While recent biographers have focused on what is perceived to be John's unhealthy attachment to his parents, Ruskin's syntactical and psychological negotiations of his two commitments are in some ways typical of this time of ritual transition. The almost excruciating balance of his sentences leveraged by the two uses of the word "still" suggests the difficulty of the transition from one psychological identification to the other. The passage opens by locating the uneasiness with his parents in Effie's mind – it is her happiness that is at stake, her happiness that will and must be deferred until the two are "indeed alone." Still, Ruskin does finally own that he is himself

---

[11] Luytens, *The Ruskins and the Grays*, p. 78 (italics in original).

"saddened" by "little things" in his parents; it is this confession that initiates a discourse of self-denial. John's pleas for that self-denial, and for an understanding of his parents, are of course backed up by what seems at the time like an inevitability: he closes with the assurance that in the end Effie will not "wish" that the journey "had been otherwise planned." The passive "planned" disguises the agency of John and his parents while committing Effie to acquiescence. Ironically, of course, all the planning – geographical and familial – on the part of the Ruskins was to be for naught. The second honeymoon to Blair Atholl was a honeymoon where Effie and John were to be, for better or for worse, "indeed alone."

The journals of Eliza Dickinson and Francis Wemyss do not include honeymoon plans, so I can only speculate about whether its unusual brevity had anything to do with a desire – this time presumably on the part of the bride – not to separate herself for too long from her family. It is unclear how much leave Francis had, but it seems unlikely that he would have been restricted to three or four days at the time of his marriage. Perhaps the short honeymoon conformed to Eliza's wishes, and the balance between its conjugality – the three days spent alone – and its proximity to family were, in fact, an attempt at negotiating conflicting feelings about her identification with Francis. Although Eliza's family were not present during the journey, Eliza was in regular communication with her mother and other family members. Eliza records a "note from mama" on the 25th and letters from her mother and Fanny on the 26th. On the 27th, Eliza writes, "a note from mama who sent the carriage for us before breakfast. I was very glad to go home & see them all again and leave Malabar Point." As we shall see, this degree of correspondence with the family of origin was not uncommon for women honeymooners.

So far we have looked at both the Ruskin and the Wemyss wedding nights as if they took place outside of time and place; in other words, as if they did not take *place* at all. This is easy to do, precisely because the ideology of the honeymoon produces an illusion of the couple in a world apart. But honeymoons are also, for the most part, acts of tourism; like all journeys abroad or out of familiar contexts, honeymoons raise the question of foreignness, of displacement, and of the negotiation of otherness, whether that otherness is embodied in actual people (for example, native populations) or in the terrain, culture, or history of the new location.[12] Like other kinds of journeys, honeymoons set up a

---

[12] For material on the touristic gaze, see, e.g., Jonathan Crary, *Techniques of the Observer: On Vision and Modernity in the Nineteenth Century* (Cambridge, MA: MIT Press, 1990); and Stephen Copley

relation of the touristic gaze and the objects of that gaze. Honeymoons, however, offer by definition two sets of experiences with the otherness of travel and two linked but not identical gazes. I argue in Chapter 2 that one task of the honeymoon was precisely to construct a purportedly unified conjugal gaze so that by the end of the journey the members of the couple would see things literally the same way. This conjugal gaze was, of course, not usually an egalitarian one; to paraphrase British marriage law, if husband and wife were eventually to see with one pair of eyes, that pair would, as it were, usually belong to the husband. Both the Ruskin and the Wemyss honeymoons provide examples of differently gendered touristic gazes and of gendered negotiations of the landscapes in which the couples found themselves.

In the case of the Ruskins, the planned honeymoon to the Continent was a journey to territory that John loved and knew well and about which he was eager to instruct Effie. His courtship letters, anticipating the honeymoon, explicitly figure the couple's future relations in a specific, if antitouristic,[13] form of sightseeing. He will teach Effie to see the architecture that is already so much a part of his own mental landscape:

This then was my thought – Methought – that your exceeding fondness of, and acquaintance with, history, might lead you to take some interest in the various edifices we should see abroad, – or indeed anywhere. That, while I was drawing or measuring – or going up on leads and tiles – and such places where you couldn't come – (Such scrambles as I have had – Effie – next to an Alpine summit – an old church roof is the most exciting thing in the world) you – in the aisle below – might be examining for me such written traditions of the place as were most interesting – and that from doing this – you would gradually come to take an interest in the expression – style and sculptured histories, of the Architecture itself.[14]

Ruskin's honeymoon fantasy – this one, too, destined to be unconsummated since Effie turned out not to like churches or architecture – is quite specific not only in its thematics of instruction but in what it reveals about how he imaginatively deploys their bodies and gazes. Ruskin sees himself quite literally as being on top and Effie as scribbling notes in the aisle below. While the fantasy gestures toward a specifically sexual iconography, it also establishes a vertically ordered gaze, associated, as we

and Peter Garsde (eds.), *Politics of the Picaresque* (Cambridge: Cambridge University Press, 1994). Both address themselves to an early period in the nineteenth century, but both take on a historically specific relation to landscape as consumable commodity.

[13] For a history of the anti-touristic, see James Buzard, *The Beaten Track: European Tourism, Literature, and the Ways to "Culture," 1800–1918* (Oxford: Oxford University Press, 1993).

[14] James, *John Ruskin and Effie Gray*, p. 59.

shall see in Chapter 2, with gendered negotiations of the Alpine peaks that Ruskin admits in his letter to finding even more exciting than the "old church roofs" where he plans to spend his honeymoon.

There is no doubt that John's fantasy of the honeymoon was explicitly connected to a specific geographical location with its ties to his personal, familial, and career histories. The actual honeymoon in Scotland became in many ways a pale echo of this fantasy, the terrain an impoverished double of Switzerland. Even before the change in honeymoon plans, John was not above making cutting remarks about Effie's native Scotland; he tells her, "I must not say any more about the Scottish *mountains* (as they are – by courtesy, I think, styled –)."[15] He was also dismissive of English topography; one version of the planned honeymoon was an initial period of time in the Lake District, followed by the continental tour. He argues that if there were to be peace in Europe, and his father were to be free to go with them to Switzerland, he and Effie should "waste no time petting each other among those Cumberland fishponds but . . . dash straight at the Alps."[16] Domestic lakes and mountains, associated with being alone with Effie and, interestingly, with "petting," are an inadequate backdrop to the honeymoon. Put another way, the Swiss tour was for John the essence of the honeymoon, as we see in the euphemistic substitution of Switzerland for marriage in his letter to William MacDonald outlining his plan to propose to Effie: "Miss Gray and I are old friends, I have every reason to think that if I were to try – I could make her more than a friend – and if – after I leave here this time – she holds out for six months more I believe I shall ask her to come to Switzerland with me next year."[17] While it is unclear in this letter whether he means to marry Effie before the trip or not (for a while John considered having Effie accompany him and his parents as his fiancée), the journey, connected as it is to Effie, is clearly the vehicle by which he expresses his affection for her. For Ruskin, the fantasy honeymoon must have been so overlaid with feelings about art, landscape, and family that it is hard to untangle one investment from another. The disappointments of the actual honeymoon also get expressed geographically; his belittling of English fishponds, even when part of a larger continental plan, are juxtaposed with a certain infantilizing tone as he imagines those ponds as the scene of "petting." Because relatively few of Effie's letters survive, it is impossible to reconstruct Effie's own erotic and geographical desires for this honeymoon. What is

---

[15] Luytens, *The Ruskins and the Grays*, p. 45.   [16] *Ibid.*, p. 94.   [17] *Ibid.*, pp. 61–2.

abundantly clear from John's letters, however, is that the fantasies of place driving the initial plans are his.

The fact that we have two (brief) accounts of the Wemyss honeymoon offers an almost unique opportunity to chart differing relations to place. Partly, no doubt, because of its own brevity, the Wemyss honeymoon seems not to have featured extensive sightseeing. At the center of each of the two diary accounts of the four days in Malabar Point, however, is what is in many ways a similar account of a visit to local caves. Here is Eliza's, written the day after the marriage:

At about 1 I took my departure ... to this place Malabers Point [*sic*]. It has been rather cloudy all day – I mean yesterday was – Today I have not done very much for the excitement of yesterday has made me very tired, I feel right now too unsettled to give my mind to anything that requires attention – took a stroll before dinner ... and made acquaintance with the European in charge of the flagstaff he is a relation of [ ] & was very civil and took me down to see the hole in the rocks which the natives believe if they enter all their sins are forgiven them & they come out regenerated [ ] Venus is now shining brightly & is beautifully clear tonight.[18]

Here is Francis's for the same day:

We are now comfortably settled here – we made acquaintance in the evening with the signalman here who is actually a native of Hanover. We found him rather amusing. We went down to look at the hole in the rocks through which the Natives pass with the idea that by so doing they become regenerated – and in some cases regain their caste when it has been lost through ceremonial omissions or some such thing.[19]

The most obvious difference between these two accounts is their use of pronouns. Eliza writes in the first-person singular, perhaps as a corrective to her fear, recorded in her diary three days before the wedding, that she would lose "every vestige of my former self." Her entry is also more clearly framed by emotional concerns and marked in a more obvious way by fatigue and stress. Her own overt reference to being "unsettled" is underscored by her confusion with respect to dates; one senses that for Eliza it has been a long time since the wedding. She devotes only one brief sentence to the caves, seeming less interested than Francis in their cultural context. The final sentence brings us back to the canonical geography of the honeymoon: Venus is shining brightly. Although it contains the same basic information, Francis's account feels quite different. Not only does he use the word "we" without comment; he seems

---

[18] Dickinson, entry for 24 January 1838, Ms. diary.
[19] Francis Wemyss, entry for 24 January 1838, Ms. diary, Colchester-Wemyss Family Papers, D36 F43.

in a general way to be more interested in the world beyond the conjugal. His entry is more focused on the sightseeing, his tone simultaneously more sociological and more dismissive of the natives. He uses a slightly more professional lexicon – "caste," "ceremonial omissions," "signal-man" – but ends with the seemingly impatient "or some such thing."

The most remarkable contrast between the two diary entries is in their very different use of the linked concepts of comfort and settlement. Although Eliza uses the word "comfort" in the phrase "everything was arranged for our comfort," it is followed quickly by a "yet." Francis opens his entry by noting they are "comfortably settled," echoing the last line of his previous entry where everything was "comfortably prepared for us." His sense of being "comfortably settled" contrasts sharply with Eliza's dominant feeling of being "unsettled" with respect to both time and place. While it is certainly possible to overread these accounts for their difference in tone, the feeling one gets from Francis is of being in place, being in the right place, even being able to place others: the sig-nalman is a native of Hanover; the natives have their place in his account; he and his wife are settled. Eliza, by contrast, seems more uneasy with place and placement, an uneasiness that comes out most strongly, of course, in the entry two days later about leaving Malabar Point.

Both the similarities and differences in the twin accounts raise the question of the relation between Francis's diary and Eliza's and, more generally, the communication between the couple. Did Francis read Eliza's diary or she his? Did he know from the diary or from other communications with her how uneasy she was about sexuality? Certainly, Francis's account of their courtship suggests that he might have shared *his* feelings with *her*. A few months before the wedding he seems to be working out a model of full conjugal disclosure in keeping with con-temporary ideals of marriage:

Dearest Eliza is less reserved than before, and appears to look forward to the change with less fear. The more I know her the more highly do I appreciate her character – I have never in my life given my full confidence to *any* one, on many points I have never [hardly?] disclosed any feelings at all – I feel that I can give *her* my fullest confidence and it is a very delightful sensation.[20]

While Francis's insistence that he can give Eliza his "full confidence" suggests that he may have shared feelings with her beyond those recorded in his diary, his underestimation of her fears suggests that she might well have kept her feelings – and thus her diary – to herself. I will address the

---

[20] Wemyss, entry for 14 November 1837, Ms. diary (italics in original).

issue of shared diaries more generally later in this chapter, but it is
impossible to tell definitively here, as in most instances, if husband and
wife wrote their entries in conversation with each other.

If both honeymoons exhibit a tension between the couple and the wider
world of friends and relatives, only one – the Ruskins' – suggests in any
sustained way the possible encroachments on the couple "alone together" of
larger social or historical events. While the Wemyss honeymoon may have
been circumscribed by the demands of Francis's job and the needs of the
Indian army, this was probably not the case. The Ruskin honeymoon offers
a real insight into what we might think of as a collision of the very private
with the very public, a collision whose contours I explore in a more general
and theoretical way in later chapters. Although the Ruskins themselves were
very much affected by the intervention of historical forces into their private
world, even John does not comment very much about the politics of the
revolutions. What is striking, however, is the way contemporary (twentieth-
century) scholars have used history in their accounts of the Ruskin marriage, moving seamlessly from the privacy of the Ruskin bedroom to topical
references where the revolutions of 1848 provide a structure of meaning for
the marriage and its failures. Luytens follows a description of John Ruskin's
wedding plans with a sentence that immediately places his desires in the
context of sweeping historical movement: "Three days after writing this on
Saturday, 26 February, news reached London which temporarily destroyed
all their hopes for the Continental tour which John had been looking
forward to far more than his wedding: revolution had broken out in Paris;
Louis Philippe fled to England; it was the end of the Bourbon monarchy."[21]
As she moves from private desire and public record, Luytens erects a frame
in which John Ruskin's hopes for his honeymoon are embedded in a
dependent clause. Indeed, in this passage there is no honeymoon, no
wedding journey; transformed by Luytens into a "Continental tour," it
participates in the public discourse of geography and war and is actually
opposed to "wedding," the only word inclusive of the private. The second
half of the sentence piles on historical events; the movement from one to
the other suggests historical inevitability, while the use of the past tense
ratifies the idea that an era – and the honeymoon? – are indeed over.

This passage is not unique in Luytens or in the works of other Ruskin
biographers in gesturing out toward history; this is partly a question of
genre. But the Ruskin marriage seems to inspire a particularly efficient
form of the movement from private to public events. Luytens, for

---

[21] Luytens, *The Ruskins and the Grays*, p. 92.

example, follows a very brief description of Effie and John's wedding ceremony with a fuller description of a Chartist rally held the same day:

On this same day, April 10, 1848, there was a great Chartist procession in London to present a petition to Parliament. There were said to be over five million signatures on the petition and a hundred thousand marchers. Bloodshed, if not total revolution, was predicted and the Duke of Wellington was put in charge of the defense of London. In the event only about twenty thousand marched. Two sympathizers who joined the procession were John Everett Millais whom Effie was to marry in the same drawing room at Bowerswell seven years later, and his friend Holman Hunt. (Mr. Ruskin was afterwards to give the danger of the Chartist uprising as an excuse for not attending his son's wedding.) There were some skirmishes between the marchers and the police but all real trouble was quenched in a deluge of rain. After the ceremony at Bowerswell John and Effie drove away to Blair Atholl for the first night of their honeymoon.[22]

History is used in two distinct ways here. First, as cause – insofar as the Ruskins, however problematically, maintained that the uprisings were responsible for their nonattendance – and second, as a symbolic juxtaposition. It is this second use of history, of course, that blurs the distinction between historical and fictional narrative: disturbances in the larger world can be read, through the literary trope of metaphor, as indications of disturbances on the level of the individual subject. The unsuccessful Chartist procession and its literal "quench[ing]" become, then, metaphors for the dampening of John's sexual desire. Phyllis Rose speaks of the wedding night as a failed revolution:

I began by discussing a revolution that did not take place and will now suggest that the sexual failure of the Ruskins' marriage can be seen as another case of revolution *manqué*, in that the young Ruskins were, like every newly wed Victorian couple, in the position of having to rebel against all their previous training. Suddenly sex, after years of being proscribed, was approved, encouraged, indeed required. What resulted was sometimes impotence and frigidity, with the attendant train of misunderstandings and hurt feelings, or, less dramatically, sex that was not very pleasurable. The Ruskins' plight was probably less extraordinary and eccentric than one might think at first.[23]

Whether or not we agree with Rose that the Ruskin wedding night was somewhat typical, it is clear that she is using history in yet a third way. While the relation between the Ruskin failed wedding night and the failed Chartist revolution is metaphoric or based on (perceived) resemblance, the relation between the Ruskin wedding night and other

---

[22] *Ibid.*, p. 106. [23] Rose, *Parallel Lives*, p. 56.

Victorian wedding nights is metonymic, deriving its meaning from juxtaposition or contiguity.

Rose's speculation about representativeness takes us to the final question about which I want to speculate here. Both honeymoons, in their
different ways, raise the issue of the representativeness of the honeymooning couples. Ruskin's fame (less great at the time of his honeymoon
than it was to become later, but very much at issue at the time of the
annulment) as well as what we might think of as his proclivities, more
dominant in later life, for prepubescent girls make his case, and thus that
of Effie, a less than ordinary one. The wealth of knowledge we have about
Ruskin and his family might, ironically, cloud or at least skew the picture
in a variety of directions. If we knew as much about the details of other
wedding nights as we know (or think we know) about the Ruskins',
would we find that many of them, like the Ruskins', did not conform to
normative narratives of consummation? Or does the fact that John
Ruskin was in many ways a remarkable figure – and of course this has
much to do with how much we know about him – make his wedding
night so exceptional that it tells us only about his proclivities and nothing
about the culture that he helped to shape? If, for whatever reason, we
agree that the Ruskins' wedding night was probably exceptional, does this
make it pathological? Are Ruskin's doubts, fears, and conflicts only
exaggerated versions of the doubts, fears, and conflicts of more ordinary
people who may (or may not) have had more conventional and con-
ventionally successful wedding nights?

The Wemysses' honeymoon is not exceptional in the same way as the
Ruskins', but it, too, raises methodological problems of over-
interpretation. Of course both the Ruskins and the Wemysses came from
situations of relative privilege; as I discuss in more detail later in this
chapter, conclusions about families like these have limited applications
outside the middle class. Even more crucial to the question of representativeness, however, is the more vexed issue of the negativity of both
the Wemyss and Ruskin honeymoons. While there are certainly more
positive and even blissful honeymoon stories I could have used to open
my study, almost all direct references to the sexual in my larger sample –
and there are only a few – are negative. Eliza certainly seems to have
thought of her experience as representative – her comment on the pain of
the honeymoon is framed as a generalization about a representative
"girl." As I mentioned earlier, we simply do not know how accurate her
sense of her own typicality might be. While the Ruskin honeymoon is
easier to put aside – marriages that ended in annulment were of course

very rare and thus perhaps unrepresentative – Rose and others suggest that nonconsummated marriages might have been considerably more common than the annulments that made them public.

THE LANDSCAPE OF MARRIAGE

As the Ruskin and Wemyss wedding journeys suggest, by the 1830s and 1840s the honeymoon was beginning to take a particular shape for middle-class couples. While I discuss details of honeymoon travel and etiquette later, it might be useful to begin with the role of the honeymoon in relation to its contextualizing institution of marriage. To do this we must go back a few centuries to a history of British marriage, a history marked on the one hand by an increasing dependence on the notion of privacy and on the privileging of individual feeling and, on the other, by movements toward regulation and bureaucratization that found their most visible expression in the Marriage Act of 1753.

Historians of marriage agree, in a general way, that some time before the end of the eighteenth century English culture underwent a shift in regard to expectations about marriage, so that among the middle and upper classes ideals of marriage came to include and indeed to depend upon ideals of companionship and romantic love.[24] Thus, a relatively new form of marriage that stressed personal liking and, often, sexual attraction competed for cultural primacy with conceptions of marriage based on financial interest and familial ties. This emergent form of marriage did not entirely replace older ideals; we can find tensions between these ideals late into the nineteenth century and, arguably, even into our own time. Still, this new marital imperative was a far-reaching one that spread *as* an imperative, if not as a reality, down the social scale. The ideals of conjugality would be most identified with the middle class and with middle-class notions of domesticity; for aristocrats, on the one hand, and for working-class couples, on the other – and for vastly different reasons – economic factors would continue to play a more important role. Still, the middle-class ideal was the one given most public currency in novels, conduct books, newspapers, sermons, and other media. While one can certainly overstate the case for this shift from one "kind" of marriage to another (surely, as critics of Lawrence Stone have

---

[24] The transition to affective marriage was most influentially laid out by Lawrence Stone in *The Family, Sex, and Marriage in England, 1500–1800* (New York: Harper and Row, 1977). Recent revisions to Stone have added nuance to the idea of transition and replacement. See, for example, Ralph Houlbrooke, *The English Family, 1450–1700* (New York: Longman, 1984).

pointed out, seventeenth-century wives and husbands were capable of attachments we would see as romantic, and certainly money played a part in many Victorian marriages, even in those with strong personal and sexual investments), it is important to think of emotions as powerful as those understood under the capacious term "love" and institutions as venerable as marriage in terms of their own histories.

There are as many names for the new marital style as there are dates for its triumph over older models. It has been variously referred to as "affective marriage," "companionate marriage," less formally as "marriage for love," and even "egalitarian marriage." While all these names point to important elements of the kind of marriage I will be discussing here, I prefer the term "conjugal marriage," or, more generally, "conjugality." "Companionate marriage" stresses the ideal that husbands and wives should be friends, that they should spend – and want to spend – time together, and that they should have shared interests. While these connotations are useful in highlighting the sharing of time, place, and ideals expected of middle-class couples in England in the nineteenth century, "companionate marriage" both overstates by implication the amount of time that husbands and wives spent together in middle-class marriages and underemphasizes the element of sexuality that, while muted in its public expression, is still very legible in Victorian accounts of what marriage should be. "Affective marriage," with its emphasis on feeling, appropriately points to the emotional investment husbands and wives were expected to make in each other, but it suggests that other, earlier models lacked feeling of any important kind. "Marriage for love" makes the same assumption in this case by introducing a term that has often been used to erase historical and cultural difference. "Love," like marriage, is a capacious term: love was always in some sense part of the marital equation; it is the kind of love prescribed for married couples – its limits, its possibilities, and its imperatives – that interests me here. "Egalitarian marriage" is simply a misnomer; while one can argue whether Victorian women had more or less power within marriage than their predecessors in earlier centuries, they were by no means equal partners in law or in practice at any stage in British history. My preferred term, "conjugal marriage," with its etymological links to joining and yoking together, suggests a powerful linking of interest between husband and wife, while seeming to acknowledge specifically sexual interest as a fundamental part of an ideal marriage. Ultimately I would like to argue that what is at stake is a specific form of what we have since 1892 but not before called heterosexuality.

All of these terms, including "conjugality," have in common a sense of the primacy of the couple – and eventually the children of that couple – over the birth family or the community more generally. For me it is most useful to see conjugality not so much as a matter of feeling as of *identification*; conjugal marriage required women and men to identify with their spouse and to carry out that identification in terms of the choices they made in their daily lives. Historians have noted the uniqueness of the expectation in Victorian culture that husbands of all classes would provide a home for their wives; this expectation played an important part in the deferral of English marriages and set up an expected physical separation between married children and their birth families. The architecture of houses followed this imperative for isolation of the couple, even, where possible, in middle-class homes. Husband and wife might or might not share a bedroom in a large house, but those bedrooms would be set off from the rooms of children and servants as well as from those with more public purposes. Isolation of this sort is closely related to ideas of privacy, a concept with its own rich and evocative history.[25] Of course, tensions between identification with the birth family and the family of marriage were not new in eighteenth- or nineteenth-century England. The biblical injunction in Genesis 2:24 that men leave their family and cleave to their wives expresses that tension by positing a solution often cited by Victorians. I would argue, however, that the texture of the Victorian solution was different and that a culture built around the conjugal unit in terms of ritual, economics, travel, and architecture began to replace older models. We might bring forward into the discussion of the nineteenth century the useful sense of paradox built into the word "cleave": meaning both "to cut" and "to join," "cleaving" suggests at once the union of the married couple and the dependence of that union on the isolation of the husband and wife from their birth families.

If expectations about the motivations for marriage increasingly emphasized linked notions of privacy and the isolation of the couple, so too did the rituals surrounding the act of getting married. Local wedding customs in England and throughout Britain continued to be varied, although old forms began to disappear, especially in urban and suburban areas. One older tradition associated with rural populations until the seventeenth century was the "big wedding." The big wedding, which might take several days or longer and unfold in several locations, was

---

[25] See Michelle Perrot (ed.), *A History of Private Life: From the Fires of Revolution to the Great War* (Cambridge, MA: Harvard University Press, 1990).

accompanied by a series of rituals, varying, of course, from one locale to another: these might include ritual leave-taking of the family; the fetching of the bride by the groom and other men from her parental house, sometimes accompanied by simulated or real violence ("rough music"); the payment of money by the groom to the community in the form of largesse; serenading of the bride and groom (sometimes with music, sometimes with more rowdy noises involving the introduction into the bedroom of noisemakers, for example, a cat shod in walnuts); and other community acts.

Three issues stand out as we contrast the big wedding with more contemporary marriage forms: time, place, and community. In most cases the big wedding was only the ratification of a betrothal; the couple already considered themselves married. There was no moment of legal marriage readily identifiable in the series of events that made up the wedding. While these weddings often ended up in church, the church ceremony was anticlimactic and often rowdy, sandwiched between other communal events. Big weddings also differed from later British weddings with respect to place. The big wedding was a mobile affair, encompassing in its rituals a variety of places and the movements of crowds of people between them. One response of the Anglican Church was to try to emphasize the special sanctity of its own space, but the big wedding proved resistant to spatial management. As John Gillis puts it, "[T]he best the established church was able to do [in their effort to control the festivities of the big wedding] was separate the feasting, music, dancing and magic from the church service itself. Denied the sanction of the church, the big wedding moved to the tavern and the village green. The processions to and from the church grew ever larger and more festive."[26] The big wedding rituals proved quite resistant over time to puritan, dissenting, and Anglican attempts to put them in their place and to draw a cordon sanitaire around the service at the altar.

The third important feature of the big wedding was the role of the community. Big weddings often de-emphasized immediate family in favor of the peer group who became the central actors in their many rituals. Often the first step in the wedding was the departure of the bride from the family home; after this, friends of the bride and groom took over the ceremonies, and the rituals continued to enact separation, in this case not so much from family but from homosocial groups of peers. Most

---

[26] John Gillis, *For Better, For Worse: British Marriages, 1600 to the Present* (New York: Oxford University Press, 1985), p. 56.

striking was the noise and spectacle of those weddings and their status as community and public events.

By the end of the eighteenth century, weddings were already much quieter, although older traditions persisted alongside newer ones. Gillis has identified a trend in the late eighteenth century toward privacy in wedding ceremonies, especially among the upper classes. He quotes Fanny Burney's recoil from the publicity of older forms:

After witnessing a "mob" waiting at the church door when an alderman's daughter wed in 1770, Fanny Burney expressed horror at all forms of the big wedding: "I don't suppose anything can be so dreadful as a public wedding – my stars! I should never be able to support it." She would have approved of arrival and departure by closed carriage, an eighteenth-century innovation, which served to protect the privacy of the couple and exemplify social distance.[27]

Privacy became part of the wedding ceremony and its attendant rituals. While ritual is by its nature social, and while marriage itself is a social and legal act, at this historical moment privacy became increasingly the idiom in which these important public acts were carried out. This is the paradox at the heart of conjugality, a belief system and a cultural practice that rewrite the public as the private and the social as the individual.

While in one sense marriage became more a matter of individual desire, in another it became far more regularized and thus more open to a different kind of public scrutiny, especially following Hardwicke's Marriage Act of 1753, which proclaimed invalid all marriages other than those celebrated in an Anglican Church or by special license. This act did away with earlier forms of marriage like the spousal, which depended only on the consent, in the presence of witnesses, between parties who wanted to marry. Hardwicke was only one highly visible moment in a long series of attempts to take marriage out of the realm of private consent and into the purview of the government. Throughout the first half of the century, parliament tinkered with Hardwicke's provisions, finally ensconcing the idea of secular (civil) marriage in the Marriage Act of 1836. These changes had the effect of shifting the meaning of marriage in two opposite directions: while, on the one hand, the legal power to define marriage moved toward the more impersonal realm of the government, on the other hand, the power to define it in day-to-day terms became the provenance of the married couple, that community of two that replaced larger and more mobile communities of friends, neighbors, and relatives.

[27] *Ibid.*, p. 137.

The shifting middle ground of communal ritual became emptied of much of its significance and social power.[28]

Hardwicke was crucial in defining a change in the character of British marriage in another way: the law had the effect of eliminating legal gray areas and producing two definitive categories: the married and the not-married. This strict binary opposition contributed to what we might think of as the climactic character of late-eighteenth- and early-nineteenth-century marriage: for the first time in British history there was no legally recognized state between being married and being single. While rare and expensive legal separations were possible before 1857, and while after the 1857 Matrimonial Causes (Divorce) Act a larger number of people took advantage of legal separations, there was – at least in theory – no doubt whether a given person was married or not.

Law, however, was not the only domain to give shape to the climactic structure of marriage. Sexual customs and ideals also supported the idea of a gulf between the married and the unmarried. As engagement became (theoretically) less accommodating to quasi-marital sexual relationships, more pressure was put on the early days of marriage to provide opportunities for sexual and other intimacies.[29]

If Victorian culture was, by and large, invested in emphasizing difference between the married and the single, then the passage from singleness to marriage was by definition a transformative one. Sexual customs and ideals supported the idea of marriage as a major transition for women and, to a substantial extent, for men. In a culture in which premarital sex was frowned upon, the sexual character of marriage became all the more pronounced, and the differences between the two states exacerbated. The public standards of Victorian culture made it quite clear that women should be virgins when they were married; it was equally clear that sex was a conjugal duty owed to the husband. There have been

---

[28] Weddings in Victorian England were, by our standards, surprisingly underemphasized. They tended to take place early in the day and to be followed by a wedding breakfast rather than an elaborate dinner or other party. This would leave time, of course, for the married couple to leave for their honeymoon.

[29] For an influential discussion of engagement and sexual intimacy, see M. Jeanne Peterson, *Family, Love, and Work in the Lives of Victorian Gentlewomen* (Bloomington: Indiana University Press, 1989). Her contention that "flirtation and more serious sexual interaction were an acknowledged part of the byplay between two engaged people" (p. 74) begs the question about what such "sexual interaction" might be. Like many sexually revisionist Victorianists, her sources are indirect. Her claims for the underestimation of the sexuality of Victorian girls, for example, are supported by a more general account of their "physical energy," their enjoyment of sports, their freedom from illness, etc. Cultural disapproval of premarital sexuality also arguably had the effect of making sex within marriage even more important.

differing accounts about sexual expectations for men in this era. Clearly there was more approval of premarital sex for men than for women, and more in aristocratic and working-class male circles than in middle-class culture. Religion, of course, complicated the picture; although certain kinds of evangelicalism that were especially inimical to premarital sex were strongly associated with the middle class, religion could and did affect people's understanding of sex in all class cultures. It is instructive to think of the case of Lord Lyttelton, an aristocrat influenced – as were many people of his class and education – by the Oxford Movement, writing an almost identical letter on the subject of sexual abstinence to each of his eight sons when they went to Eton. A letter found in his desk, which he apparently used as a model for all of them, included the following admonition:

I do not mean to go into a general lecture on this matter. You cannot doubt the sinfulness of it, and among particular motives in your case to avoid all sin, I need only mention the memory of your blessed mother – what happiness it would have been, perhaps may still be, to her, to see you leading a pure and virtuous life, and in this particular respect more than any other. On the sin itself I shall only mention one point which may not always be considered. Whatever some may think of in the *man*, no one denies its enormity in the *woman*. No one could bear to think of any woman in whom he was interested losing her character. But then it is plain no *man* can act this way without participating in the woman's sin.[30]

Lord Lyttelton was member of the lower aristocracy, a worldly man, well traveled and connected through family and close friendships with the most powerful, rich, and elite people in Britain. He seems also to have been a passionate man whose relation to both his first and second wives was defined in part by his sexual needs. No stranger to desire or privilege, he nonetheless expected of himself and, later, of his sons strict abstinence before marriage. While it is hard to say how representative Lyttelton's views on sexuality were of the aristocracy in general, he and his circle stand as a helpful corrective to blanket notions of permissive sexual mores among men of his class. Sexual mores are, of course, complex; they may or may not be coterminous with sexual behavior, and people can have vastly different standards for themselves and for other people: they can also, of course, lie or change their minds about their attitudes and their behaviors.

[30] Edith Lyttelton, *Alfred Lyttelton: An Account of His Life* (London: Longmans, 1923), pp. 15–16 (italics in original).

Victorian sexual attitudes, however they may have been realized in terms of behavior, contributed to a sense of marriage as a unique state. This is even true given the general secularization of culture and the unevenness of Victorian ideas of marriage as a sacred institution. We can see the honeymoon, then, as a bridge between two clearly demarcated sites with different legal obligations and social duties, marked for women, for example, by expected differences in body, dress, and name. The honeymoon, then, becomes a geographical and psychological site for the transformation from single to married subject, a time and place for the shifting of bodily and geographical territories, for the checking of bodily coordinates against maps and expectations.

THE CONDUCT OF HONEYMOONS

Over the course of the nineteenth century, the honeymoon became an expected part of the rituals surrounding marriage. While, to the extent that they mention them at all, other scholars have treated the honeymoon as an upper- or upper-middle-class phenomenon, my research suggests that certainly by the last quarter of the nineteenth century the tradition had infiltrated to the upper working classes. Some of my evidence for this is direct: I have found examples of shopkeepers who took honeymoons. There is also inferential evidence: for example, the remark of a Cook's tourist, George Heard, that on a trip to Europe in 1865 he was surprised when one of his fellow passengers turned out to be a major; Heard had taken him "to be a well-to-do mechanic honeymooning with his young wife."[31] For Heard, the surprise of this encounter is not that this traveling companion seemed like a mechanic but that he should in fact turn out to be of a higher class. Institutions like Cook's Tours and the general opening up of travel to the less affluent clearly had their effect on the ubiquity of the honeymoon. As we shall see, honeymoons varied in length and destination partly in terms of class, but by the end of the century, there was a range of possible honeymoon destinations from weekend trips to the country by rail to extended continental tours that had not lost their link to the eighteenth-century aristocratic grand tour. Working-class honeymoons might have both reflected and contributed to the spread of the culture of conjugality down from the middle classes throughout the last quarter of the century.

---

[31] Piers Brendon, *Thomas Cook: 150 Years of Popular Tourism* (London: Secker, 1991), p. 92.

The routinizing of the honeymoon also made for the cultural icon of the honeymooner, whose behavior was often commented upon or parodied in popular writing. This in turn helped to produce what we might think of as "honeymoon embarrassment" on the part of some bridal couples, who consciously attempted to distance themselves – with varying success – from clichés of honeymoon behavior. Georgiana Macdonald Burne-Jones was proud that the doctor who visited Edward on their honeymoon took the couple for an old married pair. In fiction, Dickens's *Our Mutual Friend* parodies Bella Wilfer's failed, but to the author's eyes charming, attempt to present herself as a long-married woman to the waiters at her wedding breakfast. Two years after the publication of the novel, a *Punch* cartoon represented essentially the same scene, complete with snickering waiters, as Amelia, "who flatters herself that [she and her husband] are taken for an old married couple," asks her new husband about what tea he takes (Fig. 1). Of course the most legible sign of the honeymooner was excessive display of physical affection: a correspondent to the *Daily News* who finds himself traveling among honeymooning couples the strictness of their judgments about the behavior of others in, so to speak, the same boat. He quotes one man proclaiming, with "a contemptuous look" at a pair of honeymooners out on one of the lakes, that he "would take care that the boat was far enough away before going on in that fashion." A female honeymooner, "a wife of three weeks," is recorded as saying, "'It is all very well to go walking in the twilight, but I think that a young lady might as well remember that a white sleeve is easily seen against a black coat.'"[32] Much of the humor of this particular piece of honeymoon popular culture derives from the fact that honeymooners tend to flock to the same places, that one can find oneself, as the correspondent to the *Daily News* did, surrounded by them at predictable spots at particular times of year.

Honeymooners were the subject not only of jokes but also of popular advice and histories of marriage that make it clear how routine the institution of the honeymoon was becoming for upper-middle-class couples. Although the *OED* gives the etymology of the term as deriving from the "honey" or full moon just on the verge of waning, Victorian sources vary regarding the etymology of the word "honeymoon." W. J. Marchant claims that the term "is said to have derived from the Teutonic custom . . . of drinking a concoction of honey for thirty days,

[32] Vacuus Viator [pseud.], "Travelling Scot-Free," *London Daily News*, 25 August 1873.

"THE HAPPY PAIR THEN LEFT TOWN——"

Amelia (who flatters herself they are taken for quite an Old Married Couple). "TELL ME, GEORGE, DO YOU LIKE GREEN TEA, OR BLACK?"
[The Waiter winks, the Chambermaid chuckles.

Fig. 1 "The Happy Pair." Cartoon from *Punch*, 16 November 1867.

or a moon's age, after a wedding feast. Attila, the Hun, is said to have celebrated his nuptials in such a glorious manner ... that he drank himself to death on his wedding day."[33] Other Victorian sources point to the "moon-age" or lunar month as the typical duration of the honeymoon phase of the relationship, and thus as a directive about the length of the ideal trip. Several Victorian accounts begin with references to Samuel Johnson, who defined the honeymoon as "the first month after marriage, when there is nothing but tenderness and pleasure."[34] While the *OED* cites Johnson, it also includes references that define the "honeymoon" as an early and ephemeral period in marriage.

Clearly, until the nineteenth century, the honeymoon was defined in terms of time; by the Victorian period, place also became an important component as the initial period of marital bliss began to coincide with the expectation of travel. While, as we shall see, Victorian conduct books often had something to say about honeymoon destinations, they also seemed to be invested in the honeymoon as a scene of departure. The 1852 *A Complete Guide to Forms of a Wedding* by David Bogue interrupts fairly straightforward advice on the logistics and etiquette of weddings with this emotional vignette:

The young bride, divested of her bridal attire, and quietly costumed for her journey, now bids farewell to her bridesmaids and lady friends. Some natural tears spring to her gentle eyes as she takes a last look at the home she is now leaving. The servants venture to crowd to her with their humble yet heartfelt congratulations; and finally, melting, she falls weeping on her mother's bosom. A short cough is heard, as of some one summoning up resolution. It is her father. He dare [sic] not trust his voice; but he holds out his hand, gives her one kiss, and then leads her, half turning back, down the stairs and through the hall, to the door, where he delivers her to her husband, who hands her quickly into the carriage, leaps in lightly after her, waves his hand to the party, who appear crowding at the windows, half smiles at the throng about the door, then gives the word, and they are off, and started on the voyage of life![35]

While the husband, who leaps lightly into the carriage with a half [ironic?] smile, is clearly the beneficiary of this ceremony, the passage lingers, like the bride herself, with the people left behind. As carriage becomes honeymoon, becomes marriage, becomes life voyage, each inexorably moving forward, the emphasis of this passage is on division

---

[33] W. J. Marchant, *Betrothals and Bridals* (London, 1879), p. 107.
[34] John Morison, *Counsels to a Newly Wedded Pair* (London: Westley, 1830), p. 7.
[35] David Bogue, *A Complete Guide to Forms of a Wedding* (London: Bogue, 1852), p. 81. A reprint of this passage, with slight changes, appears in *Routledge's Manual of Etiquette* (London and New York, 1875), p. 146.

and indecision: the half smile and the half turn that signal, perhaps, not so much doubt as hesitation.

Although in this case it is the father who most acutely feels the loss in this exemplary honeymoon narrative, other advice books use the same moment of departure to enter in more detail into the mind of the bride as she leaves her family. Again, the story tends to interrupt the most practical kinds of advice with narrative affect. One conduct book pauses in the middle of a chapter entitled "The Happy Day" to examine its own premises:

> Though we have headed this chapter "The Happy Day;" [*sic*] as it is generally looked forward to as such, and there is every reason it should be so, yet the cup of happiness is not unmixed with grief. When you stand at the sacred altar and place your snow-white hand in the warm embrace of the gentleman to whom you then vow unchanging fidelity, who can pourtray [*sic*] the feelings which agitate the mind at that critical moment? Here you stand on the threshold of a two-fold existence. This moment you are under the guardianship and protection of your parents, the next you are transferred as a trembling bride into the hands of another ... The glittering pearls may decorate the brow of the lovely bride, but how frequently are those contrasted with the silent tears sparkling with unsullied lustre upon her eye-lashes.[36]

The departure for the honeymoon often produces hyperbolic narrative and (especially) bad prose, as if the emotion of the moment breaks through the bounds of genre to suggest there are things beyond the power of conduct books to describe.

Departure for the honeymoon can also be framed less as a loss than as a form of modest withdrawal. Another conduct book instructs:

> The happy pair should not return home [after the wedding]. On leaving the church they should for a time – a honey-moon – leave the neighbourhood. She, as bride, is the object of the utmost interest; it is desirable that she should be removed from the observation of her circle ... Such a course is particularly acceptable to female modesty, and adds fresh charms to the delights of connubial bliss.[37]

Like most celebrations of modesty, this passage suggests knowledge of its opposite: that from which in order to qualify as modesty, modesty withdraws. What are we to imagine the friends and relatives would see were the bride to remain under their "observation"? And indeed, the calculus of the passage withdrawal not only takes away; it gives back with interest. Withdrawal not only promotes modesty but "adds fresh charms to the delights of connubial bliss." Bliss accumulates as "fresh charms"

[36] *The Etiquette of Love, Courtship, and Marriage* (London: Simpkin, Marshall, & Co., 1847), p. 77.
[37] A Lady, *A Manual of the Etiquette of Love, Courtship, and Marriage by a Lady* (London: Thomas Allman, 1852), pt. 3, p. 11.

and "delights" are added to it: the retreat from the public gaze into the private space of the honeymoon provides a veritable explosion of erotic rewards. The accretive calculus of female modesty is also hinted at in a passage with a very similar structure from another book: "[The honeymoon] is a practice which is highly consistent with female modesty, and we may add gives relish to connubial bliss."[38] Here "fresh charms" become perhaps more enticingly but no less obliquely "relish," while the coy "we might add" gestures once again to the accretive while suggesting stores of information and delight beyond the power of the author – or perhaps the genre of the conduct book – to specify.

Again the honeymoon puts pressure on language. Just before this particular manual says, simply enough, "[T]he place of your visit, and the length of time you devote to this happy occasion, must be dictated according to your own pleasure," it gives a spectacularly tangled justification for the practice of honeymooning:

A few weeks recreation is highly necessary as a relaxation of the mind after the *tedious anxieties and appliances of courtship*. No one can pass through the routine of courtship without great anxiety of mind. The subject is an absorbing one, and what absorbs the mind, generally affects the health. The bridal morn may disperse that feeling, but *the wedding tour will give fresh stamina to the mental structure, and an impetus to its operations*.[39]

If we can derive any meaning from this overwrought passage, it is that the honeymoon functions as a period of recovery from courtship. Courtship in this passage is portrayed, perhaps counterintuitively, as a period not of excitement but of tedium. Recovery in this one instance, then, seems to take the uncharacteristic Victorian form of an excitement and energy, as the "fresh stamina" of the final sentence might suggest. Again, while we would not necessarily look for good prose in a conduct book, the topic of honeymoons produces some of the most tangled sentences in this otherwise vanilla genre.

We have already considered the tension in the honeymoon journey between privacy and publicity, invisibility and display. Writing in 1866, one conduct book author argued that the time for an extreme form of privacy for honeymooners had already passed:

Formerly it used to be kept a profound secret where the happy pair intended passing the first few weeks of married life, and their whereabout [*sic*] was supposed to be announced by the first letter the bride sent to her mother. But as that

---

[38] *Etiquette of Love, Courtship, and Marriage*, p. 80. [39] *Ibid.*, p. 81 (italics mine).

Table 1. *Recommended honeymoon destinations*

Month	Short Tour	Long Tour
January	Torquay, South Devon	Nice, Mentone, Pau, Cannes, any part of the South of France
February	Hastings, St. Leonard's	ditto
March	Bournemouth	Rome, etc.
April	Paris	Venice, Florence, Naples, etc.
May	Brussels and a few Belgian towns	Channel Islands and Britanny
June	North Wales	The Tyrol
July	English Lakes, Cumberland, etc.	Chamoni [*sic*] and any part of Switzerland
August	Scarboro', Whitby	Scotland
September	Holland and up the Rhine	The tour of the Italian Lakes
October	North Devon	Lakes of Killarney
November	Brighton	Alexandria, Cairo, Pyramids, Nile, etc.
December	Ventor, Bonchurch	ditto

Note: Adapted from *Warne's Book of Courtship and Marriage* (London, 1886)

good lady had arranged the tour with her daughter some weeks beforehand, fiction was so transparent that the custom gradually fell into disuse, and it is now a common thing for the parties in question not only to state where they are going but to ask the advice of their friends and acquaintances as to the various places suitable for such trips.[40]

This passage suggests the presence of a community of honeymooners and potential honeymooners extending advice to each other. And indeed, I can identify several such communities or circles among my sample couples: Jonathan Abbatt relied on the positive experiences of a cousin who had taken a honeymoon in the Lake District for advice about the best place to lodge on his own wedding journey, while two of the three married Lyttelton sisters had almost identical honeymoon itineraries.

While there are not many published sources that dispense advice about honeymoon destinations, *Warne's Book of Courtship and Marriage* includes a useful chart with recommendations for "short" and "long" tours according to the month of the year (Table 1). Both the short and long tours might seem extensive to modern readers: "short" in this case means two to four weeks, while "long" means one to three months. Short tours, not surprisingly, emphasize domestic travel to the Lake District and to Wales in the summer and fall and to the English seaside in the winter.

[40] *Warne's Book of Courtship and Marriage* (London: Bijou, 1866), p. 186.

Short tours also include journeys to Paris (recommended, canonically, for April) and to Holland, the Rhine, and Belgium. Longer tours include sojourns in the south of France for the winter, Rome in March, and Egypt in November and December. When we get to the actual tourists of the sample we will see a preference for midlength continental tours and especially for journeys to France, Italy, and Switzerland.

Warne's also recommends against trying to see or do too much:

If you have but a few weeks to spare, we should recommend a trip into the country, or some quiet sea-side resort. If time is no object, doubtless a trip on the Continent will present many attractions; but even in that case, we should advise a sojourn at Dover, or whatever may be the port of embarkation, for a few days, and the selection of a fine day for crossing the channel. Above all things, avoid hurry and bustle, tearing from one place to another, and seeing all you possibly can in the time. Make up your mind if you cannot see anything comfortably, not to see it at all.[41]

Certainly, some of this advice – choosing a good crossing day and avoiding cramming in the sights of Europe – can be found in tourist manuals for more general audiences. The emphasis on quiet and on lingering at ports is, however, less pronounced in tourist guides and seems to be especially directed to the specific requirements of honeymoon travel.

The conduct sources are not explicit about whose responsibility it is to decide on a destination. Earlier, we have seen that one source imagined conversations between a bride and her mother; others seem to imply it is the decision of the groom. In my sample I found only three instances of what we might call honeymoon planning; perhaps most of this sort of thing was done in person. Jonathan Abbatt's letters to his fiancée, Mary Dilworth, suggest that he seems to have made the arrangements. He has talked with a friend, David Wilkinson, who suggested "engaging private lodging" "instead of lodging at an Inn." Wilkinson provided the name of the lodging house where Jonathan's cousins, the Jacksons, stayed, as well as a guide to the lakes. Jonathan ends the description of these plans with what may be a pro forma appeal for Mary's approval: "These plans meet my view so nicely yet if thou has any other plan to propose nothing will give me more pleasure than to fall in with it."[42] Agnes Bowers and Arthur Thorndike seem to have disagreed about the itinerary for the journey and about how isolated a honeymoon was supposed to be. I discuss their

---

[41] *Ibid.*, p. 82.
[42] John Dilworth Abbatt (ed.), *A Quaker Victorian Courtship: Lancashire Love Letters of the 1850s* (York: William Sessions, 1988), p. 232.

negotiations in more detail in the context of conjugality in Chapter 2. Ernest Roberts and May Harper apparently disagreed entirely about where to spend their honeymoon. May reported in her memoirs that she would have preferred Switzerland, while Ernest wanted to visit his aunt in Romania. They compromised by visiting Switzerland on the way back from Romania. In retrospect, May pronounced this decision "ill-advised"; she felt exhausted by all the travel and became too ill to enjoy Switzerland.[43] The persistence of May's desire to be in Switzerland (where her courtship with Ernest began) comes through in her frequent comparisons between Romania and Switzerland; a hotel in the Carpathian Mountains, for example, is approvingly described as being "like a comfortable Swiss hotel."[44]

Although the destination of a honeymoon might have been decided by either party or by both, several sources are quite clear that the exact timing of the wedding and thus of the honeymoon is up to the bride: as one book puts it, "[I]t is the lady's express privilege to fix the exact day."[45] Pat Jalland makes the interesting suggestion that this tradition might have its roots in the bride's desire to plan the honeymoon around her menstrual cycle for purposes of contraception or convenience.[46] Certainly, pregnancy – intended or not – would be an issue facing brides in planning and carrying out their honeymoon, and the bride's bodily calendar might, along with the calendar of the social and touristic seasons, be taken into account.

I can find relatively little advice on the conduct of the honeymoon itself in books of general advice. David Bogue offers the most detailed suggestions for the time following the wedding ceremony; arranged chronologically, this book's "hints" become vaguer as the wedding night approaches. In a short section entitled "Etiquette after the Wedding," the book takes on in some awkward detail the logistics of the couple's dressing for dinner: "The lady, at the proper period, retires to her apartment, and having taken sufficient time for her evening toilette, directs the chambermaid to inform her husband that his apartments are ready."[47] While this advice might seem to displace the need for information from the wedding night to an earlier period in the evening, this

---

[43] Mrs. E. S. Roberts, *Sherborne, Oxford, and Cambridge: Recollections of Mrs. Ernest Stewart Roberts* (London: Martin Hopkinson, 1934), p. 135.
[44] *Ibid.*, p. 128.   [45] Bogue, *Complete Guide*, p. 47.
[46] Patricia Jalland, *Women, Marriage, and Politics, 1860–1914* (New York: Oxford University Press, 1986), p. 36.
[47] Bogue, *Complete Guide*, p. 82.

passage comes as close as conduct books can do to providing reassurance, ritual, and order at an anxious time. Clearly, at this stage the husband and wife are imagined to be dressing separately; this might, especially before the expected sexual activities of the wedding night, have been a matter of some anxiety to a bride seeking guidance about physical intimacy. Like many conduct books, however, the use of the word "proper," as in "proper time," begs what might well have been anxious questions about etiquette: in this case about timing and propriety. "Proper time," read anxiously, might also seem to hint at deferral of sexual intimacy.

We can read for another displacement later on in this book in a section entitled "Dress of the Bride in [*sic*] the Honeymoon," where the reader is admonished that "the bride's apparel should be characterized by modesty, simplicity, and neatness. The slightest approach to slatternliness in costume – even a stray curl – not to say a visible curl-paper – would be an abomination, and assuredly stand in the future memory of the shuddering husband."[48] While I have so far tried to resist overly eroticized or psychodynamic readings, this passage, in my judgment, cries out to be read for its latent content. Like the odd passage about dressing for dinner, this one can be read as a substitution of rules about dress for unspeakable rules about undress. The word "slatternliness," also awkward enough to draw attention to itself, bridges the domains of fashion and sexuality, while the abominable "curl" also can be read in terms of what Freud would call "displacement upward." The overwrought tone of the passage – words like "abomination" and "shuddering" – points to a different and perhaps more profound version of honeymoon shock. I insist on reading for and through euphemism here because of the generic limits of advice literature; the passage here seems to be visibly struggling with these limits. These struggles may or may not be conscious on the part of the author; suffice it to say that the very topic of the wedding night produces in this book, as in others, a disturbance on the level of the writing. Victorian readers, actual women and men looking to this or other books for advice, would, I think, have absorbed not so much any specific information as a general sense of danger and of warning.

Part of the monitory structure of the preceding passage is, of course, that of metonymy, where omissions or bad behavior during the honeymoon are imagined as persisting, and perhaps increasing in effect, during marriage. The "shuddering husband" facing his slatternly wife will fix in his "future memory" (itself an interesting and somewhat ominous term)

---

[48] *Ibid.*, p. 84.

the image of the careless curl glimpsed on the wedding night. Other advice books agree that experiences during the honeymoon take on a disproportionate importance. The Countess of Blessington, for example, in her discussion of the honeymoon, contrasts the "magic mirror" of courtship where faults are overlooked or minimized to the "magnifying glass [that] seems to supply its place" in the period immediately after marriage.[49]

While many writers warn of the pitfalls of the honeymoon, including jealousy on the part of the husband, the most commonly named problem is the structure of conjugality itself. Some conduct book writers warn that couples might get bored with each other's exclusive company. The *Daily News* correspondent who finds himself among honeymooners at the Lakes boasts that he has found the solution to "living luxuriously" on "next to nothing a week": living off honeymooning couples who need distraction from each other.

A few days ago I was a lonely pedestrian, toiling along with a knapsack and staff, and regarded with suspicion by hotel waiters ... Now I am the centre and sun of a pleasant and fashionable circle, overwhelmed with invitations to drives, and dinners, and boating excursions, and having an altogether beautiful time of it at no cost. Sir, the secret of my transformation is simply this – I wandered by accident into a neighbourhood that is largely affected by newly-married couples. There are many such districts in England, and there are particular hotels, indeed, to which these young people invariably go; so that any one who wishes to follow my example may make the experiment elsewhere. All that is necessary is that you should be a modest and moderately amusing young fellow ... When you once get among these honey-moon people, they positively get hold of you and devour you. They have got so frightfully tired of the business of walking hand-in-hand, and looking at the moon, and saying nothing, that a human being who can start the most trivial subject of talk, or make the poorest of jokes, or do anything to relieve the frightful monotony experienced by the disconsolate couples, is a perfect godsend to them.[50]

The article ends with a recommended calendar and itinerary for this sort of honeymoon sponging; the correspondent claims he will plan future holidays around the peak honeymoon season – March and April – at Dover, Hastings, and Brighton, which "are very good for this sort of thing."

While the *Daily News* correspondent sees himself as being of equal help to both husband and wife, elsewhere honeymoon boredom has a gendered component. The Countess of Blessington includes in an advice

[49] Marguerite, Countess of Blessington (ed.), *Heath's Book of Beauty* (London: Longman, 1837), p. 189.
[50] Viator, "Travelling Scot-Free."

book about courtship an extended parable of two honeymooners, where it is clear that the pressures of honeymoon conjugality result in the feminization of the bridegroom. Her male protagonist, Henri, complains that he is "shut up in this retirement, away from all my occupations and amusements, leading very nearly as effeminate a life as Achilles at Syros, devoting all my time to Hermance" and longs for "a gallop, a day's hunting, or shooting; in short for any manly amusement to be partaken of with some of his former companions."[51] A similar note is struck in a *Punch* cartoon from 1862 in which the honeymooning William is overheard addressing his pipe, not his wife, as "beloved." "What a dreadful slow place the Sea-side would be," he says, "if a Fellow hadn't his Birdseye to fall back upon!" (Fig. 2). When we begin to look at some real-life honeymooners from my sample, we will find again that time can hang heavy, particularly for men who without work or male companions can become, as in the case of the Rolls-Macready or the Hotzapfel-Boycott honeymoon, merely fetchers of their wife's mail.

HONEYMOON CASES

The information about real-life honeymoons depends largely on case studies of sixty-one newly married couples whose wedding dates ranged from 1829 to 1898, with most of them taking place in the '50s, '60s, and '70s. These make up the sample from which I draw conclusions about, for example, the most typical honeymoon destinations, the duration of the average honeymoon, and the presence or absence of family members on the journey. I identified couples for my sample in a variety of different ways: through indexes to archives where it seemed that I might find letters or diaries by engaged or newly married men and women, by reading through biographies and family papers, and by soliciting suggestions from colleagues about Victorian honeymoons they had run across in their reading. These three strategies clearly skew the results of my study toward middle- and upper-middle-class couples whose family papers were deemed worth preserving, toward people who at one point achieved a certain degree of fame, and toward couples whose honeymoons have some sort of narrative interest. I explore these limitations in more detail below.

Although I did not initially set out to limit my sample to honeymooning couples, almost every couple for whom I could find a wedding date did, in fact, choose to go on a journey away from home immediately

[51] Blessington, *Heath's Book*, p. 197.

THE HONEYMOON.

WILLIAM (and who promised so faithfully to give it up, too!) "Oh! my beloved!"—"Now for a pretty speech," thinks she)—"Pipe! What a dreadful slow place the Sea-side would be, Duckey, if a Feller hadn't his Birdseye to fall back upon!"

Fig. 2 "The Honeymoon." Cartoon from *Punch*, 7 June 1862.

after the wedding. In the process of my research, always limited by the structural problems noted above, I have only come across two couples who did not travel for some period of time, however short. This speaks to me of the ubiquity of the honeymoon by mid-century for the middle- and upper-middle-class people who mostly, but not exclusively, make up my sample, although, of course, place and distance were adapted to the means and the leisure of the couples. Defining the limits of a honeymoon sometimes proved difficult: while most of my couples returned from an easily identifiable journey to set up their own home, others – for example, the Tennysons – moved among the houses of friends while they were searching for a house they could rent or buy. I have chosen in almost all cases to mark the end of the honeymoon with the couple's establishment in a house they define, however briefly they may live in it, as their first house together. The exceptions to this general rule are the few couples I discuss below, who take two honeymoon trips; in these cases it is the second, longer one I use to calculate honeymoon length.

The sources for my information about the couples range from published materials, including biographies or published memoirs or letters, to unpublished diaries and letters unearthed in various libraries and record offices in England, Wales, and, rarely, the United States. Where possible, I have consulted primary sources, even if the initial information came to me from published material. I owe much, however, to secondary sources, particularly to a number of recently published family studies that focus either synchronically on a group of sisters or female relatives or dia-chronically on several generations of a particular family.[52]

The search for primary sources has led me to what I now think of as a specific genre: the honeymoon diary or journal. With strong ties to and at times indistinguishable from the travel diary, the honeymoon diary mediates in a range of ways between personal and geographic or touristic concerns. At one end of the spectrum are honeymoon diaries like the one kept by Henry Campbell-Bannerman, whose description of his European honeymoon in 1860 is virtually indistinguishable from his European travel journals from the surrounding years. In the diary describing his honeymoon tour, his wife is mentioned, and then only by her initials, a

---

[52] Some excellent examples of this genre are Peterson, *Family, Love, and Work* (n. 29); Jalland, *Women, Marriage, and Politics* (n. 46); Sheila Fletcher, *Victorian Girls: Lord Lyttelton's Daughters* (London: Hambelton, 1997); Ina Taylor, *Victorian Sisters* (London: Weidenfeld and Nicolson, 1987); Martha Westwater, *The Wilson Sisters: A Biographical Study of Upper-Middle-Class Victorian Life* (Athens: Ohio University Press, 1984); and Barbara Caine, *Destined to Be Wives: The Sisters of Beatrice Webb* (New York: Oxford University Press, 1988).

total of two times. At the other end of the spectrum are journals like
Martha Rolls Macready's, begun a month into a four-month honeymoon
to the seaside resort of Littlehampton, in which her husband and her new
position as wife are topics regularly revisited, and indeed they inform the
vast majority of her entries.[53]

In analyzing the tone of any particular honeymoon diary, we come up
against two linked generic issues: the audience to whom it was addressed
and the broader issue of the place of diaries in general and the honeymoon diary in particular in a larger history of privacy and individuality. I
will deal with the second, more general topic first. Historians have linked
the diary or the journal to a crucial if gradual historical shift in emphasis
toward the importance of the individual. The idea of the diary as a
repository of private thoughts is a relatively modern one, dependent on
the importance of private thoughts to the construction of the individual
self. Diaries, especially but not exclusively those published or circulated,
have always, of course, negotiated the realms of private and public. Some
would argue that all diaries, even those that the writer has taken great care
to keep hidden from others, have a component of publicity as they
articulate for an imagined audience the most secret of events and opinions. Publicity and privacy get even more entangled in one another
when we take the example of the hidden diary later discovered, read, and
perhaps published by a friend, relative, or editor. If diaries in general
evoke but do not perfectly embody an ideal of private life, diaries written
during the honeymoon might raise elaborate expectations of privacy and
secrecy. This might be particularly true of Victorian honeymoon diaries,
written as they were during a period (however problematically) associated
with prudery, repression, and sexual ignorance.

While I spend some time in Chapter 3 discussing the expectations
raised – at least for this reader – by the genre of the honeymoon diary and
the carnal knowledge it seems to promise both writer and reader, I will
simply stress here that the actual diaries, despite that generic titillation,
often raise as many questions as they answer. This has much to do, of

---

[53] In thinking about the differences in degree of intimacy in the various texts, I thought at one point
that it might have something to do with whether that text was called a diary or a journal. While it
does seem that "diary" could refer to what we now might call a day planner or date book, with
preprinted dates and relatively little room to write under each, "diary" was also sometimes used by
people in my sample to describe something more expansive. The distinction between the two
terms is further complicated by cases like that of Margaret King, who used a preprinted date book
but ignored the dates, filling every page with tiny handwriting and a continuous narrative. I have
chosen "diary" – aware of the slight anachronism – as the default term because of the hermeneutic
expectations it raises in many contemporary readers.

course, with complicated Victorian ideas about sexuality, gender, and writing. We might also, for the purposes of this chapter, however, think of the choices made by the writers of these diaries in terms of their assumed audience.

It is, of course, almost impossible to deduce to what extent the diaries were seen as private to the writer and to what extent they were shared, either with the traveling spouse or with other family members on or before the couple's return. Some diaries include internal evidence of shared reading, the most obvious of which is the 1863 diary of Mary Hardcastle Collier (Lady Monkswell) of her honeymoon trip to Switzerland and Rome, where her description of the wedding day is interrupted by a brief passage written by her husband in which he playfully supplements his wife's description of a young guest's poking of Mary's ex-governess with an umbrella. Mary's diary describes the incident: "My dear old Miss Pyman I believe wept a little behind her handkerchief. She was much ill-treated by Thomas Usborne before I arrived; – he had been there some time & was getting rather bored, so he took to poking her with his umbrella between the rails!" Mary's bridegroom, Robert Collier, intervenes: "Ribs she means. Bob (that's me) happened to be looking on from his position close to the altar where he had been standing for some time trying to look unconcerned." Diaries could also be shared after their composition as part of the growing intimacy of the honeymoon: a week into their wedding journey, and after a long talk in which her husband, John, had shared his professional ambitions with her, Margaret King Gladstone offered to share her very intimate journal that included descriptions of her feelings during courtship. The episode proved to be a difficult one:

> Set free a rabbit in a trap. After tea showed J my poems & journal. Like him to know all. He did not read it but advised me not to burn it. Showed him also the printed reviews I wrote long ago & tore up one. He had really wished me not. I thought we were both in fun, & was very sorry, but we only found out how well we loved one another, & I was happier than ever before.[54]

While it is unclear why John declined to read Margaret's journal, her impulse in giving it to him seems clearly to have had much to do with her sense of what constituted intimacy and knowledge of each other. This trope of intimate knowledge is, of course, central to ideas of conjugality. Like many of Margaret's journal entries, this one begins with a

---

[54] Margaret King Gladstone, entry for 21 July 1869, Ms. diary, 1869, Papers of the King and Thomson Families, 1833–1914, PRO 30/69/852.

misunderstanding that, in its working through, deepens – at least according to her – the degree of intimacy between herself and John and thus her own happiness. The refusal to know on John's part leads, then, to greater knowledge, and the aborted gesture of shared reading becomes an important movement toward conjugality.

Some diaries I have found show more subtle traces of conjugal discussion or influence: while I have unfortunately been unable to find a diary by Charlotte Bruce Campbell-Bannerman describing her honeymoon in 1860, and thus cannot compare it with her husband's, both diaries are extant for their trip to the same location the following year. In her diary for 1861, Charley notes her husband Henry's corrections to her identifications of works of art on several occasions; it seems also that he has made some corrections and additions in his own hand. We could speculate, then, that the Campbell-Bannermans might have shared their written accounts of their honeymoon. My case studies include only one example of parallel honeymoon accounts in diaries: those of Francis and Eliza Wemyss discussed earlier in this chapter. We do not know if Francis and Eliza shared their diaries and if he read or otherwise came to know her views on sexual initiation for women.

Diaries could also vary widely in how they were used. Those least attentive to the specifics of the honeymoon as a scene of writing are by Richard Cobden, Henry Campbell-Bannerman, and (perhaps surprisingly, given her reputation for sentimentality) Emma Gifford Hardy. Cobden's letters to his brother at the time of his wedding journey read very differently from the dry factual accounts of his diary; his wife, Kate (the former Catherine Williams), is mentioned in his correspondence at every turn, the subject of admiring jokes about her adventurous spirit. Perhaps he and Campbell-Bannerman, both active in public life, saw and used their diaries differently than did women like Martha Macready: perhaps they understood the diary as a source of information, a resource for more public writings. Emma Hardy's diary is exceptional in many ways, not the least for its meticulous accounting of everyday life in France, down to details of costume, nature, and cookery that make encounters with French otherness the central concern of the piece. Honeymoon diaries written as part of a series and often bound in the same volume tend, by and large, to be more impersonal, or at least to feature the fact of honeymooning less conspicuously. The exception is the case of Julianna Taylor Fuller, whose three extant diaries, including one kept during her honeymoon, are part of the same volume, but whose honeymoon diary is marked off by photographs and intertwined locks of hair.

Another primary source for honeymoon experiences is, of course, the correspondence between honeymooners and their families. Again, it is rare to find a perfect set of materials in which both diary and letters are extant. Martha Macready's case is particularly frustrating: while she records numerous letters to her mother in her diary, I have not been able to find them. The letters might have been especially interesting given that the diary is full of references to secrets, some of which seem to have been shared by her mother. Some of Martha's diary entries *only* note that she wrote to her mother; it would be interesting to see what she found worth mentioning to her mother that she did not record in the diary. In general, the tone of letters and diary entries can be quite different; while we tend to think of diaries as the more private and thus more intimate form, this was not always the case: as I have already noted, Cobden's letters are more intimate and informal than his diary, as are Matthew Arnold's. (Part of the discrepancy might be accounted for by the wide variety of documents included under the rubric of journal or diary and how the writers imagined the genre.)

Again, the record of shared reading is tantalizing but imperfect. The most obvious example of letters shared by both members of a couple is the case of Margaret Gladstone MacDonald. A letter of congratulation on her engagement from a female friend is full of questions about how Margaret met Ramsey and what he is like: both Margaret and Ramsey have annotated the letter by answering the questions in different ink. It is hard to tell when Ramsey read this letter, whether his answers came before or after the marriage, and whether the answers were communicated in any way to Margaret's friend.[55] A somewhat similar example is a letter written to both of them during the honeymoon, in which two female friends of Margaret write alternating sentences and comment on each other's words.[56]

Although my search for letters and diaries written during the honeymoon has yielded a relatively rich archive, the research for this project has always come up against the problem of sufficiency of evidence, particularly about the sexual issues that are in many ways the center of the cultural master narrative of the honeymoon. Sexual advice is very scarce; I have come across only one explicit example, and that at second hand. Allusions to sexual activity are scarcely more numerous. While this

[55] E. Johnson to Margaret MacDonald, 23 July 1896, correspondence of Margaret Ethel MacDonald, PRO 20/69/887.

[56] Letter to Margaret and Ramsey MacDonald, 26 November 1896, correspondence of Margaret Ethel MacDonald, PRO 20/69/887.

paucity of references to the sexual was sometimes extremely frustrating, it helped direct me to larger issues of context: sex was, of course, an important, indeed a definitional part of the honeymoon, but the trans- formations implied by the assumed single act of sexual consummation must really have been far more diffuse than an erotocentric narrative of the honeymoon might suggest: new husbands and wives had to negotiate a variety of new experiences, sights, and ideas, and they have much to say about many of them. I have tried to be open to these experiences in their variety and contradiction.

It is difficult to say how representative the couples in my sample are of honeymooning or newly married couples in general. Part of the problem is, of course, the relative scarcity of material for "ordinary" couples, although, as I discuss below, "ordinary" and its corollary "exceptional" are slippery terms at best. One dimension of ordinariness is social class – and certainly my sample is skewed toward middle- and upper-middle- class couples. This issue is particularly crucial since honeymooning has been seen by most scholars as an activity limited to the upper and upper- middle classes. As I mention earlier, however, I am convinced that by the 1870s honeymoons were popular and, indeed, an expected part of the extended ritual of courtship and marriage for many sections of the lower-middle and working classes as well. It is difficult to categorize many of my couples according to class, particularly in the case of interclass marriages. It is perhaps easiest, although by no means completely satis- factory, to categorize the couples according to the occupations of the husband. This is most overtly a problem in the cases of the two profes- sional women in my sample, Elizabeth Stevenson Gaskell and Charlotte Brontë Nicholls, who are as a result of this male-oriented definition classified under "Clergy" rather than "Professional/Intellectual," but if I err it is only in following the example of Victorian ideas of marital identification.

The more general move from class to occupation allows for a more concrete set of definiteness: the men in my couples are defined in terms of what they do for a living at the time of their honeymoons, and not in terms of their own sometimes contradictory class identifications. I have chosen to focus on occupation at the time of the honeymoon, although, of course, arguments can be made that several of the younger men in this sample were preparing for very different careers whose imagined trajec- tories, even at that early moment, were more influential with respect to their sense of place in the world than their day-to-day occupations at the time. My categories are, however, capacious enough to leave room for

Table 2. *Husbands' occupations at the time of the honeymoon*

	%
Merchant/Business	15
Professional/Intellectual	44
Military	5
Clergy	16
Politician	11
Clerk	3
Landowner	3
Unknown	3

growth within them: thus I do not have to decide between, to choose a literary example, Matthew Arnold the school inspector and Matthew Arnold the poet, even though at the time of his honeymoon Arnold had not published very much. He is entered under "Professional/Intellectual." Perhaps the hardest case to adjudicate is a common one: professionals (usually barristers) who later in life became politicians. Here I have not confined myself to members of Parliament but have used my judgment to determine which bridegrooms were politically involved at the time of the marriage. John Talbot, for example, became an MP in the late sixties but was not interested in politics as far as I can see when he married in 1860. He is classified under "Landowner." Robert Collier was a working barrister, but he was already very interested in politics. While several of the male honeymooners inherited or were granted a title after the honeymoon, no one was actually titled at the time of the honeymoon.

Several of my categories cover a multitude of possibilities in terms of class and success: of the two clerks, William Halsey became an assistant to his father-in-law in India, while David Holt was in the office of the Manchester and Leeds Railway. I do not count Coventry Patmore under "Clerk," although he earned his money as a clerk in the British Library, because he was already a published poet and it was this identity that got him the job.[57] "Clergy" covers the spectrum from eventual bishop (Mandell Creighton) to curate (Arthur Nicholls). With these caveats, see Table 2 for an occupational breakdown of my sample.

[57] See Sister Mary Anthony Weinig, *Coventry Patmore* (Boston: Twayne, 1981), who explains that Mockton Miles saw Patmore's *Poems* and, as a result, "secured for him a post in the library of the British Museum" (p. 16).

The focus on occupation should not completely obscure the question of class or wealth. Of my sample, only five are perhaps not genteel: four couples who were part of a family of Lancashire Quaker merchants and businessmen (the Abbatts, Dilworths, and Jacksons), whose occupations ranged from shoemaker to printer, and the Holts (David was a railway clerk).

Another dimension of representativeness, and of the tension between ordinariness and exceptionality, has to do with the talents, the fame, and, indeed, the self-definitions with respect to these categories of one or both members of the couples. Certainly, in about half the cases in my sample, one or sometimes both members of the couple are known to history as famous authors, politicians, or scientists. Some members of my case study saw themselves as exceptional in terms of their talent and/or social position. Two factors mitigate against even the best known of these being too exceptional to be relevant to a study of honeymooning. First, many honeymooners who were later to become famous and successful were married before or soon after their first taste of success. The honeymooning Matthew Arnold had just accepted a job as a school inspector; he had not yet published the vast majority of the poems for which he would become famous. Leslie Stephen was not yet the cultural icon he was to become: he was known, if at all, as an occasional journalist and a mountaineer. William Thackeray was, at the time of his honeymoon, a struggling journalist for an obscure and (ill-fated) newspaper. Anthony Trollope and Thomas Hardy were published but were at the very beginning of their novelistic careers. Henry Campbell-Bannerman was years away from prominence in parliament. George Meredith was less successful as a writer than was his bride, Mary Ellen Nicolls, and had so far published only one poem. The exception to this rule is Alfred Tennyson, who, partly because of the length of his off-and-on engagement (ten years), was at the peak of his career on his long honeymoon, during which he arranged for publication of *In Memoriam* and was appointed poet laureate. (His wife, Emily, might be hinting either at the problem of fame or the problem of honeymoon embarrassment when she notes with relief that passersby bowed respectfully and kept out of their way.)

Ordinariness also had, of course, a gendered component. By and large, the wives of the men who were to become, or were in the process of becoming, famous saw themselves as ordinary women, both because, with one or two exceptions, they had no career ambitions beyond marriage or because they saw "ordinary" and "woman," or "ordinary" and "married woman," as synonymous terms. In some cases either the man or the woman of a given couple spent some considerable energy defending the ordinariness of the woman in question. Leslie Stephen insisted that his wife, Minnie, daughter of William Thackeray and sister of the writer Annie Thackeray, was not like her sister in being an intellectual or a bluestocking. Some women became more "ordinary" with marriage; Georgie Macdonald, who numbered among her and her husband's few financial assets her engraving tools, stopped using them soon after she and Edward Burne-Jones married.

A final way of looking at the question of fame is to see how many of these individuals are known to posterity. Of all the people in my sample, thirty-six receive an individual mention in the *Dictionary of National Biography*, twenty-three have an entry for their families (I have only counted ancestors and not descendants), and sixty-three are not mentioned. Ironically, family and not individual mentions are probably a better guide to some general sense of prominence at the time of the honeymoon.

I have identified three typical honeymoon journeys associated loosely with different classes and different relations to leisure. The first, largely for very wealthy and/or aristocratic honeymooners, or for those with wealthy or aristocratic friends, involved borrowing the home of a friend or family member. The second, for relatively wealthy couples, involved a trip to the Continent lasting, usually, at least a month. While, depending on inclination and economics, this journey could be cut short, the ideal itinerary seemed to involve a trip from Dover to Calais or some other French port; some time in Paris for sightseeing and shopping; a journey through Switzerland, often involving hiking, donkey riding, and other mountain sports differently experienced, as we shall see, according to gender; and, finally, time in Italy, culminating in a visit to Rome. The third canonical journey was shorter in terms of distance and often, but not always, in terms of time. This was a form of domestic honeymoon tourism, often to the English seaside or to the Lake District. Honeymoons like this could be weekend affairs, as they were for Arthur Hughes and Molly Thomas Hughes, or they could last for months, as in the case of Martha and Edward Macready. Clearly, this could be a cheaper honeymoon more tailored to the lives of men with regular, less flexible, jobs. This form of honeymooning was also sometimes a form of balneary or curative tourism, where one or both members of the couple took advantage of the sea or other natural resources in an attempt to improve a chronic physical condition. There are, of course, honeymoons that fall outside these three rubrics, but they do cover the vast majority of cases in my sample. While none from my sample went to Belgium or Egypt, these

Table 3. *Honeymoon destinations*

	%
Domestic only	56
Domestic & Continental	13
Continental only	26
Other	3
Unknown	2

journeys are to some extent reflected in the chart of ideal honeymoons (Table 1).

If no one went as far as Egypt, quite a few couples from my sample (twenty-four) traveled to the Continent. If we categorize the continental honeymoons by their farthest point, six went to Paris, one to Grenoble, five to Rome, four to Switzerland, three to the Rhineland/Black Forest, one to North Italy, one to Vienna (via Rome), and one as far as Romania, visiting Rome on the way. (Two continental honeymoons are unspecific with regard to location.) This means that almost all of the continental honeymooners, as far as I can tell, stayed in Paris; at least thirteen and as many as fifteen of the ones whose itinerary we know something about went to or through Switzerland. Seven went at least to Rome.

Thirty-four of the couples in my sample honeymooned only in the United Kingdom, including Ireland. Forty-two couples spent some honeymoon time domestically. Six spent at least part of their honeymoons in ancestral homes in England. Of those who did not spend time in ancestral homes (thirty-six), eighteen went primarily to the seaside and eighteen stayed inland. (For the purposes of this reckoning, unspecified journeys to Scotland are counted as inland since there were few seaside resorts in Scotland, even at the end of the century.) Five of the inland couples went to the Lakes and thirteen took trips to other inland destinations such as Leamington Spa. Seaside honeymoons took place at resorts big and small up and down the seaside on both coasts from Torquay to Folkestone, although most couples stayed south of London. I characterize two honeymoon destinations as "other": the Dickinson/Wemyss honeymoon that began in Bombay and the Thackeray/Shaw honeymoon that began in Paris and ended in its suburbs. There is one honeymoon in my sample for which I have not been able to locate a destination (see Table 3, and Maps 1 and 2).

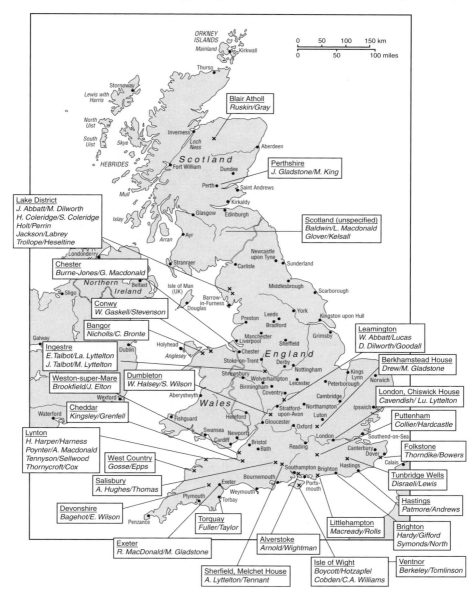

Map 1 British honeymoon destinations listed according to longest known stay.

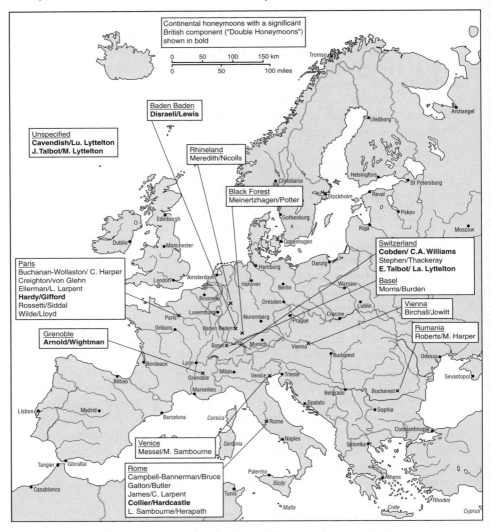

Continental honeymoons with a significant
British component ("Double Honeymoons")
shown in bold

0   50   100   150 km
0   50   100 miles

Baden Baden
Disraeli/Lewis

Unspecified
Cavendish/Lu. Lyttelton
J.Talbot/M. Lyttelton

Rhineland
Meredith/Nicolls

Black Forest
Meinertzhagen/Potter

Paris
Buchanan-Wollaston/ C. Harper
Creighton/von Glehn
Ellerman/L. Larpent
Hardy/Gifford
Rossetti/Siddal
Wilde/Lloyd

Switzerland
Cobden/ C.A. Williams
Stephen/Thackeray
E. Talbot/ La. Lyttelton

Basel
Morris/Burden

Vienna
Birchall/Jowitt

Grenoble
Arnold/Wightman

Rumania
Roberts/M. Harper

Venice
Messel/M. Sambourne

Rome
Campbell-Bannerman/Bruce
Galton/Butler
James/C. Larpent
Collier/Hardcastle
L. Sambourne/Herapath

Map 2 Continental honeymoon destinations listed according to furthest point.

Several of my honeymooners took a double honeymoon: the first usually shorter and domestic, followed by a longer one – usually to a more distant place. The Arnolds' week-long honeymoon to Alderstoke was followed by a second month-long trip to Paris and Switzerland. Charlotte Brontë and Arthur Nicholls visited Cornwall and then went on to Ireland to visit relatives. The three Lyttelton sisters and their husbands lived out a tradition of double honeymoons associated with the wealthy: in each case they borrowed the house of an aristocratic connection for a short time, came back for a visit to their birth family, and then went to the Continent. Meriel and Lavinia borrowed the same house ten years apart: the first part of each sister's honeymoon was spent at Ingestre, the seat of Lord Shrewsbury. The socially prominent Colliers also borrowed a mansion before departing to the Continent. Margaret King took a double honeymoon for different reasons: she and John Gladstone spent the first ten days in Perthshire, returned to John's home for five days, and then departed with John's children from a previous marriage for a month-long holiday in the West Country. Another category with only two entries is the aborted honeymoon. The Burne-Joneses were supposed to go to Paris to join the Rossettis, but due to Ned's illness they stayed in Chester. Readers of this chapter will already be familiar with the aborted Ruskin journey.

Although some scholarship has suggested that Victorian honeymoons did not isolate the couple from their birth families as they typically do today, the majority of my couples (forty-three) honeymooned alone. Six used the honeymoon to visit their families, while six divided their honeymoon between an initial period alone together and time with family members. Martha and Edward Macready spent a month together at Littlehampton and were joined for a few weeks by Martha's mother, who left them together to complete their five-month honeymoon stay. The Boycotts were also joined by the bride's mother at the seaside, while the Jonathan Abbatts were joined by "friends" (probably relatives) after only one day in the Lakes. Relatives of Clarissa Larpent James joined the couple in France after the Jameses spent a four-month honeymoon à deux, while Lavinia Lyttelton Talbot's unmarried sister visited her in Switzerland toward the end of the honeymoon. Meriel Lyttelton Talbot spent part of her honeymoon alone with her husband in a borrowed house, then came home to her sisters before leaving for the Continent. As I noted above, Margaret King Gladstone and John Gladstone made two honeymoon trips – one with and one without John's children. The Harpers, who traveled further than anyone else in my sample, followed the canonical

Table 4. *Family presence during the honeymoon*

	%
No family	70
Meet family/friends	10
Stay with family	10
Unknown	10

honeymoon trail to Italy alone but visited the groom's aunt in Romania. I do not know the family situation of six couples (see Table 4).

The length of the honeymoon varied, of course, according to the means and leisure of the couples – this usually meant in practice the means and leisure of the groom. Honeymoons ranged from a weekend to nine months, with thirty-six out of sixty-one – more than half the sample – lasting one month or more. (Calculating honeymoon length can be tricky; I did not have enough information to discover the length of twelve honeymoons.) What this tells me is that the sample is biased toward the wealthy and that the ideal honeymoon of the period was probably two months long. Some bridegrooms, like Matthew Arnold, deferred long honeymoons until they were sure of a job; others like Coventry Patmore, Edmund Gosse, and David Holt may have deferred marriage until they were able to take a honeymoon. Even among less wealthy and/or less privileged people we have examples of substantial honeymoons. Several of the newlyweds in the Abbatt circle of Quaker merchants and shopkeepers took two-week honeymoons, while the wealthiest member of this group, George Glover, took a honeymoon that lasted two months. Printer David Dilworth, an Abbatt cousin, went for one week to Leamington, Warwick, and Stratford-upon-Avon (see Table 5).

It is interesting to speculate about sexuality and the honeymoon and also about the couples' reproductive futures. The records tell us something about how many couples conceived a child on the honeymoon. These calculations depend on the availability of certain kinds of information from honeymoon length to a family tree as well as on a list of limiting assumptions. Honeymoons must be fairly long to be able to make any kind of credible guess about conception. I am also ignoring the possibility of unrecorded miscarriages and assuming full-term births. With these caveats in mind, I find that eight women became pregnant on their honeymoons, thirty-one did not, four are probable, one unlikely, and two possible. In ten cases the honeymoons were too short to tell, and in five cases there is

Table 5. *Honeymoon length*

	%
Less than 1 week	3
1–2 weeks	13
2 weeks – 1 month	7
1–2 months	36
2 months +	23
Unknown	18

insufficient information to make any kind of calculation. Of the ten where the honeymoons were too short, there are several possible "yeses": Brontë/ Nicholls, Coleridge/Coleridge, Harper/Buchanan-Wollaston, Harper/ Roberts, King/Gladstone, Thomas/Hughes, Shaw/Thackeray, and von Glehn/Creighton. If we consider only honeymoons lasting more than two months, five out of thirteen became pregnant; one additional is possible. We have one recorded miscarriage (Mary Gladstone Drew), but it is difficult to say how far along in the pregnancy this took place. The consistently mysterious Martha Macready tantalizingly fainted in church, but the couple never had children, so if this were indeed a symptom of pregnancy in middle-aged Martha, it must have ended in a miscarriage (see Table 6).

HONEYMOON FICTIONS

Despite the centrality of the sample couples to my understanding of the honeymoon, this book is by no means exclusively a study of real-life honeymooners. In order to identify the cultural work expected of a honeymoon, one must also look at the honeymoon as an ideal operating in a variety of cultural contexts. Literature is one such context. I focus particularly closely on novels because so many of those written in this period can be defined as marriage-plot novels, in which the narrative is shaped by the quest of one or more pairs of heroes and heroines for a happy marriage. In the vast majority of these novels, a successful marriage ends the narrative; in an important minority, however, the story continues beyond the wedding. These are the novels that are by definition most interesting for the purposes of this project. I find that for this subset of marriage-plot novels the honeymoon tends to be represented in one of two contrasting ways: as a blank space, often between chapters that depict the wedding and the return home, or as richly detailed narratives. In both cases the honeymoon is often of great thematic importance; textual

Table 6. *Honeymoon conceptions*

	%
Yes	13
No	51
Possible	3
Probably	7
Probably not	2
Unknown	8
Insufficient data	16

silence about the honeymoon is by no means an indication that it is of no interest – often quite the opposite is true. Unrepresented honeymoons are often unnarratable in D. A. Miller's sense: the import of the honeymoon often exceeds the power of representation and language.

In invoking the marriage plot, I want also to stress a connection between fiction and nonfiction that can be articulated through the concept of narrative. The marriage plot is obviously a narrative structure that shapes fiction, but it can also be thought of as a structure that works to shape real-life experience; in other words, it is a cultural as well as a purely literary plot. I am speaking here of the stories men and women told themselves about what was proper and desirable to imagine as a life story; certainly in the Victorian period (and to a large extent today) marriage was central to culturally sanctioned life stories. Women in particular were expected to marry and to structure their imaginative futures around that indicative act. There is an intimate relation, of course, between cultural and literary narrative: the reading of novels can influence and even shape lives. The Victorians were particularly sensitive to this; the connection surfaces most clearly in antinovelistic discourse where critics argued that reading novels or reading a certain kind of novel would give young women unrealistic and dangerous expectations of what marriage should be and of the necessary role it should play in their lives. The reality that many middle-class Victorian women remained single did not alter – indeed may be said to have fed into – the power of the marriage plot in daily life.

One final way of thinking about the cultural marriage plot is as what I am calling a master-narrative, a culturally powerful story with a predictable shape against which individuals are encouraged to evaluate the course of their lives. The master-narrative for middle-class women of the period would feature marriage as one of its climactic moments and the births of children – especially the first few – as others perhaps equally powerful. Any departure from this master-narrative would be marked, however subtly, as a failure calibrated by the distance from this ideal.

The idea of the master-narrative brings together fiction and real life by acknowledging the power of certain culturally sanctioned stories over individual choices, whether they be authorial or personal. Certainly, Victorian women could choose not to marry, but that choice would be remarked upon and, in most cases, negatively construed; novelists could write novels in which their heroines did not marry, but these endings outside the marriage plot would often be criticized. These endings would also be difficult to write. One thinks of Charlotte Brontë acceding to her father's request that she hold out hope that her heroine, Lucy Snowe, would marry at the end of *Villette*. One might think also of the self-imposed challenge of Anthony Trollope, who, in writing *Miss Mackenzie*, deliberately set out to produce a heroine who did not marry. Trollope took care to make Miss Mackenzie middle-aged and not terribly attractive; he also gave to her and to the eponymous novel a title indicative of her single status. Despite Trollope's initial intentions, Miss Mackenzie married at the end of the novel, as it were, against the will of her creator.

If the master-narrative of both fiction and real life was shaped, particularly for women, around marriage, the honeymoon functioned slightly differently within that narrative in fictional and real-life contexts. Both stressed transformation and portrayed the honeymoon as a liminal space in which conjugality could be negotiated or rehearsed, but the symbolic nature of novels emphasized the honeymoon as a narrative space in which the alert reader could (and should) read for clues about the future of the marriage in question. Novels join conduct books in seeing honeymoons as metonymic, as inevitably indicative of the success of a marriage. The Wemyss honeymoon, discussed at the beginning of the chapter, indicates that in real life a problematic honeymoon did not inevitably lead to an unsuccessful marriage. On the other hand, the Collier honeymoon, discussed briefly earlier, in which the bride and groom seemed so at ease with each other that the husband could write jokes in his wife's diary, turned out to be a failure. In other words, in real life the master-narrative was powerful but not definitional and the climactic nature of the honeymoon was mitigated by years of marriage and family life that typically followed. Nonetheless, as my case studies repeatedly show, the honeymoon was a time of serious cultural pressure, relatively easy for some to negotiate and visibly painful, as we shall see, for others.

CHAPTER 2

Reorientations

LEAVING HOME

The honeymoon diary of Juliana Taylor Fuller almost perfectly embodies what I have argued was the central task of the Victorian honeymoon: the transfer from one kind of identity and identification to another. While in its content the diary neither holds out nor fulfills promises of intimate revelation, it adheres closely in its shape to the honeymoon's underlying story of transformation. The honeymoon diary is actually one of three accounts of journeys in the same album: Juliana and her husband honeymooned at Bath and Devon in 1866, traveled to Switzerland in 1867, and visited Wales in 1868.

The first – honeymoon – account is marked off from Juliana's narratives of the couple's subsequent journeys by a symmetrical frame of photographs – one on the first and one on the last page of the journal for 1866. The first photograph is of Grovelands, the home of Juliana's birth family; the second, of Hyde House, the ancestral home of her husband, John Stratton Fuller. At the very beginning of the diary, before the photograph, are two entwined locks of hair tied with blue ribbon. If we read along with the architecture of the diary, then, we can see the Fuller honeymoon not only as a journey to the touristic sites of the south of England but as a journey from one home, one family, to another. This journey takes its inspiration from the almost talismanic emblem of conjugality: the locks of hair that initiate the movement from one place to another. The final placement of Juliana in Hyde House, the replacement of one home with another, tells, at least on the surface, a tale of seamless transition from single to married life.

Partly because of the class to which the Fullers belonged, the ending of the diary adds another layer of transition, an opening out from the couple to the community. Hyde House represents a particular form of conjugality no less focused on the couple, but one that places that couple at the center of a small world of dependents, friends, and family:

Great was our pleasure in seeing our own apartments newly furnished with the kind presents of our relatives and friends. In the evening we were serenaded by the ringers of Chesham Church who performed upon handbells in the hall producing a very harmonious effect. Some of them also sang very nicely and departed to their homes after receiving the old English cheer![1]

Represented through their gifts, "relatives and friends" join tenants and neighbors in a chorus of voices that blesses and authorizes the marriage. Significantly, these are not permanent presences; the musicians "depart" "to their homes," leaving husband and wife alone together with the memories and reminders of the broader community.

Juliana's pair of photographs, separated orthographically by the length of the honeymoon narrative, assures the reader of the stability of a structuring concept of home. Although the location and the physical features of her home change as she exchanges one for the other, by the end of the diary there would seem to be no doubt that Julia feels *at* home in Hyde House. While her emotionally sketchy account of the honeymoon does not help us to see what made this process possible, we can read back from its triumphant results to imagine her honeymoon as embodying the Victorian ideal of transformation, where a journey away from familiar territory allowed for change to be redefined as a return.

For many of the other couples in my sample, the transition to marriage and from one home to the other was not so easy a matter. In quite a few cases the birth home and family continued to exert a nostalgic pressure, as different identities, identifications, and expectations clashed. The honeymoon, for many couples, was a period of negotiation between past and present, the familial and the conjugal, homosocial and heterosexual. Following the visual landmarks of Juliana Taylor's diary, this chapter traces a double movement required by the Victorian idea of conjugality that was often worked through on the honeymoon: this process involved, first, a turning away from the birth family and, subsequently, a turning toward a new family and a new set of identifications. Together, these movements accomplished, when successful, what I am calling "*reorientation*," a movement that, appropriately enough perhaps for a process involving literal travel as well as psychological journeying, suggests movement through space with reference to particular landmarks. The term also registers, however briefly, a prior moment of possible *dis*orientation as familiar points of reference recede and are replaced by new ones.

The first part of this chapter, "Leaving Home," describes the first movement as it was attempted by a variety of different couples from my

---

[1] Juliana Taylor Fuller, entry for 27 November 1866, Ms. diary 1866–67, Juliana Taylor Fuller Diaries, M993 EHC 195.

sample. It looks at struggles on the part of men and women to *turn away* from their former lives, their birth families, and their identity-conferring roles within those families. The second part of the chapter moves on to the second stage that can be seen as a *turning toward*; this section focuses on the construction of conjugal identification on the honeymoon and, in particular, on its relation to landscape and sightseeing. The work of reorientation is not done until men and women find a place for their birth families in their new identities as married individuals and their new joint identity as a married couple. What I am describing, of course, is my model and a Victorian ideal. These stages could unfold simultaneously, partially, or not at all. Conjugal identification could sometimes occur, as we shall see, as early as the engagement period, or it could be deferred until later in marriage. Nonetheless, I would argue that the honeymoon served as a useful time and place for the undertaking of linked transformations on the part of Victorian men and women.

Many members of my sample experienced tension between their birth and conjugal identifications. Predictably, these conflicts were more acute for the women in my sample than for the men, although the example of John Ruskin is an exception in this as in many other regards. Sometimes these tensions produced conflicts between husband and wife or between the husband and his in-laws. The conflicting identifications for the women in my sample did not necessarily correlate with untroubled relations with their family of origin. Quite the contrary: as we shall see, in the two fullest examples of honeymoons dominated by relations with mothers and sisters, those relations were often far from peaceful.

One measure of how this tension was negotiated is, of course, to look at how often members of birth families were included in the honeymoon. As we saw in Chapter 1, this record is somewhat mixed, with the vast majority of honeymoons being couples-only affairs. If we look more closely at the texture of these honeymoons and the courtships that preceded them, however, we can come up with a more nuanced picture of the obligatory transition from birth to conjugal family and become alert to a less literal and more diffuse, if no less anxious, sense of the presence of the birth family and of other friends in the relationship between husband and wife.

In some cases, we can see in the record traces of a negotiation between husband- and wife-to-be over the location of the honeymoon and, by extension, over the degree to which it was assumed to be a time of withdrawal from friends and family. Although only one side of the late-courtship correspondence has been preserved, we can infer from the letters of Arthur Thorndike to his bride-to-be, Agnes Bowers, that they might have had quite different ideas about how private a honeymoon should be, and about what distance a honeymooning couple should maintain from friends and public activities. Arthur opens the discussion of their honeymoon destination by proposing a sojourn to the seaside:

> Another thing, dear, I have been thinking about ... don't you think, dear, it would be much pleasanter to go to Hastings or Dover or some seaside place than going to London. I think myself, it would be infinitely more pleasant. In the first place London is a most doleful place to go to, especially in September when nothing is going on and there is no novelty to either of us to go there and there are so many friends about town who we should be bound to go and see, though I should not care at all to do so, nor do I think she [*sic*] would. Whereas at Hastings or Dover we should have *novelty* – no *friends* and good sea air ... I do not think we should find it any more expensive and to my mind more enjoyable [*sic*], but, dear one, I feel I am very selfish in saying all this, if you have thoroughly made up your mind that our honeymoon must be in London.[2]

Agnes obviously answered in part as Arthur wished. She apparently agreed to an amended version of the seaside trip, but, interestingly enough, maintained the London connection by assuming they would go by train via the city. Arthur answers by asking her to abandon the idea of London altogether and to plan a different route:

> I was so glad to get your letter this morning and to find that it is no disappointment to you to give up going to spend our honeymoon in Town. I like the idea of Folkestone quite as much as Dover or Hastings and if we found it dull at Folkestone, we could go to Dover. But, dear, I do not see the necessity of going to London to go to Folkestone. I have not looked out the trains but should have thought it would be much quicker to go by the coast line thro' Brighton. Will you look it out, dear, and see which will be the shortest journey.[3]

In one of the few examples I was able to find of honeymoon planning and negotiation on the part of an engaged couple, there seems to be some possible disagreement about the function of the honeymoon: Arthur looks for novelty and occupation, but always in the context of isolation from people toward whom he might feel a social obligation. We do not know directly what Agnes's views were on either of these dimensions of the journey, but we can surmise that her sense of the roles of "friends" in the transition to conjugality might well have been different. We also

---

[2] Patricia Casson (ed.), *"My Dear One": A Victorian Courtship: The Letters of Agnes Bowers and Arthur Thorndike* (London: MacRae, 1984), p. 108 (18 August 1881; italics in original).
[3] *Ibid.*, p. 111 (20 August 1881).

know that if this was in fact a conflict, Agnes "won": Arthur's letters close to the wedding date imagine them leaving for London.

Maud Tomlinson Berkeley's diary offers a more explicit – and more humorous – account of conflicts over the role of privacy in honeymoon arrangements. Immediately after noting that the weather at Ventnor, the site of her 1892 honeymoon, was "unremittingly bad," she records the fate of her suggestion that she have friends join them to make things more lively:

> Suggested we telegram to Lilian and Steakie and ask them to visit us one day. Surprised to find dear Jim adamant that they should not. He takes the nature of the honeymoon rather more seriously than do I. I thought it would be fun to give the girls a treat. And they would certainly liven up the Bonchurch Hotel. There is a particular soda syphon on the sideboard in the dour dining-room here which simply cries out to be used in some piece of horseplay. The Colonel [her husband], I could see, was not amused when I mentioned this. It seems that married ladies do not behave with that lack of circumspection on which Lilian and Steakie and I had always prided ourselves.[4]

While Maud's humor exaggerates the difference between herself and the colonel, as well as between married and single woman, the honeymoon here is clearly operating as a scene of instruction in conjugality and decorum. The "girls" who have been so important to Maud's ten years as an adult single woman have no place on the honeymoon. Relations to place have themselves changed; in this case, the Bonchurch Hotel, for Maud a potential scene of horseplay, becomes a backdrop to a more "circumspect" set of behaviors and expectations.

The fact that only a small minority of the sample honeymoons included family or friends means, of course, that by far the majority of the couples honeymooned, in the instructive paradox of conjugality, "alone together." But preoccupation with the concerns of, and identification with, the birth family was, of course, not simply a matter of the family's physical presence or absence. At issue is the larger context of reorientation, complete or partial, successful or not. A certain wistfulness about life with the birth family, a certain "homesickness" for women and sometimes for men caught between two homes, is quite common throughout the sample. From the brief but evocative postscript to a happy letter "home" to her father from Fanny Wightman ("Flu") Arnold – "Only second time I have been away on your birthday"[5] – to the more

---

[4] Flora Fraser, *Maud: The Illustrated Diary of a Victorian Woman* (San Francisco: Chronicle, 1987), p. 122 (entry for 2 January 1892).

[5] Cecil Y. Lang (ed.), *The Letters of Matthew Arnold*, vol. 1 (1829–59) (Charlottesville: University of Virginia Press, 1996), p. 219 (19 September 1851).

clearly melancholic comments of Susan Miers – "How I wished for my dear parents, particularly that one dearest of all, who would have been the one to give me to Frank"[6] – we see that marriage for some represented, among other things, a real loss of connection.

As the last example shows, the periods of engagement and marriage before the honeymoon could also be times when identifications could be, and often were, negotiated. The letters of William Thackeray to his fiancée, Isabella Shawe, show, perhaps more acutely than any others, the double identificatory pull experienced by many women in my sample. Thackeray's problems with his mother-in-law were legion; his engagement letters, however, vacillate between an identification with Mrs. Shawe as a stand-in for him and a powerful sense that, as Isabella's husband, he will soon, in the natural course of things, replace her mother. On 18 April, four months before his marriage, Thackeray speaks of the "change" Isabella must go through, but he passes on kisses to his fiancée through her mother:

And now shall I tell you, how I think of you mornings, and dream of you nights, how happy I am at this prospect of independence, and of marriage – wh[ich] must very soon take place now dearest, for there is little use that I can see in delay – You must make up your mind to the change, dear Woman, and I do believe though I say it that shouldn't, you will have as good a husband as ever a little Woman had. Ask your dear Mother to bestow 10000000 kisses on you and place them to the account of your obedient Servant. W. M. T.[7]

In this letter Thackeray imagines, or claims to imagine, that Isabella's mother can act for him. This suggests, not only that the transition from the familial to conjugal might be seamless, but that the two kinds of love are literally accountable to one another in a system of equivalent exchange in which Thackeray's kisses get transformed into a debt to his mother-in-law. This notion of equivalence quickly disappears in Thackeray's response to Isabella's next letter:

Your Sunday letter dear Puss has just reached me, and very happy I was to receive it – but what in God's name have I been saying to hurt you (for I see you are hurt) and your Mother? What a scoundrel should I be were I to endeavour to weaken such a tie as exists between you two – The separation to wh[ich] I alluded did not go further than the bedroom – If I recollect rightly this was the chief object of my thoughts at the moment, and I opined that you would be unwilling to quit your bedfellow, and your present comfortable home for another with me.

---

[6] Susan Miers, entry for 14 October 1850, Ms. diary, 1850, S. M. Miers Diary, M795 EHC 27.
[7] William Makepeace Thackeray, *Letters and Private Papers of W. M. Thackeray*, ed. Gordon Ray, vol. 1 (Oxford University Press, 1945), p. 307 (18 April 1836).

If you are my wife you must sleep in my bed and live in my house – voila tout – I have no latent plans – no desire for excluding you from those whom I sh[oul]d think very meanly of you, were you to neglect.[8]

Here, of course, despite his protests, the idiom of replacement dominates over the idiom of continuity, culminating as it does in the highly charged image of Isabella exchanging her sister's bed for her husband's. It is perhaps not surprising that, at the end of this long letter, which includes a response to one from Isabella received in midcomposition, that the language of sexual rivalry deepens and becomes more explicit. As Thackeray says in his closing, he has "grown to such a pitch of jealousy, I was quite angry at your Mother's telling me that you were so well & happy – I was in a rage that you were not more miserable like myself."[9]

For William Thackeray, at least, the honeymoon did much to resolve the problem of conflicting identifications. He is able both to joke to his aunt, in a letter accepting her invitation to spend part of the honeymoon journey with her, that Mrs. Shawe has "come to pay us a visit of condolence"[10] and to assert Isabella's identification with him: "WE, (does it not sound very magnificent?) shall be delighted to occupy your pretty little rooms, and stay with you a few or many days – for this place [Versailles] has a certain dulness [*sic*], in spite of my peculiar situation, and I shall be too glad to pass a little time in your pleasant country villa." The capitalized "WE" suggests the primacy of their union, a theme carried out both in his description of Isabella in the signature of the same letter as "that diminutive individual, who bears the name of your affte. Nephew W. T. Thackeray," and in his calling her, in another letter written at the same time, "that diminutive part of me." Of course, the union is not a symmetrical one: she is "diminutive," "part of" him, part of his signature. Moreover, after the brief "visit of condolence" from Mrs. Shawe and a day or two of being alone with his bride, Thackeray announces his relief at the prospect of moving from "the certain dulness" of Versailles to a house occupied by members of his family of origin.

While Thackeray's attempt to come to terms with his wife's identificatory struggle is perhaps the most vividly rendered, other husbands from the sample responded with varying degrees of sympathy for the conflicts their wives were experiencing. Charles Kingsley accused Fanny Grenfell

[8] *Ibid.*, p. 309 (21–25 April 1836).   [9] *Ibid.*, p. 312.
[10] William Makepeace Thackeray, *Selected Letters of William Makepeace Thackeray*, ed. Edgar F. Harden (London: Macmillan, 1996), p. 37 (25 August 1836).

of falling into a family pattern of "deifying emotion" when she explained how hard it was to part from her sisters,[11] while Arthur Thorndike spoke of the transition away from the family home in far more sympathetic terms:

This day fortnight we shall be just starting for London feeling very queer, I have no doubt, with heaps of rice down our backs and our hearts overflowing with love and gratitude. You will be feeling sad at leaving your parental roof where every comfort and happiness has been yours; where you have been made so much of as you so richly deserve; where high, low, rich and poor loved you. Darling, you will be leaving all of this for love of me. I often wonder at your love and think how *true* it is, to be able to give up so much to "Come and live with me and be my love."[12]

Of course, not all women felt the same degree of attachment to their birth families or resolved conflicts, if any, in the same way. Margaret King Gladstone wrote to her mother three times on a ten-day journey to Perthshire and took her husband to stay with her mother immediately afterwards. In one of the letters, however, in answer to complaints of neglect, Margaret warned her mother to expect fewer letters because of her new duties toward her husband and household.[13] Margaret had obviously set her priorities and aligned herself strongly with her new home. A dramatic moment of transition seems to have occurred on the honeymoon:

[T]he loneliness and pain grew, and more and more as we walked to the Falls of Bracklinn. He was speaking of the Presidentship of the Royal Society, we were looking at the view, but my heart was aching sorely. I was thinking too of the going to Penbridge Square so soon, and fearing the mistress's duties, when we sat down on a large stone at the falls. I told John a little and some tears fell, but I felt still as if he did not understand me and oh so sad that it was possible to be lonely walking by his side, and wondering if it must often be thus through life, till half before tea half after sitting at his feet I told him all, and was comforted "as one whom her husband comforteth" and understood his love better and was understood and not thought foolish, and the sorrow and loneliness were gone, replaced by utter rest and peace.[14]

Here we have the characteristic coordinates of the honeymoon: the honeymoon scenery with its powerful links to events and emotions; the

[11] Susan Chitty, *The Beast and the Monk: A Life of Charles Kingsley* (London: Hodder, 1974), p. 85.
[12] Casson, *"My Dear One,"* pp. 118–19 (2 September 1881).
[13] Patricia Jalland, *Women, Marriage, and Politics, 1860–1914* (New York: Oxford University Press, 1986), p. 123.
[14] Margaret King Gladstone, entry for 26 July 1869, Ms. diary, 1869, Papers of the King and Thomson Families, PRO 30/69/852.

new home anticipated sometimes with excitement, sometimes with anxiety, often, of course, with a mixture of the two; and, finally, the space and time "alone together," a time carved out of the newly conjugal ritual of meals and walks, "half before tea half after," in which conversation takes place. This transition is, of course, a happy one in the diary: it is a triumphant example of reidentification. In the larger context of Margaret's relationship with and letters to her mother, however, the invocation of the new household in Penbridge Square retained some of its associations with conflict.

While many of the difficulties of transition center on the figure of the mother, sisters also represented a powerful, enduring – and often con-flictual – link to earlier identities. The three married daughters of Lord Lyttelton – Meriel, Lucy, and Lavinia (whose mother died before the eldest, Meriel, was married) – experienced their own marriages, and those of their sisters, in terms of sororal loss. With their sister May, who never married, they formed an intragenerational chain of loss and replacement: when one sister married, another took her place as mother of the family, mourning the presence and the abilities of the previous one. The sisters' honeymoon letters to each other as well as their diaries at the time of separation reveal the importance of the sororal bond, even in the context of remarkably loving and indeed sensuous relations with their husbands.

The centrality of sisters to the transition to conjugality is revealed in the structure of the Lyttelton honeymoons themselves: in each case, the bride and groom would spend the first part of the honeymoon at a borrowed mansion; then they would return to visit a family home before departing for the Continent. The leaving after the ritualized return, often figured by the sisters left behind as a more difficult parting – a "second wrench" as Lucy called it – emphasized the interplay between departure and return, identification and disidentification, that it was the work of the honeymoon to accommodate. Sororal presence on and in the honeymoon took other forms as well; not only was May one of only two sisters in my sample to join a honeymoon in progress, but Meriel and Lavinia spent the first part of their individual honeymoons in the same borrowed house: each spent time at Ingestre, a family seat, before the trip home and then to the Continent. The honeymoon, then, became a scene for the interplay of sameness and differences between sisters that I have elsewhere called "sororophobia."[15] In this case, sexual difference, as represented by the

---

[15] Helena Michie, *Sororophobia: Differences among Women in Literature and Culture* (New York: Oxford University Press, 1987).

connection to the husband, is expressed as both departure from and identification with sisters who have already taken the same journey.

On one side of this paradox is the palpable sense of loss felt by both the honeymooning sister and the sister left behind. Lucy writes to the honeymooning Meriel of the pain she feels entering her sister's room and looking at her new signature. She teases Meriel about her infrequent replies to Lucy's almost daily letters, telling her sister that "we don't expect [letters] every day from Mooners in Honey."[16] Lucy's half-joking tone, typical of the Lyttelton family idiom, is not totally convincing. As Lucy herself notes, she is not sure "why I get facetious ... I suppose it's hiding my feelings under a sickly mask of mirth."[17] Although we do not have Meriel's letters to tell us something of the experience of the sister who leaves the family, we do have Lucy's comments four years later as she departs for her own wedding journey. A few days before the wedding, Lucy again mourns leaving the room she shared with a sister – this time Lavinia, the next in line. Although the day before the wedding Lucy, now in London, seems more cheerful, she still speaks of "indefinable clouds" as well as of the "sunshine" of her impending marriage: "The blessed thought to me is of all the sunshine which is in my heart breaking out bye and bye [*sic*] and scattering all these indefinable clouds. He [her fiancé, Frederick Cavendish] is so gentle and tender with me and when he is with me they do a little scatter!"[18] Lucy continues with this metaphor on the honeymoon itself, writing to Meriel that "[t]he sunshine is beginning to scatter the clouds. That sounds melancholy for a honeymoon letter, but you know exactly what I mean by it."[19] If Lucy charts the tension between conjugal joy and familial loss in terms of weather, Lavinia, at this point the sister left behind, chooses the more intransigent idiom of time to mark out a calendar of loss: "Last Sunday with Lucy,"[20] she writes. Four years earlier Lucy had also marked time in this way, noting the first "sisterless birthday"[21] soon after Meriel's marriage.

Completing the chain of substitution and subtraction, Lavinia's accounts of her own marriage are marked by her grief over leaving May. Her departure from "the darling old home"[22] is haunted by a "vision" of her sister alone. Like Lucy's, Lavinia's letters home are equivocal, celebrating her union with her husband while articulating a real sense of loss. Writing home for things she has inadvertently left behind, Lavinia describes herself as "umbrella-less, watch-less, clockless, workless, and

---

[16] Sheila Fletcher, *Victorian Girls: Lord Lyttelton's Daughters* (London: Hambleton, 1997), p. 62.
[17] *Ibid.*   [18] *Ibid.*, p. 99.   [19] *Ibid.*   [20] *Ibid.*   [21] *Ibid.*, p. 62.   [22] *Ibid.*, p. 154.

hat-less."[23] While she does not add "sisterless," we can perhaps hear an echo in the grammar of loss of Lucy's earlier plaint. Predictably, May's own sense of something missing is less humorous: "terrible ... one-legged feeling," she says, echoing her aunt's letter to Lucy at the time of Meriel's wedding, where Aunt Yaddy sympathized, "I can well believe how one-handed you feel."[24]

The transition to conjugality was not by any means registered only in the idiom of loss. Lucy's climatic metaphor also allows for an articulation of what seems to be profound sexual feeling as she writes on her honeymoon of her relation with her husband: "A sort of rocking on bright waves before launching out on new seas – which I know is never to come again; but as long as this wonderful sunshine is poured round me – I mean the great new sunshine of our love for each other – all the coming waves must look bright to me."[25] The sisters are also often able to integrate their conjugal experiences into a narrative of female identification and transmission. After Lavinia's wedding, for example, Lucy, now married for six years, writes: "All that is agitating and overwhelming gradually loses itself in a love that learns more and more to trust and give itself up to the great answering love ... [A]s our own Mammy used to say, there is a halo round the honeymoon that ... can never come again."[26] Lucy's identificatory advice to her sister is framed as a transmission from their mother whose happy marriage all three sisters use as a model for their own.

The Lyttelton sisters were unusual in many ways, from the closeness of their family identifications to the remarkable worldly and emotional successes of their early marriages. (Lucy's ended quickly and tragically when she died in childbirth.) Although the sisters all married men of considerable status – Lucy married into the immediate family of the Duke of Devonshire and one of her many homes was Chatsworth – they seem to have negotiated the demands of marriage with relative ease. Perhaps not coincidentally, they also were among the most successful at integrating sororal and conjugal love.

Other people in my sample were not quite so successful. Louise von Glehn Creighton, for example, reported that her identification with Mandell (Max) Creighton, which began before marriage, placed a strain on her relation with her sisters:

It is not easy to write much about the time of our engagement. We were absolutely absorbed in one another and in the wonderful discoveries we were

[23] *Ibid.*, p. 156.　　[24] *Ibid.*, pp. 156, 162.　　[25] *Ibid.*, p. 105.　　[26] *Ibid.*, p. 156.

continually making in one another. On the whole our tastes and interests were wonderfully alike, and to discover this was an ever new delight ... I cannot imagine a more perfect companionship of mind than we enjoyed during those months of our engagement. Besides this, he was a very ardent lover.[27]

The couple's mutual absorption came, however, at a cost. Louise's identification with Max divided her emotionally from her family, especially from her sisters. When she turns from a celebration of her relationship with Max to a discussion of her sisters, her tone changes dramatically. No longer are the "months of her engagement" a time of "perfect companionship of mind." Instead, only a few pages after her initial euphoric description, she shows us the other side of this story of gain and loss: "I do not feel as if those months were very happy to me. I doubt whether such a transition time as an engagement is ever happy for a girl ... I expect that I was unduly sensitive & exacting, but I certainly found both Mimi & Olga very unsympathetic at this time."[28]

Perhaps because she identifies the months of engagement as a time of "transition," Louise's account of the couple's honeymoon in Paris is quite matter-of-fact. In the *Memoir* it is portrayed as almost entirely domestic, a time of shopping for the new household:

We were only to have about a week's honeymoon & thought Paris would be the best place to spend it in. We visited picture galleries & churches, & looked a great deal in shop windows, hunting for various things for our house. We wanted to have as few ordinary things as possible & looked everywhere for some different kind of dinner knives, & also for brass fireirons. We were troubled because the sets being made for wood fires never had a poker, & we could not discover the French word for poker so as to ask for one. Our chief purchase was a moderator lamp made out of an oriental vase, which was long our chief lamp.[29]

The repeated "we"s structure this passage as a story of conjugal unity; the objects for which they search, even those for whose names they search together, cast, like the moderator lamp, a domestic light on the honeymoon. In this account, although not in Louise's more official *Life* of her husband, the sights of Paris are quite literally the sights of the new home: the transition to conjugality precedes the honeymoon and its experiences.

In assessing the role of the birth family on the honeymoon, I have looked at the literal presence or absence of family members on the honeymoon and also at often isolated expressions of affective loss and gain. By looking more closely at two honeymoon stories, alert to

---

[27] Louise Creighton, *Memoir of a Victorian Woman*, ed. James Thane Covert (Bloomington: Indiana University Press, 1994), p. 40.
[28] *Ibid.*, pp. 44–5.   [29] *Ibid.*, pp. 45–6.

many kinds of often competing identifications, we will be able to consider the honeymoon in ritual terms as an event with specific relations to time and place that dramatizes and attempts to resolve some of the conflicts I have described above. The two honeymoons on which I have chosen to focus, those of Charlotte Hotzapfel Boycott and William Boycott, who were married 27 August 1831, and Martha Rolls Macready and Major Edward Macready, who celebrated their wedding 1 August 1840, have several key elements in common: the presence of the bride's birth family on part but not all of the honeymoon, a vexed but central emotional investment in the birth family on the part of the bride, and the centrality to the honeymoon experience of communications by letter and parcel between the bride and the birth family. Both honeymoons are shaped by the rhythm of correspondence between the bride and her female relatives, the groom acting as mediator in this emotionally charged communication. The Boycott and Macready honeymoons, then, are epistolary in form and content, the brides noting in their diaries the receipt and sending of frequent letters and packages establishing a link to old homes. Even the locations are similar: in choosing the British seaside – the Boycotts honeymooned at Guildford and the Macreadys at Littlehampton – the couples took their wedding journeys within relatively easy reach of their birth families. Both couples were eventually joined on the honeymoon by members of their families; Charlotte's day-to-day description of the honeymoon in her multivolume diaries ends after two weeks with the arrival of a large family party, while Martha's honeymoon diary begins a month after their wedding when her mother and a female companion arrive at a hotel in Littlehampton near the Macreadys' lodgings.

Because the letters of Charlotte's older sister Caroline are available dating as far back as 1813, and because we have diaries of Charlotte's many years before and after the honeymoon, we have far more direct information about Charlotte than we do about Martha. In fact, Edward Hall, in whose collection the Hotzapfel papers can be found, at one time intended to publish the diaries and letters up to 1820 under the title "Love and Freindship [*sic*] in Regency London: Hotzapfel Diaries and Letters (August 1813–August 1820)." Hall dismisses the later diaries as lacking in the "Regency spirit" and the intrigue of those written before 1820; he seems particularly dissatisfied in his editorial correspondence with Charlotte's marriage to the "shadowy William Boycott" and with her frequent comments about her own health, including what seems to him to be an extended and self-indulgent description of her giving birth in, as

he exclaims, "two different rooms!"[30] Hall clearly prefers the younger
Caroline and Charlotte, who compete with each other for lovers; spread
rumors about themselves, each other, and third parties; and contradict
themselves from page to page.

Charlotte's account of her honeymoon, then, postdates the decline of
her "Regency spirit" and is characterized, like Martha Macready's, by
attention to the minutiae of ill health and by a generally anxious tone. It
does, however, extend the sense of the earlier entries that she and her
sister have a deeply sororophobic relationship, in which identification and
closeness are in constant tension with disidentification and rivalry. The
relationship, vexed as it is, is clearly central to Charlotte, as is the relationship with her mother and, to a certain extent, with other members of
the birth family.

The first honeymoon entry on 28 August, describing the activities of
the previous (wedding) day, ends with a notation that Charlotte has
"begun a letter home in the evening." She had also received letters and
parcels that morning. In a letter written the same day, she slips when
noting that she has finished the letter begun the evening before: "I finished my home [sic] for home, William took it in the evening to the post
office after which he read one chapter of Father Clement [sic] aloud."
"Home" in this honeymoon account, as in most if not all of my other
examples, always means the birth family; the slip of "home" for "letter"
in a diary otherwise free from such mistakes suggests, if nothing else, the
intensity of Charlotte's family ties. Charlotte's investment in these ties is
further ratified by a connective ritual she describes in the same entry:
"[D]inner at 4 oclk at 5 oclk precisely took a glass of wine to all friends at
home according to a promise made, that they would do the same at the
same moment."[31] Like the letters, the ritual of simultaneous wine
drinking temporarily bridges the gap that the honeymoon as an institution is working to create.

The role of the "shadowy William Boycott" in this careful choreography of separation and union is difficult to untangle. He appears in the
diary as a walking companion and reader but most often, as we have seen
earlier, a deliverer of mail or, more generally, an intermediary in the
family correspondence. For example, the entry for 4 September begins:
"William rose at 6 oclk, drove over to Newport for a letter from home.

---

[30] Edward Hall, notes to file, Charlotte Hotzapfel Ms. diary, Hotzapfel Diaries, D/D2 EHC 122, 34,
M 890–902.
[31] Charlotte Hotzapfel, entry for 28 August 1831, Ms. diary, 1831, D/D2 EHC M 890.

I overslept myself and did not rise until 10 minutes to 10 oclk ... dreaming of home. I wrote a letter home in the morning ... [H]e returned from Newport about 2 oclk bringing letters ... with which we were much delighted."

Not all of the letters from home are delightful. On 1 September Charlotte "received a letter from Caroline which pained me much as it appears to convey reproach, I sat down to answer, but was induced not to send what I had by William as he reminded me that what I had written would perhaps make them unhappy. Wrote another letter – could not go out it rained heavily all day." Here we see hints of the conflict that marked the sisters' relationship in the earlier materials. Significantly, William intercedes in, but by no means displaces, the centrality of the sororal relationship. Conflict with Caroline is later replaced by worry about her:

William went before breakfast to the Post Office for letters, got one from Jacques saying Caroline had a head ache [*sic*] which together with our not having heard from her at the same time occasioned us ... consternation, which happily was put an end to by a letter written with her own hand which had been routed to [their former hotel] the Dolphin.[32]

The "us" of "caused us consternation" and the "we" of "we were much delighted" suggest that, from Charlotte's point of view, William has become part of the family nexus, identified primarily with her concerns and feelings with respect to the rest of this close-knit family. He also stands far enough apart to advise her – apparently, in her opinion, wisely – about her relations with her birth family. Perhaps more importantly, he is a facilitator; he walks to the post office while she sleeps and dreams of home; he walks further than she is able to to acquire the letters that so regularly punctuate her experience of the honeymoon. Despite the anxiety that plays through these entries, there seems to be no overt tension between William and her family, between former and present self. The accommodation of her new life to the old takes the form, literally, of a correspondence between them.

At the end of two weeks, letters are no longer necessary. The usually sluggish Charlotte rises at 6:30 and breakfasts "before 8" so they can leave Southampton and join a family party in a cottage at Twickenham: "Father, Julia, Caroline, Anne and Jacques came to give us the meeting and spend 2 weeks together, never was there such a happy meeting and hearty welcome as we received from them all ... I felt sick, and my head very bad during the ride, my side ached much in the evening."[33]

The month-long honeymoon, then, is split neatly in two: two weeks of solitude à deux, two weeks of togetherness with family members. The account of the honeymoon works toward the happiest synthesis of conjugality and family loyalty. The last sentence of this triumphant entry might give us pause, however: Charlotte ends her description of the honeymoon safely reensconced in her role of family invalid. While Charlotte certainly reports feeling regular pains and sickness in her two weeks with William, her final comment suggests that illness itself might have been a way of forging an identity that could bridge two family roles.

Martha Macready's diary, like Charlotte's, refers throughout to a mysterious and unnamed conflict with her family, in this case her mother and sister. Like Charlotte's, the diary locates that conflict outside the relationship between birth family and husband. Martha's eagerness to see her mother after a month of honeymooning at Littlehampton is absorbed smoothly into a narrative of conjugality. On the day before her mother returns home, leaving her daughter with her new husband in Littlehampton, she takes farewell of her mother by talking to her about the joy she takes in being married to Edward: "Dongan washed my hair. Mama sat with me, and we talked of my unbounded happiness – Indeed – I am most blessed in the love of one, whom I love with the whole strength of my being – and he – dearest love – how truly does he love me – and how fond am I of his affection."[34] During her mother's month-long stay in Littlehampton at a neighboring hotel, mother and daughter exchange visits on a daily basis; Martha often takes tea with her mother (also a Martha; it is presumably for this reason that the daughter is called "Patty" by her mother and husband) while Edward takes long walks.

Mother and daughter apparently cannot bear to take leave of each other when the time comes: on 7 October Martha writes: "Were going over to see them off when Robert met us with a note saying they would rather not say adieu – Edward went over to them. A lovely day too warm for a bath. Wrote to Mama." Edward, like William Boycott, acts as a mediator here, in this case taking on the emotional burden of farewell. Later on, the alliance between Edward and his mother-in-law shows a slightly less benign side: after a conflict with her daughter over a mysterious "Mr. S.," the elder Martha writes not to her daughter but to

---

[33] *Ibid.*, 21 September 1831.
[34] Martha Rolls Macready, entry for 6 October 1840, Ms. diary, Rolls Family Papers, D361 F/P 6.9.

Edward. The younger Martha blames herself: "Only Edward had a letter from Mama – I am so vexed she has been so annoyed and all through my fault."[35] The cause of the conflict is what Martha earlier describes as "a most unsatisfactory and extraordinary letter from Mr. S." Martha unites mother and husband in her self-reproach: "This matter has bothered me more than I can describe because I have been the cause by my thoughtlessness, of annoying the two persons dearest to me – I have been quite ill about it."[36] From earlier hints in the journal it seems that Mr. S. is a jilted or rejected lover; he becomes part of a conjugal narrative by Martha's repeated insistence in the diary that she has never been in love before and that her happiness with Edward is complete.

Martha's relationship with Edward is itself more conflicted – and more fully fleshed out – than Charlotte's with William Boycott. The diary vacillates between blissful ejaculations of love, punctuated with Martha's characteristic dashes and exclamation marks, and equally exclamatory entries in which she tries to come to terms with Edward's bad moods. Both blissful and desperate entries unfold, however, in the idiom of conjugality, through which Martha repeatedly describes a complete identification with her husband. When Edward is, as he often seems to be, depressed, Martha notes her dependence on Edward's moods. Her diary entry for 28 September makes this explicit: "Edward was not himself this afternoon – I know not why – but when he is thus it makes me feel so utterly depressed I can scarcely contain my tears. My spirits depend entirely upon his, and rise and fall with them."

While I will address the possible causes of Edward's low spirits in Chapter 3, and in a different way in my speculative final chapter, I would like at this point to stress Martha's conjugal identification with her husband, an identification that may or may not have been reciprocal.

For Martha, as for Charlotte, however, conjugality was triangulated through a perhaps almost equally identificatory relation with the birth family – in this case, of course, with Martha's mother. "Mama" clearly knew something about the mystery of Mr. S.; it is also possible that Martha confided to her the fact of or even the reason for Edward's persistent "low spirits." Since we do not have copies of the almost daily letters from Martha to her mother, we cannot know. We do know, however, that mail from her mother or sister – expected or delayed – had the potential to make Martha feel physically ill, and that she struggled against submitting to this kind of illness. The entry for 19 November

---

[35] *Ibid.*, 17 October 1840.   [36] *Ibid.*, 13 October 1840.

suggests some of this conflict: "Mama's parcel not arrived. It has made me very sick and nervous. I wish I could get over this turning of the stomach when some thing annoys me." Today we would identify Martha as a person struggling with boundary issues; the honeymoon diary indicates that these boundaries could be breached from two directions. Traditional accounts of the honeymooning body with their focus on sexual crossing, joining, and transgression account for only part of Martha's mysterious but ever-present physical troubles; her bodily illness and health were defined by familial as well as by conjugal expectations.

At crucial moments and anniversaries, particularly toward the end of the honeymoon, Martha struggles to summarize its effects. Her entry for her thirty-sixth birthday on 15 December, the day before she and Edward were to leave Littlehampton, is a triumph of honeymoon geometry as she celebrates the solid triangulated relationship of mother, self, and husband: "My 36th birthday – and what a happy one. E wrote M such a dear, dear letter." Her final honeymoon entry the next day produces a slightly different geometry and a slightly different geography as she celebrates instead the primacy of her connection with Edward: "Little Hampton [*sic*] – dear Little Hampton! Where we have spent four blessed months as mortals can desire, and sufficiently proved that we are all in all to eachother and independent of the world."[37] Here, Littlehampton is framed not as a bridge between two families and two identities, but as a place to the side of "the world" and, by extension, the birth family.

Martha's reentry into the world, and specifically into the world of her family and Edward's, is marked by small conflicts. Martha suspects that Edward's sisters do not like her and engages in more mysterious quarrels with her mother. Her diary entry for 31 December takes stock of the previous year by alluding to seemingly more serious problems:

And so ends the year 1840 – the most eventful of my life and the most blessed. Although in its commencement I suffered perhaps more than anyone can imagine – and from the conduct of women – it is a certain and most unpleasant fact that women are capable of the most cruel behaviour towards eachother and seem often to delight in marring eachother's [*sic*] happiness – but finis coronat opus – I am happy in spite of all attempts to blast my hopes – am blessed, and I hope am the cause of happiness to the best of husbands.

The diary identifies neither the source of Martha's suffering nor the women who she claims have caused it. We know for certain that the women in question were those of her own family. The valedictory

---

[37] *Ibid.*, 16 December 1840.

structure of this final entry, however, suggests a movement away from a world of women to an explicitly conjugal one: to a relationship described as an ending that crowns a period of emotional work. This is, in part, the shape of the Victorian marriage plot, although as various critics have suggested, relations with female relatives, even and perhaps especially in novels as devoted to marriage as Jane Austen's, remain crucial. Martha's valediction writes an ending to the story of 1840 that might be undone in the very first days of 1841.

Martha's story is not, of course, the only one that could be told. We have no record of Edward's feelings about the honeymoon. We do, however, have the diary of another Martha, our Martha's mother. Mrs. Rolls's account is disappointingly a diary in quite another sense, consisting as it does of one-line entries listing her social engagements. The monumental period in her daughter's life is remarked as follows:

June 23 Called at Carleton Terrace (home of Edward's relatives)
July 15 Major Macready dined
July 31 Macreadys dined
August 1 Patty's [Martha's] Wedding Day
August 3 a letter from Patty and the Major
August 18 The E. Macreadys went to Little Hampton[38]

While the tone derives explicitly from the genre of this diary, it is hard for at least this reader not to see an imbalance in the relationship between mother and daughter, as the Macready name, to paraphrase George Henry Lewes, "swallows up" her daughter's. The nominal shifts from "Patty's wedding day," to "Patty and the Major" to "the E. Macreadys" tell a story of easy progress toward conjugality; the elder Martha's diary seems unconcerned with looking back.

I end this section on leaving home with the story of the mother – however sparse and unsatisfactory it may be – to give a sense of the complexities of disidentification. Martha's mother may have longed for her daughter, or she may have been glad to get her out of the house. She may have looked forward to her own journey to the Macready honeymoon, or she may have felt embarrassed or impatient. The younger Martha's identification with her mother is no less mysterious, no less fraught, than that other identification sometimes seemingly accomplished by the honeymoon. The sons and daughters of these honeymoon stories are not necessarily moving, however they might want to frame it in this way, from a place of

---

[38] Martha Rolls (senior) entries for July and August, Ms. diary, 1840, Rolls Family Papers, D361 F/P 3.5.

solidity and peace to something less stable. They are constantly in negotiation with many possibilities – and with the idea of place itself.

COMING TOGETHER

The first part of this chapter focused on departure, on the imperative
literally and figuratively to leave the birth family behind. This section
takes as its subject the second step that completes the process of reorientation, moving us forward in time and in space to conjugal identification and to the replacement of one set of coordinates with another.
Because of its spatial inflection, reorientation takes us into the two linked
realms of the geographic and the visual; if nothing else, the cultural
imperative to honeymoon emphasized new landscapes and focused on
new visual experiences. This is true, of course, even of couples who were
revisiting places that they had seen before. Honeymoons forged an intimate relationship between the cultural and psychological landmark of
marriage and the landscape of the wedding journey: however familiar the
places and destinations of that journey, they were by definition being
visited as though for the first time by people experiencing themselves in
terms of distance from previous selves. At the same time, honeymoon
tourism, like other forms of travel, was never innocent of previous
journeys, previous cultural investments in particular places. The canonical
sights of Europe were in some sense familiar even to those who had never
left England; paintings, photographs, guidebooks, novels, poems, and
plays had turned the most culturally significant sights of the Continent
into visual icons, and visits to them were, in some sense, examples of déjà
vu. This would be particularly true, of course, for cities like Paris and
Rome or for natural sights like Mont Blanc that had been frequently
reproduced in visual and verbal form. I will be looking in this section
both at first visits and at revisitations, registering, in the former case, a
rich visual and textual history that made first visits into revisitations and,
in the latter case, a sense of a new relation to familiar sights. Honeymoon
tourism must be understood simultaneously in relation to time and place,
to narratives of individual lives marked by the climactic changes of
marriage and by acts of traveling through and coming to terms with
physical space. For this reason this chapter emphasizes honeymoons as
journeys through and in space.

Recent work on tourism has made it impossible not to consider
journeys to unfamiliar territory as, among other things, acts of looking.
Honeymoon tourism has its own special relationship to the visual and to

the act of sightseeing that were often part of its day-to-day experiences. This chapter will follow the linked but by no means identical gazes of particular men and women as they looked at churches, mountains, and works of art at this crucial time in their lives. It will consider both the culturally charged category of scenery and what were for the Victorians, as for us, visible signs of culture: the great "sights" of European art and architecture.

As we imagine honeymoon couples confronting, consuming, and negotiating the sights of Europe, we must imagine them undertaking these tasks in relation to maps of various kinds. While literal maps and guidebooks were obviously an important resource for honeymoon tourists, we can think of mapping in a broader sense that includes cultural artifacts like paintings and literary texts. Novels in particular, I argue, articulated a prescribed relation of honeymooner to the sights of Europe: the déjà vu of symbolic revisitation became, in addition, a form of déjà lu, where tourists on their wedding journey traveled in the footsteps not only of other real-life honeymooners but of fictional married couples as well. Marriage-plot novels must have served in some sense as maps or guidebooks to appropriate behavior or, more generally, to an appropriate orientation to landscape, aesthetics, and sexuality. It is for this reason that I juxtapose literary and nonliterary sources in trying to understand the moralized and sexualized landscape of the honeymoon and the various acts of looking that constituted sanctioned relations to the sights of Europe.[39]

If we consider the act of looking on the honeymoon we cannot ignore – as the Victorians also could not – the honeymoon's constitutive sexual act. We have seen in the case of the Ruskins that looking or choosing not to look had consequences in the realm of the sexual. In the Ruskins' case the relation between the sexual gaze and the touristic gaze was especially complex; if we believe that Ruskin was disgusted by the difference between Effie's body and the classical female nude, the connections between sexual looking and sightseeing become very powerful. While these connections might be less explicit in the case of most of the

---

[39] It is interesting to speculate why fictional honeymoons should be, by and large, grimmer than the representations of real-life wedding journeys. Certainly, there would be cultural pressures to report that one's honeymoon was a success – and to convince oneself that this was the case. More specifically, however, as I discuss in Chapter 1, honeymoons in fiction are often used as foreshadowings of marital breakdown: there is, in other words, a powerful generic use of the honeymoon as metonymy. While it is sometimes tempting (most markedly, I think, for the reader of novels) to read real-life honeymoons this way, I have tried to resist teleological readings even and especially when I knew that bad honeymoons were followed by bad marriages. I have tried to respect the immediacy of those accounts that are not retrospective.

honeymooners in my sample, I would argue that they are nonetheless present and at issue in many cases.

"Reorientation" also suggests a link to what we now call "sexual orientation." I will argue that sexual orientation, broadly defined, changed in a profound way for the men and women who undertook these honeymoon journeys in the nineteenth century. My use of the term – and of "sexual *re*orientation" – is capacious: it includes but is not limited to a movement from what we would now call the homosexual to what we would now call the heterosexual. Rather, I argue that all couples, whatever their attractions to men or women, were relocated by the demands of the honeymoon to a relatively recent and indeed narrow form of heterosexuality *avant la lettre*, a kind of heterosexuality I also call, in the first chapter of this book, the "conjugal."

Before discussing specific examples of the relation between the turn to conjugality and geography, I would like to offer one last observation that both attempts to justify my emphasis on sexual orientation and points to difficult issues of methodology and reading. To put it simply, I have found in many of these accounts a profoundly sexualized relationship to landscape. Sometimes this relation between the erotic and the geographical is temptingly simple: reading about Swiss honeymoons it is impossible to avoid entirely the specters of mountains and the most literal-minded of readings of men's and women's different relations to them. While I have tried to avoid seeing all mountains simply as phallic symbols, a mountain, in these accounts at least, is rarely just a topographical formation. It can serve as a testing ground, a reminder of a previous way of life, an object of aesthetic inquiry or debate, a site of terror or challenge, or a place of gender definition. Again, I want to move from the narrowest kind of sexual interpretation to a fuller reading that still takes into account a sense of the erotic and of gender difference. Sexual reorientation is, then, not simply a matter of specifically sexual activity; it describes a realignment of sexual and gender identifications that may or may not be expressed within the confines of "the" sexual act.

In what follows I look at travel and sightseeing as privileged instances of possible reorientation and at the touristic register of the honeymoon as literally making visible the efforts involved in the reorientation process. I begin by considering a case of self-proclaimed failed reorientation – the honeymoon of John Addington Symonds and Catherine North Symonds – and go on to use the failures and refusals that constituted that honeymoon to open up the links between reorientation and geography as they are expressed in the taking in of continental "sights." I narrow my focus to two geographical settings central to one version of a typical middle- to upper-middle-class honeymoon: the historical and antiquarian sights of continental cities – particularly in this case, Rome – and the mountain scenery of the Swiss Alps. For each place I attempt to document some of the psychological, sexual, and visual investments that linked sightseeing with the cultural work of the honeymoon. In the case of the Roman honeymoon, I begin with negotiations, fictional and nonfictional, of touristic sights and end with a juxtaposition of two Roman honeymoons from two different kinds of cultural sources: the infamous wedding journey of Dorothea Brooke and Edward Casaubon as described in George Eliot's 1872 novel, *Middlemarch*, and the honeymoon tour of Emily Jowitt and Dearman Birchall one year later, as reported in Emily's diary. The difference in tone between the disappointing and indeed terrifying *Middlemarch* example and the euphoric account of travel, sightseeing, and marriage in the Birchall diary is, in a rough sense, typical of differences between fictional accounts – almost all negative – and accounts from diaries and letters, which tend to be more positive, at least about the relationship between the couple. Birchall's diary is remarkable, however, for the length and geographic scope of the honeymoon it records, as well as for its sustained tone of blissful intimacy.

Finally, I turn from the historical sights of Europe to nature, as it was embodied for Victorians in the Swiss Alps, and to the less clear-cut negotiations of sightseeing and tourism that composed the honeymoons of Leslie Stephen and Minny Thackeray Stephen in 1867 and of Matthew Arnold and Frances Lucy ("Flu") Wightman Arnold in 1851. Both these honeymoons register a profound and gendered ambivalence about travel, about scenery, and about the relation between these aspects of tourism and conjugality itself. While both the sections on Rome and on the Alps focus on sexual reorientation, the Roman material emphasizes the cultural demands placed upon the woman honeymooner in the effort to align herself with her partner and with the educated touristic gaze. The section on the Alps also takes on the reorientation required of the male partner. While I will return briefly to the example of Symonds, whose relations to Switzerland involved repeated reorientations of his sexuality in the most conventional sense, I will linger on the case of Stephen, whose return to Switzerland for his honeymoon was figured in his writing as a turn *away* from the mountains and mountaineering toward a more domestic and (in his terms) feminized life. Finally, the discussion of Matthew and Flu Arnold will propose a more complex case, in which turning away – from one's partner and from the landscape – becomes crucial in establishing gendered agency.

My first example of sexual reorientation in a chapter that deals largely with heterosexual couples honeymooning in the Swiss Alps and in Italy invokes the experience of a self-identified homosexual man who, it seems, made a deliberate choice to avoid Switzerland as the site of his wedding journey with his wife. Looking back on his honeymoon in his *Memoir*, John Addington Symonds stepped back from the narrative of his complex sexual identifications to make a more general point about Victorian erotic culture:

Truly we civilized people of the nineteenth century are more backward than the African savages in all that concerns this most important fact of human life. We allow young men and women to contract permanent relations involving sex, designed for procreation, without instructing them in the elementary science of sexual physiology. We do all that lies in us to keep them chaste, to develop and refine their sense of shame, while we leave them to imagine what they like about the nuptial connection. Then we fling them naked in bed together, modest, alike ignorant, mutually embarrassed by the awkward situation, trusting that they will blunder on the truth by instinct. We forget that this is a dangerous test of their affections and their self-respect; all the more dangerous in proportion as they are highly cultivated, refined and sensitive.[40]

Symonds is important, not because he is a "typical" Victorian honeymooner, whatever that might mean, but precisely because his self-situation with respect to normative modes of Victorian sexuality can help us both to defamiliarize that norm and to feel anew its familiar pressures. Symonds, who throughout his life saw himself as primarily attracted to men, and who in his later years was to make male homosexual relations the topic of his research and autobiographical writing, might seem an odd – even a perverse – choice as an exemplary honeymooner. What Symonds's experience and his own analysis of it allow us to see, however, is the cultural work performed by the ideal Victorian honeymoon, by the ideal *of* the honeymoon: its heterosexualizing imperative, its work of reorientation, even for couples who approximated its canonical sentiments more closely than Symonds was willing and, in his terms, able to do.

The work of reorientation is laid bare by the language of instruction and acculturation that characterizes the passage from Symonds. Such language is particularly remarkable because of Symonds's own conflicting uses of the word "natural" with respect to his sexuality. Symonds, for instance, was at

---

[40] John Addington Symonds, *The Memoirs of John Addington Symonds* (Chicago: University of Chicago Press, 1984), p. 158.

once able to make fun of his "innocence" in thinking that his decision to marry would take care of "the necessity of growing into a natural man"[41] and to refer unironically to the "superior naturalness and coolness" of his first heterosexual passion.[42] His strong, if intermittent, sense that men and women could and should be educated into conventional sexuality fore-grounds the honeymoon as the privileged scene of instruction.

The Symondses' honeymoon is also instructive with respect to another important trope of reorientation: the rich and pervasive lexicon of place. Again, Symonds's experiences gesture obliquely, if topically, to a powerful norm. A lifelong lover of the Alps, who associated the mountain scenery with his first heterosexual romance with a Swiss girl named Rosa as well as with his later engagement to Catherine North, a man who was to be instrumental in popularizing the Alps as a winter resort for British invalids, Symonds went against the habits of his class and his own habits of place to take his honeymoon in Brighton. His daughter Margaret, writing from their eventual home in the Alpine resort of Davoz Platz, remarks the oddness of this choice: "[T]hey did not go to the Alps which both of them loved so dearly; they did not even go to Italy – they went for some quite unimaginable reason to Brighton."[43] While in the memoir Symonds does not offer a reason for the choice against Switzerland and for what was even then a fading seaside resort, he does link the embar-rassments of the honeymoon specifically to place:

It requires all the romance of a Romeo and Juliet to make a double bedroom in an English town hotel appear poetical. The first joys of nuptial intercourse ought not to be remembered in connection with places so common, so sordid, and so trivial. I shall not forget the repulsion stirred in me by that Brighton bedroom or the disillusion caused by my first night of marriage.[44]

For Symonds, already provided with a rich lexicon of erotic transfor-mation derived from the Swiss Alps, Brighton served as a shorthand for the impossibility of reorientation. Symonds's eroticized map of Europe was not merely a result of his personal experiences with the men, the women, and the mountains that he had encountered there before his marriage. While the European continent has frequently been represented in British literature as a place of illicit sexuality, it was also the primary location of appropriate erotic transformation within marriage. The sights of Europe – natural and historical – served as landmarks in reorientation.

[41] *Ibid.*, p. 135.   [42] *Ibid.*, p. 144.
[43] Margaret Symonds, *Out of the Past* (London: John Murray, 1925), p. 86.
[44] J. A. Symonds, *Memoirs*, p. 156.

Again, we might turn to failed transformation, in this case a literary one, as a way of understanding cultural ideals.

Wilkie Collins's *The Woman in White* contains perhaps the most efficient novelistic discussion of how the honeymoon was expected to work. Through the negative example of Laura Fairlie, we can gain insight into a cultural script perhaps more easily legible in a marriage plot novel than in a diary or a memoir. In Collins's novel, Marian Holcombe becomes anxious because the letters her sister Laura writes her from her wedding journey to Europe show no sign that the transformation Marian has hoped for and that the community in which she lives seems to expect has taken place:

I cannot find that [Laura's husband's] habits and opinions have changed and coloured hers in any single particular. The usual moral transformation which is insensibly wrought in a young, fresh, sensitive woman by her marriage, seems never to have taken place in Laura. She writes of her own thoughts and impressions, amid all the wonders she has seen, exactly as she might have written to someone else, if I had been travelling with her instead of her husband . . . Even when she wanders from the subject of her travels . . . her speculations are busied with her future as my sister, and persistently neglect to notice her future as Sir Percival's wife . . . In other words, it is always Laura Fairlie who has been writing to me for the last six months, and never Lady Glyde.[45]

In this passage, geography and tourism are intimately entangled with nominal and personal change. The change would have been, of course, more acute for the bride for whom marriage was both a sign and a vehicle for a change in legal and sexual status. Although in earlier times in public (but not legal) usage a married man assumed the title of "master," as opposed to "lad," by the Victorian period it was only women who were renamed by marriage. This gendered nominal transformation was often figured as a rebirth or, with only a slight shift in valence, as a death. Victorian novels are filled with scenes like the one in Emma Guyton's *The Wife's Trials*, where Lilian tells her sister, Elizabeth, with a mixed sense of loss and pride, that upon her marriage she "will be Lilian Grey no longer!" Her sister's response, "You will be Lilian Hope, dearest!" suggests the powerful psychodynamics of a new beginning, a literally hopeful birth into a different identity.[46]

In my sample I find that many women and men remarked the name change in letters or diaries. Some, like Susan Miers, who is not included in my case studies because she traveled from London to Rio de Janeiro to

[45] Wilkie Collins, *The Woman in White* (New York: Oxford University Press), p. 181.
[46] Emma Guyton, *The Wife's Trials* (New York: Garland, 1976), p. 2.

marry her shipbuilder husband in lieu of taking a honeymoon, do so with apparent excitement; Miers practiced her name and new signature, followed by exclamation points, in the margin of her diary beside the entry for her wedding day. Eliza Wilson Bagehot focused on the loss of her old name but found herself "surprised" that she was not "more sad at losing" it.[47] Arthur Thorndike writes to Agnes Bowers in 1881 in an idiom that echoes the doubly valenced passage from *The Wife's Trials*: "This will be the last time you will be able to say on August 31 'I am Miss Bowers.' This month will never see you again under that title. Fancy, dear, only 15 more days."[48] Despite the forward-looking tone of the last sentence, Arthur constructs a calendar ultimately based on loss. Perhaps the most somber of the honeymooning women in my sample, Eliza Dickinson, who, living in India with her military family, married Captain Francis Wemyss in 1838, speaks directly – and mournfully – of the loss of self. Her last visit to church before her marriage is a "melancholy" occasion: "I did not like the feeling [of] the complete change in my life which is soon to take place, I sense the signal for every vestige of my former self to depart." On her wedding day she notes that "I did not recognize myself under my new name."[49]

Laura Fairlies's failure to become "Lady Glyde" is, of course, a symptom that something is deeply wrong with her marriage. The topography of the honeymoon has also failed to do its transformative work, as the problem of incomplete naming gets projected onto the honeymoon landscape. The "wonders" Laura has seen, the sights of the Continent, cannot act as supports to the legal project of renaming; there has been no "moral transformation." Laura's refusal to "notice her future as Sir Percival's wife" introduces a visual idiom that links the two projects of nominal and touristic reorientation.

If the *Woman in White* depends on the absence of visible signs of reorientation to hint at the failure of the novel's central marriage, Anne Brontë's *The Tenant of Wildfell Hall* offers us, through the diary of its heroine, Helen Graham, a visible struggle over her honeymoon's "Continental scenes." She writes retrospectively in her journal a few months after their marriage:

But Arthur is selfish – I am constrained to acknowledge that ... The first instance he gave was on the occasion of our bridal tour. He wanted to hurry it

[47] Mrs. Russell Barrington, *The Love Letters of Walter Bagehot and Eliza Wilson* (London: Faber, 1933), p. 201.
[48] Casson, *"My Dear One,"* p. 117.
[49] Eliza Dickinson, entry for 21 January 1838, Ms. diary, vol. III, 1838, Colchester-Wemyss Family Papers, D36 F35.

over, for all the Continental scenes were already familiar to him: many had lost their interest in his eyes, and others had never had anything to lose. The consequence was, that after a flying transit through part of France and Italy, I came back nearly as ignorant as I went, having made no acquaintance with persons and manners, and very little with things, – my head swarming with a motley confusion of objects and scenes – some, it is true, leaving a deeper and more pleasing impression than others, but these embittered by the recollection that my emotions had not been shared by my companion, but that, on the contrary, when I had expressed a particular interest in anything that I saw or desired to see, it had been displeasing to him in as much as it proved that I could take delight in anything disconnected with himself.[50]

Helen's journal imports into fiction a popular cultural rendering of the ideal honeymoon as a learning experience in which the husband figures as a guide. Again, the points of view of husband and wife are rendered with a literal attention to sight: "the Continental scenes" have lost their charm in Arthur's eyes; Helen's own untutored gaze produces a "swarming" and "confusion" that amount to a distortion of vision. The successful honeymoon is imagined as producing a change in the bride's fundamental perception as well as in her relation to "persons," "manners," and things.

WHEN IN ROME

Of all the continental destinations that appear in both the fiction and the nonfiction of the period, the two most evocative in terms of the density of their cultural investment were Rome and the Swiss Alps. While only seven couples in my sample went to Rome, it still arguably functioned as an ideal, if expensive, capstone to a wedding journey. It is, of course, very difficult to summarize "Victorian" attitudes toward Rome, and not only because of the many changes in travel, in aesthetics, and in politics that took place over the relevant period. Certainly, the struggle for and eventual unification of Italy over the middle decades of the century required the sometimes difficult reimagining for British tourists of Rome as the capital of a modern nation state. But Rome was already a city of layers of visible contradiction: statues of classical gods and Christian saints in the Parthenon, Christian churches built visibly on top of Roman temples, ruins and squalid apartment buildings. As Italy thrust its way onto the political stage, the English had to deal not only with different versions of the past, not only with the contrast between past and present, but with the relationship between the past and a not entirely

---

[50] Anne Brontë, *The Tenant of Wildfell Hall* (Oxford: Clarendon Press, 1992), p. 204.

comprehensible future: Rome as the epicenter of both papism and nationalism, as an eternal city frozen in time and the place of new and powerful movements.

The contradiction between modern and ancient Rome, both before and after the unification of Italy, revealed itself most acutely in British and American comments about the dirtiness of the city and its people. Roman dirt and "Roman fever," indissolubly linked in the British mind, were often portrayed by tourists as barriers separating them from various incarnations of the Roman past, as a literal and figurative patina over the canonical sights of the city. Tied to this sense of contradiction is one of disappointment, a motif to which many travelers returned. William Hazlitt, for example, set the tone for a century of deflated expectations, noting, in 1825,

an almost uninterrupted succession of narrow vulgar-looking streets, where the smell of garlic prevails over the odor of antiquity, with the dingy melancholy flat fronts of modern-built houses, that seem in search of an owner. A dunghill, an outhouse, the weeds growing under an imperial arch offend me not, but what has a greengrocer's stall, a stupid English china warehouse, a putrid *trattoria* . . . to do with ancient Rome? No! This is not the wall that Romulus leaped over; this is not the Capitol where Julius Caesar fell.[51]

For Hazlitt as for tourists who followed in his path, the "real" Rome was the Rome of the ancients; modern Roman life was something, by and large, to be ignored or endured by the practice of a touristic tunnel vision.

Despite the many disappointments recorded by, among others, Ruskin and Dickens, Rome continued to assert a powerful aesthetic force on English tourists, many of whom framed that disappointment as a contrast between what they had seen in paintings and engravings of Rome and the experience of traveling to it. Augustus Hare, one of the few Victorians to fall unabashedly in love with the city and the author of *Walks in Rome*, the most comprehensive Victorian guidebook to the capital, captures some of this contrast in the second paragraph of his guide:

An arrival in Rome is very different to that in any other town in Europe. It is coming to a place new and yet most familiar, strange, and yet so well known. When travelers arrive at Verona for instance, or at Arles, they generally go with a curiosity to know what they are like; but when they arrive at Rome and go to the Coliseum, it is to visit an object whose appearance has been familiar to them from childhood, and long ere it is reached, from the heights of the distant Capitol, they can recognize the well-known form: and as regards S. Peter's, who

---

[51] Brian Barefoot, *The English Road to Rome* (Upton-upon-Severn: Images, 1993), p. 163.

is not familiar with the aspect of the dome, of the wide-spreading piazza, and the foaming fountains, for long years before they come to gaze upon the reality?[52]

The Victorian experience of Rome, then, cannot be limited to actual journeys; to understand its significance for Victorian tourists and would-be tourists we must appreciate it as not only containing examples of great art but as a subject of art, not only as a place to trace the history of art but as a signifier of art itself. The visual economy of Rome was, for the British, necessarily complex, involving negotiations of climax and anti-climax, expectation and disappointment – even, as we shall see later, expectations of disappointment.

In order to untangle the relation between honeymoons and touristic narratives of expectation and disappointment, I turn to two different kinds of sources, the fiction of George Eliot and the diary of Emily Jowitt. Eliot's novel *Middlemarch* can, of course, make Dorothea Brooke's experience of Roman art and architecture a metaphor for failure in other aspects of the honeymoon. For real-life honeymooners, I am not suggesting a one-to-one correlation. Instead of emphasizing a scheme of equivalence, I want to return to the imagination of day-to-day life on the wedding journeys: the pressures to understand and appreciate canonical sights, the pleasures of learning and seeing that might or might not be shared with a new partner, and the feeling perhaps, if this were a first trip to Rome, that a long-held dream might finally have come to pass. These feelings, and others that we might imagine, begin to flesh out relations between tourism and conjugality that move beyond substitutive readings. Nonetheless, Eliot's literary rendering provides a structure of seeing and feeling that makes intelligible – Eliot's charged word here – experiences of real-life honeymoons.

Published in 1872 but set forty years earlier, *Middlemarch* explicitly figures Dorothea's honeymoon experience in Rome, "that city of visible history," as a visual assault that clarifies for the reader the opposing points of view of husband and wife. For the novel's heroine, the sights of Rome violently transform the worldview she has brought with her on her wedding tour:

To those who have looked at Rome with the quickening power of a knowledge which breathes a glowing soul into all historic shapes and traces out the sup-pressed transitions which unite all contrasts, Rome may still be the spiritual center and interpreter of the world. But let them conceive one more historical contrast: the gigantic broken revelations of that Imperial and Papal city thrust abruptly on the notions of a girl brought up in English and Swiss puritanism, fed

[52] Augustus J. C. Hare, *Walks in Rome* (London: Strahan, 1871), p. 1.

on meagre Protestant histories and art chiefly of the hand-screen sort . . . Forms
both pale and glowing took possession of her young sense, and fixed themselves
in her memory even when she was not thinking of them, preparing strange
associations which remained through her after-years . . . In certain states of dull
forlornness Dorothea all her life continued to see the vastness of St. Peter's, the
huge bronze canopy, the excited intention in the attitudes of the prophets and
evangelists in the mosaic above, and the red drapery which was being hung for
Christmas spreading itself everywhere like a disease of the retina.[53]

The sights of Europe produce in Dorothea a terrifying distortion of
vision. I have argued elsewhere that the recurring nightmares sound very
much like the horrifying and repetitive dreams of rape survivors and that
the visual violations of St. Peter's and of a spectacularly carnal imperial
city suggest the more overtly sexual violations of marital rape. What
concerns me here, however, is Eliot's explicit use of the trope of sightseeing as a way of registering sexual and social dislocations associated with
the failed honeymoon.

Dorothea's terrified gaze is contrasted to three others in the novel. The
first is signaled by the address at the beginning of the passage quoted
above: "To those who have looked at Rome with the quickening power of
a knowledge." Here we have an audience whose look is defined in terms
of a diffuse but potent knowledge of Rome and its history, a look so
powerful that it brings ruins and ideas to life. The knowledge that
accompanies this look, "which breathes a glowing soul into all historic
shapes and traces out the suppressed transitions which unite all contrasts," undertakes no modest visual task; it is the audience with this
knowledge that is asked to imagine into visibility not only world-making
historical forces but also the impressions of Dorothea, whose own gaze is
brought to life by the injunction to "conceive one more historical contrast." What is remarkable about the gaze that activates these imaginings
is the ease with which it moves between categories: between past and
present, between protestant and cosmopolitan historiographies, between
terror and pleasure. This ease is, of course, not of the same sort as that
which marks a more canonically touristical gaze, invoked dismissively by
the narrator when she explains that "the weight of unintelligible Rome
might lie easily on bright nymphs to whom it formed a background for
the brilliant picnic of Anglo-foreign society, but Dorothea had no such
defense against deep impressions."[54] The "bright nymphs" who relegated
Rome to the background of a "brilliant picnic" participate in a sort of

[53] George Eliot, *Middlemarch* (New York: Oxford University Press, 1988), pp. 159–60.   [54] *Ibid.*

touristic glare that confuses background and foreground, self and other, in a movement that does not so much connect as erase. Ignorant of the histories that could make Rome legible, too intelligent and too sensitive to ignore what she does not understand, Dorothea remains outside the visual economy of educated and uneducated tourism.

Perhaps most painful is the disjunction of her gaze from her husband's. Casaubon infamously spends the honeymoon in the labyrinthine libraries of the Vatican, leaving his wife to see the "sights" that are no longer new to him. The separation between them is a matter not merely of their physical separation but of what we might think of as a temporality of the gaze. Eliot embeds a piece of Casaubon's personal history in what is otherwise a condescending and indeed sinister invocation of the sights of Rome. Toward the end of the honeymoon, Casaubon somewhat awkwardly expresses the hope that Dorothea's "time" in "Rome" "has not passed unpleasantly." He turns the wish into a scene of honeymoon instruction with the following "little speech":

Among the sights of Europe, that of Rome has ever been held one of the most striking and in some respects edifying. I well remember that I considered it an epoch in my life when I visited it for the first time; after the fall of Napoleon, an event which opened the Continent to travellers. Indeed I think it is one of several cities to which an extreme hyperbole has been applied – "See Rome and die": but in your case I would propose an emendation and say See Rome as a bride, and live henceforth as a happy wife.[55]

In a novel so attentive to histories both national and personal, it is interesting that Casaubon should mention his own first "epoch"-making journey to Rome "after the fall of Napoleon." Casaubon's gaze is separated from Dorothea not only by gender, not only by his professional investments, but also by generation. If, for Casaubon, his first visit to Rome represented an "epoch" in his life, what about this revisitation, this honeymoon? By setting the climactic moment of his climactic narrative of tourism back in time to "after the fall of Napoleon," Casaubon is emphasizing the difference between himself and his wife. His personal story, marked and made significant by its associations with public events that took place when Dorothea was a child, cannot be Dorothea's. Her "epoch"-making journey is the honeymoon, the novel's historical present; his Roman narrative of transformation took place before the events of the (already historical) novel. If Casaubon has already been transformed by

---

[55] *Ibid.*, p. 163.

Rome, there is little or no place on this second journey for a second, conjugal, transformation.

And there is no doubt, by the end of the "little speech," that Casaubon's sense of transformation has a visual component. He ends with a proverb about the power of sight, although his amendment, "See Rome as a bride, and live henceforth as a happy wife," cannot finally free itself from the sinister implications of the original and succeeds only in aligning the happy wife with death and bridal transformation with changes more sinister. The act of "seeing" retains its power through both versions, both endings; if we think back, through Dorothea's recoil from the red hangings to the Ruskin honeymoon, it is seeing that both substitutes for and prevents consummation. While critics have long assumed that Casaubon was impotent and the Casaubon marriage unconsummated, his preoccupation with "forms" suggests to me a rigid adherence to conjugal duty. *Middlemarch* records both a series of assaults on Dorothea's vision and the impossibility of bringing that vision into alignment with appropriate touristical and conjugal requirements.

Emily Birchall's experiences, reported in her meticulous honeymoon journal of 1873, provide a spectacular contrast to Dorothea's. She records a five-month wedding trip – to France, Switzerland, Italy, Vienna, and Budapest – whose visual center, like that of the *Middlemarch* honeymoon, is St. Peter's. Despite a radical difference between her tone and the Eliot narrator's as Birchall describes her loving and companionable relationship with her husband and the joy she takes in visiting touristic sights, Birchall's account shares with Dorothea's experience a profound investment in the visual as it is embodied in St. Peter's and, more generally, in Rome. Birchall's journal entry for the couple's first day in Rome takes for granted the significance of Rome for educated tourists:

In Rome! the first thought when we awoke this morning, as it was the last when we closed our eyes last night. It seems almost too good to be true that the longing dreams of one's whole life should actually be realized. And the morning is so fresh and bright and sunny that Rome appears to us first under the most charming circumstances possible. It is far far more delightful in every way than either of us expected, high as were our expectations. It is such a bright, healthy feeling, *cheerful* city, such a *clean* place, so orderly, that even had it no historic associations, no monuments of art or antiquity whatever, it would still be, I think, the very pleasantest, charmingest spot on the face of the earth.[56]

[56] Emily Jowitt Birchall, *Wedding Tour, January–June 1873, and Visit to the Vienna Exhibition*, ed. David Verey (New York: St. Martin's, 1985), p. 22.

More telling than the "charmingest" superlatives with which this passage ends, more telling even than Emily's most unusual use of the words "clean" and "healthy" to describe a city that other Victorians associated with filth, beggars, and fever, are the pronouns that authorize Birchall's point of view. By the time the couple arrives in Rome, the gazes of husband and wife are completely aligned: the two open and close their eyes together, look at Rome together, and, finally, evaluate their experiences in the same way. We do not, of course, have the advantage of Dearman Birchall's direct testimony, but this is beside the point: we can watch as Emily carefully constructs a joint point of view from which she is able to assert a "we" and an "us" that come to life in the act of looking. Emily's sole use of "one" ("the longing dreams of one's whole life") does not so much separate her from her husband as suggest a universality to her dream that extends beyond even this couple's sleeping and waking.

Emily brings the conjugal gaze with its attendant "we" to bear upon what for her is clearly a synecdoche for the touristic experience of Rome, the canonical visit to St. Peter's:

The first place we go to is of course S. Peter's. Who could be twelve hours in Rome and keep away from her Cathedral? We walked to it, guided by Perrini ... over the Ponte di S. Angelo where the first glimpse of the Dome came to us, and far from feeling the least touch of that disappointment which, so many say, accompanies the first sight of it, it filled me with wondering imagination. It was grander, huger, vaster than my dreams of it. We walked on till we stood in the glorious Piazza, with S. Peter's in front of us, its splendid colonnade on either side, and the Vatican to our right. We went into the cathedral, and we stood still in sight of its vastness, breathless with awe and wonder. Dearman said he never felt so excited in his life, and my feelings were certainly beyond description.[57]

Like *Middlemarch*, Emily's journal represents sight as a point of entry into the body; the hugeness of St. Peter's has the power to take one's breath way. Of course, in this case, it is not one but two bodies that are simultaneously and identically affected. Emily's own "wondering imagination" melds, several lines later, with a shared experience of "awe and wonder." In the context of a honeymoon diary, and particularly of one as unusually attentive to the physical as Emily's – she jokes at one point about Dearman's "nudity" when he takes off his waistcoat to walk along the French coast – the excitement Emily attributes to Dearman and the

more generalized "feelings" she claims for herself take on an erotic register. The contrast with Dorothea's experience is stark.

Of course, Rome was not the only city to make it possible to produce
the visual reorientation embodied in the conjugal gaze. The city's hyperbolic status as a visual icon is useful in that it foregrounds the problems
and the pleasures associated with sight. Rome, in my account, becomes
not only a city to which a relatively small portion of my honeymooners
traveled but a place where the hopes and disappointments of some Victorian honeymooners could, with the help of novels, guidebooks, and
other cultural artifacts, begin to be made visible.

ALPS ON ALPS

If representations of honeymoons in European capitals yoke sexual
transformations to discourses of history and architecture, the Alpine
honeymoon brings to bear upon both male and female bodies the resonant discourse of the sublime. It is this high-cultural discourse that
enabled, more broadly, the linking of romantic love with the touristic
category of "scenery." The intimate relation between canonical scenes of
Alpine tourism and sexual love took a variety of cultural forms: from
Matthew Arnold's and Symonds's actual romances with young Swiss girls
to novels like Dinah Mulock Craik's *Young Mrs. Jardine*, in which the
hero meets his future bride in Switzerland. Here is Symonds in a diary
entry for 1863:

Rosa has become part of me, as no woman, no one else perhaps before was. She
has stirred true feeling, and has made Switzerland my soul's home. The memory
of Murren will endure like a great symphony, multitudinous with thought and
motives – storm, sun, and mist, and snow; unfathomable moonlight nights; calm
mellow evenings and cold sunrises; the greenery of the pine-croned [*sic*] alps [*sic*],
the glaciers and the precipices, the wrecks of avalanche and raving winds; all
combined, controlled, and brought into harmony by the thought of Rosa.[58]

And here is a scene from Craik's novel:

The Jungfrau in the sunset, spiritualized by a clear amber glory, till it resembles
nothing earthly, only that New Jerusalem "coming down from heaven like a
bride prepared for her husband" – Roderick gazed and gazed, almost out of
himself with ecstasy, thinking of nothing, seeing nothing, though there was a
little group beside him gazing too. But he never noticed them, till stepping
backward, he came against somebody, and said, "Pardon, madame" – then

---

[58] J. A. Symonds, *Memoirs*, p. 144.

turned and saw it was no madame at all – mademoiselle. She had not observed him – not in the least. Her eyes too were fixed upon the mountains in entire absorption – large, calm, blue, almost English eyes.[59]

Marjorie Hope Nicholson's *Mountain Gloom, Mountain Glory* usefully traces a series of perceptual and cultural shifts in the eighteenth and early nineteenth centuries that made it possible, in the imagination of elite travelers and viewers, to uncouple mountains from their traditional association with barrenness, isolation, and hard work and to enshrine them at the center of an aesthetic of the sublime. Leslie Stephen unconsciously charts a similar history in his 1871 classic collection of essays, *The Playground of Europe*, which, in bringing together articles he wrote for mountaineering and less specialized journals, monumentalized both a phrase and a series of mountain passes for the common reader. Stephen's essays recapitulate two themes that James Buzard has identified in his book on British tourism, *The Beaten Track*: the first, which is Buzard's central concern, is the antitouristic discourse of much elite writing about travel; the second, to which Buzard devotes much less time, is the gendering of the touristic landscape. Stephen combines both impulses in his repeated insistence that, despite the "invasion" of Switzerland by the British, "there are innumerable valleys which have not yet bowed the knee to Baal, in the shape of Mr. Cook and his tourists" (p. 48). In naming and narrativizing these valleys, Stephen sets up two Switzerlands, two Alpine experiences, one of which is literally on a higher plane than the other:

Suppose that we are standing upon the Wengern Alp; between the Monch and the Eiger there stretches a round white bank, with a curved outline, which we may roughly compare to one of Sir E. Landseer's lions. The ordinary tourists – the old man, the woman, or the cripple, who are supposed to appreciate the real beauties of Alpine scenery – may look at it comfortably from the hotel. They may see its graceful curve, the long straight lines that are ruled in delicate shading down its sides, and the contrast of the blinding white snow with the dark blue sky above; but they will probably guess it to be a mere bank – a snowdrift, perhaps, which has been piled by the last storm. If you pointed out to them one of the great rocky teeth that projected from its summit, and said that it was a guide, they would probably remark that he looked very small ... Now a mountaineer knows, to begin with, that it is a massive rocky rib, covered with snow, lying at a sharp angle, and varying perhaps from 500 to 1000 feet in height.[60]

---

[59] Dinah Mulock Craik, *Young Mrs. Jardine* (New York: Harper, 1880), p. 46.
[60] Leslie Stephen, *The Playground of Europe* (London: Longmans, 1871), p. 277.

This account depends, of course, as much on an identification *with* the mountaineer's corrective vision as on the idea of the misidentification *of* the ridge from the hotel room. And it is this central identification that constitutes the collection's construction of an audience: in the introduction, which works to provide a context for the various essays, Stephen apologizes for his tone – in particular for the slang and the jokes that he sees as a prominent feature of the essays' address. He offers the excuse that the essays were originally addressed to "companions," who come to life in the course of the introduction as the more-than-implied readers of his book:

Most of [the essays] were written for a small and very friendly audience; and while the pen was in my hand, I had a vision before my eyes of a few companions sitting at the door of some Swiss Inn, smoking the pipe of peace after a hard day's walk, and talking what everybody talks from archbishops to navvies; that is to say, what is ordinarily called "shop."[61]

The vision, conjured up here as it is elsewhere in *Playground* through a wreath of smoke, works through the twinned processes of exclusion and inclusion: navvies, archbishops, mountaineers, if they do not speak the same language, speak severally from within a specific language system of which mountaineering "shop" talk is only an example.

The final essay of *Playground*, "Regrets of a Mountaineer," records for posterity the struggle of separation without disidentification. The title's assertion of Stephen's continuing identity as a mountaineer does not so much belie as memorialize the project's central identity-conferring term:

But I have long anticipated that a . . . day would come for me, when I should no longer be able to pursue my favorite sport of mountaineering. Some day I should find that the ascent of a zigzag was as hard as a performance on a treadmill; that I could not look over a precipice without a swimming in the head; and that I could no more jump a crevasse than the Thames at Westminster. None of these things have [*sic*] come to pass. So far as I know, my physical powers are still equal to the ascent of Mont Blanc or the Jungfrau. But I am no less effectively debarred – it matters not how – from mountaineering. I wander at the foot of the gigantic Alps, and look up longingly to the summits, which are apparently so near, and yet I know they are divided from me by an impassible gulf.[62]

While there are no satisfactory explanations of the construction of this "gulf" that separates Stephen from his beloved mountaintops, this mental topography suggests an impenetrability more profound than that of the mountain passes themselves. This change, this loss, is figured as the

[61] *Ibid.*, p. vii.   [62] *Ibid.*, p. 265.

unbridgeable crevasse. And the bridge to the unbridgeable, as we shall see presently, is marriage.

If we map out, with Stephen, a terrain and a vision so presumptive of masculinity that gender becomes visible only as a gap in class inclusiveness, what then would it mean for a man, say Leslie Stephen, and a woman, say Minny Thackeray Stephen, to honeymoon in the Alps? What it meant for Leslie Stephen was, it appears, a realignment of his gaze with the hotel window. A letter to Holmes, dated from the honeymoon, asserts in equivocal form the language of loss that so marks the end of *Playground*:

I was married on June 19 [1867], and to avoid all folly of breakfasts, &c., we got it done at 8 A.M., and started by the Folkestone and Boulogne train for Paris ... We went to Switzerland and visited my dear old mountains, and to you – being out of the possibility of peaching – I may whisper that I felt certain pangs at staying at the bottom, instead of bounding from peak to peak across the fathomless abysses of the glacier. However, I had, as you may well believe, a glorious time notwithstanding.[63]

In tracing the language of loss, I am, of course, allowing the shifts in Stephen's point of view to construct the story. This is, as George Meredith puts it in *The Egoist*, only the half-written story of the honeymoon, the bachelor's side. But what of Minny, whose access to the passes is mediated not only by Leslie's special preparations for her comfort but also by his experiences as he and others presented them to her?

We have only a few clues from this half. Stephen's most recent and sophisticated biographer, Noel Annan, inserts the activity of mountain climbing into a euphoric honeymoon story:

They went for their honeymoon in the Alps and the spirited letters they both wrote to Anny [Minny's sister] showed the joy they found in each other. Minny declared that crossing three passes a day was well enough except for the fact that it was obligatory to eat a meal of bread and honey at the top of these. Leslie teased her for saying that she had seen the place where the Rhine flows into the Rhone "showing the effect of crossing three passes on a weak mind." She called him Lez and he nobly restrained himself from climbing more than one or two Alps. But she was content to be left to read in the hotel and to make uninhibited comments on her reading. "Poor old Queen, what a time the Prince must have had with her," was her comment on the Queen's life of Prince Albert.[64]

Minny's letters force us to inhabit, in this case both literally and figuratively, the view from the hotel. Figuratively, Leslie Stephen's own

---

[63] Frederic William Maitland, *The Life and Letters of Leslie Stephen* (New York: Putnam, 1951), p. 196.
[64] Noel Annan, *Leslie Stephen: The Godless Victorian* (New York: Random, 1984), p. 63.

point of view has aligned the hotel with misidentification; even when
Minny is out among the mountains, she misreads the landscape. Perhaps
more important, because more mundane, is what happens when Minny is
literally left behind. In reading and telling the story of the uppity queen
("what a time the Prince must have had with her"), Minny announces her
own willingness to spend time *without* her husband. What a time, we
might think, the mountaineer must have had without *her.*

Midcentury honeymoon narratives, both historical and fictional, are
filled with negotiations between men and women about place on the
Alpine terrain. Sarah Tytler's *The Honeymoon's Eclipse*, written in 1899
about what it identifies as a distinctively 1850s honeymoon, features as
one of the first signs of marital discord the fact that Tina, the bride, not
only disdains Alpine scenery and wants to shop in Paris but refuses to stay
at the inn while her husband makes the obligatory ascent of one of the
peaks: "He had intended to persuade Tina to remain at one of the hotels,
while he hired a guide and made his 'prentice attempt at Alpine
mountaineering that he might judge for himself how much harder the
effort, how much grander the reward than he had known when he
climbed Ben Ledi."[65] As we shall see, questions of placement grew more
acute during Matthew and Flu Arnold's extended honeymoon, when
Matthew famously, or at least productively, spent the night at the
monastery of the Grande Chartreuse while Flu slept at a lodging outside
the monastery gates.

Whatever the compromises with and to desire any of these women
might have made, we must not imagine Minny Stephen's point of view as
betokening a simple desire to move outside the hotel. She writes to a
friend: "I am trying not to look out of the window, for if I do I shall see
the Matterhorn with the moon shining on it and you can't think how
horrid it looks, like a great hooky sort of gleaming ghost. I always think it
will come and poke its great hook nose into the window."[66] This refusal
of the gaze is here a deliberate misidentification. While she gets the name
of the mountain right, she refuses to see it from the point of view of the
mountaineer: it is a ghost; it has a nose; from the now protective window
of the hotel it assumes a gothic form. Like the dome of St. Peter's, which
for the honeymooning Dorothea Brooke becomes a nightmare vision
imprinted on her retina, this natural "sight" of Europe threatens to cross
the boundary between spectacle and body.

[65] Sarah Tytler, *A Honeymoon Eclipse* (London: Chatto, 1899), p. 20.
[66] Annan, *Leslie Stephen*, p. 63.

A different, but perhaps equally evocative crisis of vision seems to have occurred during the honeymoon of Matthew Arnold and Flu Wightman. Their honeymoon involved two journeys several months apart: the first, to Alverstoke on the English coast and, the second, to Paris, through the Alps, and on to Italy. The two honeymoon journeys are usually seen as having produced two important poems: the first, of course, the poem that might be placed at the center of the honeymoon canon, "Dover Beach," and the second, "Stanzas from the Grande Chartreuse." The identification of the honeymoon with the production of Matthew Arnold's poetry highlights one sort of cultural work at the expense of another: even those biographers who linger on more private aspects of the wedding journeys – the extent to which Matthew loved Flu, his general views of women or sexuality, the vexed question of his virginity – tend to read the journeys through the poems and thus unconsciously to see them as productive only of literary and indeed canonical forms of meaning. In the only analysis to foreground Flu's letters, Flu's point of view, James Broderick uses Flu's comments – many of them about weather – as a local corrective to the poems and as a sign of Arnold's transformative poetic powers. He acknowledges Flu's irony and the fact that her letters can be read as "frank testimony to the cost of poetry on the other side of the wicket," but he ends his brief discussion with a comfortable reestablishment of a reading community unsurprised by that cost and, presumably, accustomed to paying it:

We are not surprised that Arnold excludes direct reference to his bride or her discomfort. In the elegies for his pets he does not allow himself to be very specific and intimate in referring to his own family; and the special success of a minor poem like "Geist's Grave" depends on its relaxed mingling of the literary and the homely. But in his serious poems where the grand pathos of the age is his theme, his principle of selection is just, albeit somewhat stiff.[67]

I do not want to linger on the analogy with pets but prefer instead to move from making an analysis that depends on the poem as a product to thematizing poetry as an interpretive frame. What might it mean, then, for Flu to honeymoon in the Alps with someone who was, in the best scenario, always on the verge of producing a poem that would embody, however stiffly, "the grand pathos of the age"? What would this sense of one's husband being on the verge do to one's journey through the terrain

[67] James H. Broderick, "Two Notes on Arnold's 'Grande Chartreuse,'" *Modern Philology* 66.2 (November 1968), 158.

that represented for him not only the site of his sexual past and the poems he was currently writing about it but the potential locus of future fame? It is tempting to see the answer as a form of vertigo. This is Flu in a letter to her sister, describing a mule ride across the mountain pass from Beaufort to Les Chapieux:

Quite dark nearly all the way. I never was more alarmed, & altogether quite lost my nerve and behaved dreadfully. It was so dark & I was perched on an enormous mule, with no saddle, only a kind of pack made up with hay & my shawl, so that I felt very insecure & the guide walked about two yards in advance holding the end of a long rein. The path was very narrow & the mule crawling along the edge. Then I had my legs hanging over the edge at the most frightful height, with nothing for hundreds of feet below. I never was more glad to get to any place than Chapiu [*sic*].[68]

The disorientation of the journey is borne out in what Stephen might recognize as misidentification: the "Chapiu" to which this nightmare journey tends is Les Chapieux. Matthew's own diary, despite its confident adherence to facts, makes an even more singular error of place: "Sunday, September 7, 1851 Grande Chartreuse"; "Monday, September 8, 1851, Chambéry"; "Tuesday, September 9, 1851, L'Hopital [*sic*] Conflans"; "Wednesday, September 10, 1851, Chapon."[69]

Matthew Arnold's disorientation, usually framed as a reorientation away from his unsuitable attachment to the mysterious Marguerite and toward the accommodations of bourgeois married life, has been amply documented in biography and criticism. His poetry, in particular the "Grande Chartreuse," has been seen as an attempt to come to terms with sexual conflict. As Alan Grob puts it, "In contradiction to what we know biographically, that after staying overnight at the Grande Chartreuse

---

[68] Matthew Arnold, *The Letters of Matthew Arnold*, ed. Cecil Y. Lang, vol. 1 (1829–59) (Charlottesville: University of Virginia Press, 1996), p. 217. This scene of honeymoon vertigo for women on mules is repeated in several accounts. Richard Cobden writes to his brother of a similar episode involving his bride Kate:

Kate bore the fatigue like an Amazon – there was only one drawback to her fame as a frigid heroine – and it arose from inexperience at the beginning of our excursion – The mules are used in ascending the steepest parts, to zig-zag, from side to side; & just as we were at the edge of a precipice Kate's mule turned its head right athwart the road, and to her amazement instead of going straight up as before, he walked firmly for the side – A tragic scene followed, much to the amusement of the guide – The screams were not loud enough to disconcert the mule backed(?) at his wanted distance from the edge of the precipice . . . A slight fit of hysterical laughter and all was right again. But you would be astonished at the courage that a week's riding has given her – I caught her eating a biscuit(?) with her bridle dropped over the animal's back at a point off the road near Chamonix, where we should have shuddered at the outset of our journey (Richard Cobden to Fredrick N. Cobden, 30 June 1840, Richard Cobden Letters 1833–1865. Collection 1040 Box 1, Folder 6).

[69] Arnold, *Letters*, p. 216.

Arnold did return to life in the world, to marriage, and to work, the fantasy of childhood that concludes the poem provides him with an imagined and perhaps wishful scenario in which he is finally able to forsake those obligations."[70]

For better or for worse, *for* Matthew Arnold, we have the evidence of the poem. What happens to the vertigo, the sense of verge, when there is no poem to record it? We have "only" the following words from Flu:

The Grande Chartreuse I was not going to turn my back upon; as women are not admitted I was lodged in a small house not far from the monastery where I spent rather an uncomfortable time as it was bitterly cold. Matt was allowed to have supper with me, but at 1/2 past 7 he was turned out and went into the monastery where he had a cell to sleep in.[71]

The turns of this passage are many and curious. Flu's insistence on orienting herself *toward* the monastery – "The Grande Chartreuse I was not going to turn my back upon" – suggests an agency denied to her husband: "Matt was allowed to have supper with me, but at 1/2 past 7 he was turned out." Flu's emphasis allows us to look at what Broderick might see as "the wrong side of the wicket": to reorient ourselves with respect to the language of exclusion. As in the case of Minny Thackeray, it is hard to tell who is leaving, who is turning away from, whom: we have here perhaps a deliberate or partly conscious misidentification, not of landscape, but of its traditional hierarchies.

This is not to pass over the real terror we can read in these honeymoon journeys: the hook-nosed Matterhorn coexists with the life of Prince Albert; the hotel room is both sanctuary and scene of potential or achieved violations. While it is tempting as a historian of sex to continue to ask binary questions about their Victorian subjects – Did they or didn't they (do it)? Did she or didn't she (enjoy it)? – those subjects, too, speak from both sides of the wicket.

I would like to end as I began with the instructive case of John Addington Symonds: cultural authority and self-proclaimed sexual deviant, loving husband and lifelong lover of men, lover of Switzerland, lover *in* Switzerland, and domestic honeymooner. Symonds returned from his Swiss idyll with Rosa to a complete physical and mental breakdown. After consulting, among others, William Acton, he found with his father's help an "excellent surgeon," who, as Symonds puts it,

[70] Alan Grob, *"A Longing Like Despair": Arnold's Poetry of Pessimism* (Newark: University of Delaware Press, 2002), p. 521.
[71] Arnold, *Letters*, p. 216.

"gave me a simple remedy for my eyes – vinegar and water for a lotion, and the prospect of recovery through time and perseverance. For my constitution, he recommended cohabitation with a hired mistress, or what was better, matrimony ... As by inspiration, the memory of Catherine North returned to me."[72] This return, this deliberate reorientation, took Symonds, among other places, to Brighton. Symonds's description of his honeymoon oscillates characteristically between a sense of his typicality and his isolation. Once again:

It requires all the romance of a Romeo and Juliet to make a double bedroom in an English town hotel appear poetical. The first joys of nuptial intercourse ought not to be remembered in connection with places so common, so sordid, and so trivial. I shall not forget the repulsion stirred in me by that Brighton bedroom or the disillusion caused by my first night of marriage.[73]

Symonds's turn toward the Brighton bedroom came, of course, at a tremendous cost, although he was always to maintain his love for his wife and his family life in Switzerland. He was always clear about this. For Fanny Arnold, for Leslie Stephen, and even for the fictional Dorothea Brooke, we can begin through their travels to articulate the more hidden costs of reorientation.

[72] J. A. Symonds, *Memoirs*, p. 152.   [73] *Ibid.*, p. 156.

CHAPTER 3

Carnal knowledges

MARTHA KNOWS

Of all the men and women in my sample of honeymooning couples, I feel that I know Martha Rolls Macready the best. Part of this feeling comes from what I can express only in the idiom of ownership; unlike many of the other honeymooners about whom I have substantial information – Effie Ruskin, say, or Flu Arnold, or even Emily Birchall – Martha (as I find myself unable not to call her) is my discovery. And this, in turn, has something to do with how, and in what form, I "discovered" her. Although Martha's diary does not have the generic markers of Juliana Fuller's – no blue ribbon, no locks of hair or photographs – it speaks the genre of the honeymoon diary in other ways: its careful daily entries, its meticulous attention to and vocabulary for emotional life, and, most of all, its foregrounding of the vocabulary of the conjugal. Its topics and its language are inflected throughout by the lexicon of privacy, affect, and, finally, of secrecy. Of all the honeymoon diaries I have read, Martha's is the most novelistic, the most like a Victorian novel, both because of its linked interest in quotidian detail and interior life and because of what we might think of as its narrative structure.[1]

Martha's is also one of the least touristic of the diaries. She writes from the small seaside resort of Littlehampton, where she has gone, it seems, in part for her health. Hers is not a honeymoon of continental scenes: there is no St. Peter's on the horizon of her wedding journey, no mountain peaks. Despite its length, this is a contracted honeymoon: unlike her counterparts who honeymoon in Europe, moving from museum to museum, Martha focuses on one painting she sees near the end of her stay. Scenery, in the context of this honeymoon, means the same few stretches of beach traversed many times a week. Martha keeps a weather

---

[1] Martha Rolls, Ms. diary, 1840, Rolls Family Papers, D361 F/P 6.9.

eye out for changes in the sky, the texture of seaweed, or signs of approaching storms. Her movements, as she records them, are localized, scaled down: although her husband, Edward Macready, walks to Arundel, some five miles away, she waits on the beach with her mother. The one place-name to interrupt the sense of placelessness is the village of Rustington, one mile away. Martha notes – without apparent interest in its sights or indeed in the accurate spelling of its name – that all walks seem to lead to "this village." Adventures come slowly as the honeymoon unfolds; unlike Kate Cobden or Minnie Thackeray, Martha does not scale peaks or encounter the sublime; her encounters with nature involve a ritual of slow immersion in which she is gradually moved, over a period of many weeks, from a warm bath into a bathing machine and thus into the sea. The scale of the honeymoon suggests the theme of the diary: intimacy, its approaches and limits. In this minimalist landscape, stripped almost bare of landmarks, the relationship between Martha and Edward is, to borrow Martha's words, "everything." We can read the diary as a daily exploration of how well one person can know another, of the pleasures, the pressures, and – for Martha, painfully – the limits of the conjugal.

Martha's diary, despite its many detailed entries, points to a series of secrets: a mysterious family feud; an unidentified but crucial Mr. S., with whom Martha may have had a previous romantic relationship; an unnamed illness; and, finally, the biggest mystery of them all, the secret of Edward's persistent "low spirits." The story unfolds gradually as about two months into the honeymoon, on 28 September, Martha notes that all is not well with Edward: "Dearest Edward was in very bad spirits all the evening – he said he was quite well – but evidently something was the matter – which made me very unhappy." The link between his "spirits" and hers becomes more explicit and, indeed, more hyperbolic with the passage of time. Two sequential entries for 14 and 15 November show Martha's absorption in Edward's state of mind. On the fourteenth Martha writes: "Edward was not himself this afternoon – I know not why – but when he is thus it makes me feel so utterly depressed I can scarcely contain my tears. My spirits depend entirely upon his, and rise and fall with them." In this passage, we can feel Martha's frustration as she substitutes conjugal empathy for conjugal knowledge. Although Edward is "not himself," the diary hints at the possibility that Martha is or should be Edward, that their identification should be so complete that she must feel with him.

It might be useful at this point to step back from Martha's identifications and Martha's frustrations to the expectations of the reader of this diary – in other words, in this particular context, to mine. These expectations come from two linked sources: the novel and the archive. As we shall see in Chapter 4, the honeymoon novel is in some sense about the discovery of secrets, as two characters, isolated from the rest of the world on their wedding journey, confront each other's often horrific sexual and financial pasts. And we do not need the specific genre markers of the honeymoon novel to desire and, indeed, to expect full revelation. As I read Martha's diary entries for November, the heft of the pages to come hinted at the kind of full knowledge and resolution one might expect from a novel of psychological realism, a novel called *Martha* or, perhaps, with some attempt at distance, *Littlehampton*.

The expectations of the archive are equally if differently compelling. The genre of the diary and the subgenre of the honeymoon diary seem to hold out the promise of intimate revelation. In this instance, the fact that Martha is *not* a character in a book suggests an authenticity itself tangled up in expectations that a diary can tell us more than a novel, that readers of and in the archive can finally literally hold in their hands the key to that always elusive enterprise of Victorian sexuality. As an obsessive reader of Victorian novels turned in middle life into an archival scholar, I was susceptible to the epistemologies that structure both novelistic and archival relations to the secrets of Victorian life.

Imagine, then, the moment when I turned to Martha's entry for 15 November. For some reason Martha's handwriting, admirably clear to this point, became harder to read. I could just make out "The cause of Edward's depression which I have now learnt has made me still more uncomfortable – indeed truly unhappy" and then, even less legible, "I must do all in my power to remedy it and I think I shall succeed – God grant it." End of entry. Despite the promise of the archive; despite the tools and skills for examining it that I had learned over time; despite having found the records office containing Martha's family papers and having traced its renamings; despite having learned the names and nicknames of Martha's family, the intricacies of her handwriting, her system of abbreviation; despite having looked up local histories, maps, and histories of the British seaside and having traced her few political references; despite having located her mother's diary, her husband's account book, her brother's political cartoons – I was not to know what Martha knew. Despite my identification with Martha and my experience in reading novels and characters on paper, I was not going to be able to give a name to the causes of Edward's low spirits or to understand the nature of Martha's prayer for help with the burden and privileges of her knowledge of them. Despite my literary training in reading beyond and around silences, I was left to inhabit this one. I was not to know Martha.

SCENES OF INSTRUCTION

In other chapters, I have looked at the honeymoon primarily as a time and place of transformation or reorientation from one identity to another, conjugal one. If we think about the conjugality produced in and through the honeymoon, however, we come up inevitably against the question of knowledge. On the most obvious level, the geographical displacements of the honeymoon required not only adjustments of ideas and identities but a kind of learning as well. While the idiom of instruction is, predictably enough, strongest in accounts of Continental honeymoons, where men and women were at pains to absorb information about cultural landmarks, other kinds of learning also took place. Martha Macready is once again modestly instructive: she and Edward read to each other and shared their views on what they read. Martha struggled to learn self-knowledge, framing her diary as a series of reminders to herself about appropriate behavior. Martha's honeymoon was also, as we have seen, about getting to know Edward and of coming to a sense of the limits of her knowledge.

These kinds of knowledge, or knowledges, are not of, course, those that are privileged by Victorian or contemporary narratives about the honeymoon, which depends so heavily for its narrative and social structure on the assumed event of sexual consummation. So far, I have insisted that these knowledges be read in conversation with the sexual requirements of the honeymoon: in other words, I argue in Chapter 2 that the various activities of the honeymoon that are not indicatively or overtly sexual be read as crucial to the project of sexual reorientation. For the purposes of this chapter I want to linger on specifically sexual meanings and identifications, granting to the honeymoon the hegemony of the sexual and reading with the grain of the cultural demand that the honeymoon be an initiation into specifically sexual knowledge.

What can we know of Martha in this context? Although reading the diary gives us a rich sense of the importance of Martha's body and Edward's as they walked or failed to walk; swam or balked at swimming; felt better, worse, faint, or in pain; applied leeches and drank medicine, there are no overt references to sex. The structure of Victorian sexual reticence and also the structure of archival readings for carnal knowledge suggest that the places to look for sex are in the silences that make up so much of Martha's diary. In this context it is perhaps significant that the diary begins one month into the wedding journey; we have no written trace of the wedding night. The diary, in fact, begins, for all its insistence on conjugality, with what might be thought of as the semipublic phase of the honeymoon: the arrival of Martha's mother with a friend precipitates the honeymoon into written form as implied audience and family come on the scene together. Did Martha write of her wedding night?[2]

What of other silences in the diary that might be significant, that might indicate, not omission, forgetfulness, or boredom with the task of writing, but the vivid presence of something that, to Martha's mind, could or should not be spoken? And here I must refer once more to the temptations of the archival reader, to the temptations of reading honeymoons *with* cultural expectations and *for* sex. The truth is that all of Martha's prevarications and silences can be read as oblique references to the sexual, and that all of her mysteries can be "solved" by recourse to it. One could, for example, read Martha's several honeymoon illnesses as part of the sexual and reproductive plot that shapes our understanding of the honeymoon. On 2 October, when Martha reports, "Not well. Very faint after breakfast, Better after dinner," the temptation is to look for signs of pregnancy. This suspicion might be supported by her notation, about two weeks later on 20 October, that she was "[u]nwell in Church – obliged to come home," and by the fact that once again she seemed better in the evening. Diagnosing morning sickness at this distance of time and culture is, in one sense, ludicrous, but the power of the reproductive plot and of sexual discovery makes it difficult not to read Martha's body for symptoms of the sexual and Martha's prose for symptoms of repression. Readings of the honeymoon for the signs of pregnancy are doomed, however, to disappointment: Edward and Martha will have no children. (The persistent reproductive reader, however, would note, with truth, that Martha might have had an early miscarriage during the period covered by the diary – or a late miscarriage or even a stillbirth in the period after the diary ends. Martha's age – she was thirty-six – can be offered as evidence for or against this possibility.)

It was, for me, equally tempting to read Edward's "low spirits" as having some kind of sexual component. Martha's refusal to spell out the problem once she discovered it suggests that the problem, whatever it

---

[2] Of course this question opens the way for another powerful archival fantasy: the discovery of the crucial missing letter or other document that will not only fill in gaps but will make the story cohere. We can no more know the answer to this question than we can imagine with any accuracy what she might have written; this deferred beginning is the silence that structures everything.

might have been, was too private to be confided even to a diary. Since Martha seems not to wince at other possibly taboo subjects – her bad moods and bad behavior, conflicts between herself and family, indigestion, and so forth – it is very possible to conclude that the answer to the mystery lies in one of the few areas Martha never mentions. While there is much that cannot be known about Martha, the kind of knowledge the Victorians might have called carnal is an area of aggravated ignorance, perhaps for Martha, and certainly for the reader of her diaries.

This chapter moves the term "carnal knowledge" from its immediate context and revises it into plural form in order to suggest the multiple kinds and levels of information about sex available to us and to the Victorian cases we study. This chapter consists of three parts, each a different kind of thought experiment. The first, "Knowledge Tree," is an attempt to outline, again in some realist detail, the accretion of partial and contradictory knowledges that undergird what we think of as "sexual knowledge" and to organize them schematically as a tree, or series of levels. The second section, "The Knowing Victorians," consists of a discussion of recent trends in the scholarship on Victorian sex and in the revisionary narratives of Victorian sexuality associated with Stephen Marcus, Peter Gay, and Michael Mason. I then test the figure of the sexually positive Victorian against the availability of sources and, ultimately, against my sample. In the final section, "Transmitting Knowledge," I turn to two figures from that sample, Margaret Gladstone MacDonald and Maud Sambourne Messel, to speculate in more detail about what different kinds of information about sex might have been available to two late-Victorian women from different strata of the professional middle class. As in the section on the knowledge tree, I stress the multiplicity of sources, information, misinformation, and euphemism. The discussions of Margaret and Maud do not form themselves neatly into a tree; my speculations about Margaret are more like a series of widening circles as I begin with direct evidence of her knowledge about sex and move to a more speculative array of possibilities about information potentially available to her. In the case of Maud Messel, competing knowledges take the more intimate form of a dialogue between herself and her mother as her honeymoon letters to her mother negotiate sexual knowledge and sexual ignorance through an intense and intensely private vocabulary of the erotic. Rather than moving out from Maud's situation to speculate where she received her sexual knowledge, my discussion of Maud's experience lingers in the context of family and of a relationship based, as I read it, partly on sexual and epistemological competition.

KNOWLEDGE TREE

I argue earlier in this book that different kinds of knowledges can compete or overlap; in the case of John Ruskin, for example, his expertise about the female body as it was rendered in classical sculpture was a form of sexual knowledge that could be understood, according to most understandings of his marriage, to compete with his knowledge of the actual female body and to defer indefinitely his acquisition of carnal knowledge in the traditional sense. In this chapter so far, I have focused on two kinds of knowledge: what a Victorian woman might have been able to find out about sex from a variety of sources and what contemporary Victorianists might be able to know – that is to find out – about how much such a woman might know. Before turning to actual examples of sexual knowledge, I would like to pause long enough to consider the many kinds and levels of knowledge that might contribute to a substantive and nuanced epistemology of Victorian sex.

I like to think of my model as a knowledge tree – not only because the multilevel structure of epistemology resembles the cantilevered branches of a simplified evergreen (think of a child's drawing of a Christmas tree), but because the link between sex and knowledge embodied in the story from Genesis and in its central icon of the tree of knowledge is itself an important context for all Victorian and twentieth-century knowing in a Judeo-Christian tradition. Thus the connection and the resonant story of the Fall form one of the largest and lowest branches of my tree. In what follows I take the example of female orgasm and the knowledges that surround and contextualize it as a way of thinking (down) through the levels of the tree and producing a multilayered rendering of Victorian sexual epistemology.

I assume, for the purposes of this tree of knowledge, a Victorian heterosexual couple and a community of modern readers or scholars. While I understand that some couples might be quite different from one another, I pose these differences as various possible ways of answering the questions that form the branches of the tree. I also understand that there would and have been differences among scholars of the Victorian period; the capacious "our" on the other side of the barrier that divides Victorian actors from modern interpreters (represented in this model as a black line) is meant as a starting point that produces questions to be answered differently by different Victorianists. Here are some levels we might want to consider:

- What a particular Victorian woman would have known about sex. We might start, simply enough, with "experience" as opposed to "knowledge," but the category of experience itself immediately involves us in the problem of knowledge. Did this woman know what an orgasm was, whether or not she had had one? Did she know how to simulate one? Did she know not to? Was orgasm part of her vocabulary, her mental and/or erotic lexicon?

- What her husband or partner would have known about sex. We might also think of the husband or male partner and his forms of knowing in a variety of senses: did he know about the existence of female orgasm? Did he know what role it might or might not play in reproduction? Did he know whether his partner was orgasmic? Marie Stopes's concerns about simulated orgasm take us to the question of the sources of his knowledge:[3] Did it derive from books? From experiences with prostitutes? From experiences with his partner?

- What the man and the woman would have known – or would have thought they knew – about each other. Both partners might have had ideas about whether female orgasm was necessary for reproduction; those ideas might have been different or the same. Their ideas about whether women could or should have orgasms as part of a sexual relationship might likewise have differed. They might or might not have known how to talk about these differences; they might or might not have shared a common sexual language. The knowledge of each partner about the other would also have been affected by their general ideas about the "opposite" sex.

- What the couple had learned from informal advice networks. What would the man and the woman have learned from their friends and families? Could they have distinguished misinformation from good advice? What investments might those families have had in their own ignorance or in the ignorance of the imaginary couple? Might the woman's family have competed or clashed with the man's in setting the terms of the couple's sexual knowledge? Would there have been generational differences between the couple's younger friends or siblings and their parents or grandparents? How would individual members of the couple and the couple as a unit have negotiated rebellion and identification in their assimilation of sexual knowledge from the previous generation?

- The knowledge of the family physician who might have advised one or both members of the couple. How much would a woman's doctor have

---

[3] Marie Stopes, *Married Love: A New Contribution to the Solution of Sex Difficulties* (London: Putnam's, 1918).

known about female orgasm? What would he, for example, have thought the connection was between reproduction and female orgasm? Would he have shared knowledge about spontaneous orgasm with his patient? Would he have said different things to patients of different genders? Would he have expected a husband to be the one to impart information to his wife? Would a woman have known what questions to ask her doctor? And would he have known how to answer her so she understood?

- The knowledge of the scientists and more academic doctors who published articles on sexological topics read by family physicians. Academic doctors would have been more aware of research cutting off orgasm from reproduction. Some did and some did not publish about this; many equivocated. Where did academic doctors get their knowledge? (Lawson Tait, for example, interviewed husbands about female pleasure in women with ovariectomies, but he did not ask the wives themselves.)[4] Again, how would the husbands in this study have known how to represent their wives' sexuality? How would the doctors have known what questions to ask? Would information from sexologists have reached the couple (if at all) through the scientist himself? Through scientific or popularized articles? Through the family doctor?
- Our knowledge about all of the above.
- Our belief about the state of our possible knowledge – metaknowledge – our sense of epistemology.
- Our sense about the state of our own sexual knowledge and our narratives about scientific progression. (These might be challenged or enriched, for example, by the recent discovery of a slight but persistent link between female orgasm and reproduction.)
- Our sense about what is, was, or should be pleasurable.
- Our sense of what is moral, natural, acceptable, or normal.
- Our sense of the Victorians and of Victorianism. Which historical narrative(s) of Victorian sex we believe in.
- Our sense that sex and knowledge are linked. (For example, the Judeo-Christian context for using sex as a metaphor for knowledge and knowledge as a euphemism for sex.)
- Our sense that sex and knowledge are opposed through a cultural linking of knowledge to the brain and sex to the body.

---

[4] Lawson Tait, "Lawson Tait on Oöphorectomy," *British Gynecological Journal* 4 (1888), 3107.

THE KNOWING VICTORIANS

Victorian sexuality has been a topic of recent scholarly interest as, slowly over the last fifty years, old ideas about Victorian prudery competed with, and in some cases were replaced by, what we might think of as more sex-positive accounts of Victorian culture. From soon after Victoria's death – which consecrated a reign into a historical era until the 1960s and beyond – the adjective "Victorian" connoted sexual prudery and innocence, even to scholars of the period. Today the picture is more complicated; although the specter of the prudish Victorian is still viable in popular culture, it coexists in scholarship with other stories and images, like those that formed the basis for Steven Marcus's 1964 study, the hauntingly titled *Other Victorians*, which noted that the period was marked as much by the proliferation of brothels and pornography as by sexual recoil. Still, with Marcus, these sexually active Victorians remained "other" to official discourse; perhaps ordinary middle-class men visited prostitutes and consumed pornography, but they did this by living two parallel lives, by living in private an identity, in fact, "other" to their public selves.[5]

The supposed prudery of the Victorian period was even more famously undermined by Michel Foucault, not himself by any means a Victorianist, whose introduction to the first volume of his *History of Sexuality* posited European discursive practices at odds with their own stated prudery. For Foucault, the sexual sciences that flourished in the Victorian period were only one example of the proliferation in the nineteenth century of sexual discourses, many of them restrictive, but all displaying a deep cultural investment in representing sexuality and in circulating those representations throughout a given culture.

These two influential studies – Marcus's and Foucault's – initiated two powerful trends in the representation of Victorian sexuality by late-twentieth-century scholars: first, that Victorian sexuality was paradoxical, that despite a surface adherence to restrictive norms, the culture was obsessed with sex. For some scholars this paradox was absorbed rather easily into dominant narratives about Victorian sexuality by recourse to the idiom of hypocrisy: Victorians became, in effect, both prudish and insincere. For others, like Marcus, the contradictions in Victorian attitudes were resolved by the idea of the opposition between culture and subculture; Marcus's most important contribution is his sense of the

[5] Steven Marcus, *The Other Victorians: A Study of Sexuality and Pornography in Mid-Nineteenth-Century England* (New York: Basic Books, 1964).

fluidity of these two cultures and how easily – or at least how frequently – an individual or indeed an idea about sexuality could slip from one to the other. Some scholars saw the paradox in terms of a cultural double standard: this would show up not only in the classic gender opposition between middle-class and upper-class men with relative sexual freedom, on the one hand, and their more cloistered wives, on the other, but also in class terms. Scholars of working-class culture, like Françoise Barret-Ducrocq, documented a rich sexual working-class culture at odds with middle-class erotic norms.[6] For Foucault, however, the paradox of sexual expression and restriction adhered in the very nature of sexual language itself; Foucault maintained that even, and perhaps especially, antisex rhetoric as it extended into public and private life necessarily produced new ways of representing and thinking about the sexual.

The second trend in this kind of study was to see the Victorians as in need of rescue from a past scholarship that underestimated the degree of their sexual activity, knowledge, and pleasure. This rescue has been played out over and over again in scholarly works of the late twentieth century, in which it is repeatedly announced, as if for the first time, that the Victorians were more knowledgeable, sexually enlightened, and indeed interesting than we had previously thought. We might begin here with Foucault's famous parody of the "repressive hypothesis" in the opening section of volume 1 of *History of Sexuality*:

For a long time, the story goes, we supported a Victorian regime, and we continue to be dominated by it even today. Thus the image of the imperial prude is emblazoned on our restrained, mute, and hypocritical sexuality. At the beginning of the seventeenth century a certain frankness was still common, it would seem. Sexual practices had little need of secrecy; words were said without undue reticence, and things were done without too much concealment; one had a tolerant familiarity with the illicit . . . [I]it was a period when bodies "made a display of themselves."

But twilight soon fell upon this bright day, followed by the monotonous nights of the Victorian bourgeoisie. Sexuality was carefully confined; it moved into the home. The conjugal family took custody of it and absorbed it into the serious function of reproduction. On the subject of sex, silence became the rule.[7]

This parody of a devolutionary historiography, which celebrates a freer sexual past and denounces a Victorian legacy imagined to persist until a problematic present, is all the more persuasive in that the historiography

[6] Françoise Barret-Ducrocq, *Love in the Time of Victoria: Sexuality, Class, and Gender in Nineteenth-Century London* (London: Verso, 1991).
[7] Michel Foucault, *The History of Sexuality*, vol. 1 (New York: Parthenon, 1978), p. 3.

it seems to be undermining is one that through his other works became associated with Foucault himself. The history of sex here is also specifically a history of a class; according to how "the story goes," it is the bourgeoisie that in becoming a dominant cultural force created and carefully maintained sexual silence.

The first volume of *Education of the Senses*, Peter Gay's capacious inquiry into the life of the bourgeoisie of nineteenth-century Europe, reaches into the heart of bourgeois culture to refute, through case studies, the narratives of middle-class repression parodied by Foucault. Gay offers us a small and intimate series of encounters with bourgeois men and women who clearly enjoyed their sexual experiences. Ranging over the cultures of the United States, Germany, France, and England, Gay presents a gallery of bourgeois sexual subjects, individuals who prove (in the old sense) the rule of nineteenth-century sexual silence. Of course, Gay's subjects were exceptional individuals who not only experienced sexual pleasure but took the time to write extensively about it. As Gay acknowledges about his only extended female example, "[W]hen the historian finds someone like Mabel Loomis Todd, leisurely and uninhibited enough to keep an exhaustive record of her erotic life and leave it to posterity intact, he can only express his gratitude and quote at length."[8] Gay acknowledges exceptionality as an issue while defending something like the representative nature of his informants: "Explicit erotic notations like Mabel Todd's journals are rare, but not unique. Similar entries, whether shamefaced confessions or glowing memories, punctuate the diaries and correspondence of others, now and then, here and there. True, not all of the experiences they record were gratifying."[9] While others have critiqued Gay's study for the small size of his sample, I see his work as producing a kind of knowledge different from that produced by the survey or the statistical analysis: the slice of bourgeois life he offers is a close-up, an exploration of possibility. And this possibility is explicitly figured against what Gay calls "received wisdom." After quoting at length a letter from David Todd to his wife upon discovering her pregnancy, Gay notes:

This letter is something of a historic document. David Todd, to be sure, was working in an ancient tradition when he endowed maternity with sanctity; it was certainly the common coin of respectable rhetoric throughout the nineteenth

---

[8] Peter Gay, *Education of the Senses*, vol. 1 of *The Bourgeois Experience from Victoria to Freud* (Oxford: Oxford University Press, 1984), p. 71.
[9] *Ibid.*, p. 111.

century. What is striking is that he joined piety about motherhood with enthusiasm for sexuality. The received wisdom has long been, we know, that the nineteenth-century middle-class male split his love life in two, that some of his women were angels, others were whores. But the conduct and the sentiments of the Todds contradict this prevalent perception.[10]

Like the passage from Foucault, this one relies on knowledge of received history. Gently taunting his reader with the "we know" of received wisdom, Gay asserts a counternarrative that derives from declaredly individual experience, in this case the articulate and sensual voice of the woman who was to become the editor of Emily Dickinson's poetry and the lover of Dickinson's brother, Austin. So much depends, of course, on whether one can generalize from Mabel Loomis Todd to other Americans, to other American women, to other Victorians. So much depends on the use of the word "historic" in the phrase "historic document" that opens the passage quoted above. Is David Todd's letter "historic" because it is paradigm-breaking, earth-shattering: historic, in other words, in the sense of "first"? Or is it historic in what might, under the pressure of some arguments, be seen as the opposite sense: "historic" in the sense of a return to a new and more scrupulous history, one that is attentive to the lives and voices of the not-yet-famous? Gay's rescue of Mabel and her husband from the "you know" of Victorian history posits a different kind of knowledge, not only for his nineteenth-century subjects but for historians of the period.

Foucault published the first volume of his work in 1976; Gay, in 1984.[11] Together, these books and others written around the same time opened the way not only for a new Victorianism but for a new Victorian, a newly interpellated figure always defined against an older and grimmer figure of a prude. Perhaps the older figure was difficult to erase; perhaps our culture, for reasons of its own, needed to hang on to the image of the Victorian prude. It is certain, however, that the rescues of Victorians by historians of sex in the seventies and eighties, did not, as it were, "take." The Victorians had to be rescued again, in the 1980s and the 1990s, and continue to be rescued, with almost heroic determination, into the twenty-first century. The book jacket of Patricia Anderson's *When Passion Reigned: Sex and the Victorians*, published in 1995, offers a blurb from James Kincaid, himself a supporter of sex-positive Victorianism: "A rollicking, subversive, and massively entertaining account of Victorian passions. Anderson takes the usual cliché about prudish Victorian sexual

[10] *Ibid.*, p. 89.   [11] Foucault's *The History of Sexuality*, vol. 1, was translated into English in 1978.

repression and stands it on its head – skirts flowing downward, bum exposed." This literalizing – and eroticizing – of the trope of inversion depends once again on the "usual cliché"; once again, Victorians need to be turned upside down in order to be rescued into sexual delight.

My own coming of scholarly age coincided with the second wave of Victorian rescues. On the one hand, I read Gay, Foucault, and Marcus; I believed their accounts, believed in their jovial and indeed carnivalesque Victorians. On the other hand, I, like many of my teachers who had also read (and assigned to me) the same canon of sex-positive texts, began my Victorian classes with examples of Victorian prudery. We were all particularly enamored, it seemed, of two stories: first, the one about Queen Victoria advising her daughter to endure sex by lying back and thinking of England and, second, the one about Victorian chair and piano legs having to be swathed in material to avoid visual reminders of forbidden body parts. The first story is true as far as it goes, although the evidence suggests that when it came to her own relationship with Albert Victoria was a great deal more positive about erotic possibility. The second story is, regrettably for many Victorianist lectures and lecturers, apocryphal. I suspect, however, that both continue to be told.

Despite the rescues I have mentioned above, and those by Michael Mason in his two meticulous studies of Victorian sexuality,[12] there is still substantial scholarly doubt about the sex-positive version of Victorianism, a doubt that, despite my investments to the contrary, I have come to share. While we will always be "discovering" more Victorians who talked freely about and enjoyed sex, there is also evidence that many Victorians knew very little about it. The work of Marie Stopes in the early twentieth century suggests, at least in her analysis, a profound ignorance about sexuality on the part of many of her readers and of her implied audience. While her work is post-Victorian, many of her subjects grew to maturity in the Victorian period. And, unless we posit an actual decrease in sexual knowledge from the late-Victorian to the modern period, we would have to assume that many of her conclusions applied to earlier times as well.

Stopes's famous and popular book on sexuality, *Married Love* (1918), assumes a general sexual ignorance among both men and women. "Man," she says, "is also the victim of the purblind social customs which make sex-knowledge taboo." According to Stopes, this ignorance can have terrible long-term consequences. In a somewhat gothic rendition of

---

[12] Michael Mason, *The Making of Victorian Sexuality* (Oxford: Oxford University Press, 1995) and, by the same author, *The Making of Victorian Sexual Attitudes* (Oxford: Oxford University Press, 1994).

what she sees as an all-too-typical wedding night, Stopes, like John Addington Symonds, blames female sexual ignorance and the society that cultivates it for a variety of ills:

It has become a tradition of our social life that the ignorance of woman about her own body and that of her future husband is a flower-like innocence. And to such an extreme is this sometimes pushed, that not seldom is a girl married unaware that married life will bring her into physical relations with her husband fundamentally different from those with her brother. When she discovers the true nature of his body, and learns the part she has to play as a wife, she may refuse utterly to agree to her husband's wishes. I know one pair of which the husband, chivalrous and loving, had to wait years before his bride recovered from the shock of the discovery of the meaning of marriage and was able to allow him a natural relation. There have been not a few brides whom the horror of the first night of marriage with a man less considerate has driven to suicide or insanity.[13]

Stopes offers no support for the harsh assessment with which this passage ends. But she does go on to tell stories of women with whom she has dealt in her practice who knew little or nothing about sex or pregnancy at the time of their marriage. She also discusses the phenomenon of male ignorance, particularly that which derives from experience with prostitutes. Stopes argues that if too much of men's knowledge comes from prostitutes, they will find their wives cold and unresponsive by comparison.[14] Stopes's comments point once again not only to gendered differences in knowledge but to the different kinds of knowledges that can accrue around sex. Men may have "known" prostitutes and, by having experienced the sexual act, they might know more about sex than their wives, but they might not know enough to understand that prostitutes often feign orgasm. Some kinds of knowledge, as we have seen in the example of John Ruskin with which this book begins, get in the way of others.

Of course, Stopes has an investment in public ignorance about sex; the usefulness of her writing and of her practice depends on it. Like many of the sex manuals I will discuss below, *Married Love* relies on tropes of ignorance and enlightenment and on the identification of the author with the bringing of knowledge. Even so, we must allow the evidence of Stopes's accounts of ignorance some weight. Perhaps more convincing about general sexual ignorance are the letters from readers Stopes received in response to the publication of *Married Love*; while the people who were inspired to write to Stopes constitute a self-selected group, and while

---

[13] Stopes, *Married Love*, p. 52.   [14] *Ibid.*, p. 54.

Stopes's own principles of selection and preservation are not always clear, these letters do testify to the prevalence of ignorance about sexual matters among men, among women, and even among doctors. One correspondent, an anonymous French woman, expresses her wish that she had read *Married Love* "before I was married." She tells Stopes, "[Y]ou [*sic*] advice would prevent quite a lot of mistakes." The woman notes that, presumably because of her reading of *Married Love*, she went to her doctor to get fitted with a pessary, but that her doctor did not know what one was.[15]

The men who wrote to Stopes did not seem on the whole to be more sexually sophisticated than the women. A fifty-nine-year-old man, who obviously came to sexual maturity in the Victorian period, claims he "married at 33, knowing nothing & thinking the greater the spirituality the greater the suppression of sex, so I went thro' the honeymoon without (although occupying the same bed)."[16] Another male correspondent, a science teacher at a grammar school, wrote to Stopes to tell her that her book persuaded him against his past convictions about the dubious value of sexual knowledge. Noting that this was the first time he had read a book "of the character 'what a young man should know,'" he explains that for a long time he resisted sexual knowledge on principle: "I always preferred to think that whenever I married I should not want to know anything in advance and I hope that my wife would not [crossed out] anything either. We should just be a couple of innocents walking into our Garden of Eden."[17] This willful ignorance of sexual matters takes us back to Stopes's critique of the cult of female "flower-like innocence"; in this case at least, the privileging of innocence extends to the man as well. Additionally, this reader's reference to the genre he calls "book[s] of the character 'what a young man should know'" suggests the centrality of epistemological questions to sexual ones, not only for him but for a society that produces so many examples of the genre whose cultural power this individual man has for so long resisted.

Of course, with Stopes as with other experts, Victorian and contemporary, we come to the state of her own knowledge. Although Stopes knew, by our standards, quite a lot about certain aspects of sexuality, especially female pleasure in certain sexual acts, she, like many of her contemporaries, believed that masturbation was morally and physically dangerous for both sexes. She was alert to monthly cycles of female

[15] Letter to Stopes from French woman, 8 June 1920, Marie Stopes Papers, PP/MCS/A54.
[16] Letter to Stopes, no date, Marie Stopes Papers, PP/MCS/A55.
[17] Letter to Stopes, 3 November 1919, Marie Stopes Papers, PP/MCS/A54.

receptiveness, but again, like many nineteenth- and early-twentieth-century "experts," she saw menstruation as a particularly fertile and sexually receptive time for women. In any account of Victorian sexual knowledge we must think, not only about ordinary men and women and how they understood the knowledge available to them at the time, but also about the knowledge of Victorian experts and what *they* knew in relation to the sexual "truths" of the twenty-first century.

In this section of the chapter, I have moved – if not seamlessly, then without remark – between two kinds of sexual knowledge: what the Victorians knew about sex and what we know about how much they knew. While I will try to complicate this picture further in a later section by introducing other levels and other kinds of knowledge, I want here to address directly how much contemporary scholars know or can know about Victorian sexuality – including the state of Victorian knowledges about sex.

As Lesley A. Hall points out in an elegant and useful article "Sex in the Archives," scholars of Victorian sex have been limited to a few kinds of sources.[18] Hall lists personal diaries or accounts, papers of societies or groups of people devoted to sexual topics or to an articulated idea about sex, as well as records of foundling hospitals or other institutions devoted to the regulation of sex. I would add medical and other "advice" literature and pornography. All these sources give a biased picture: personal diaries, because they, by definition, tell the story of articulate people who imagine that their ideas and experiences are worth preserving; papers of groups like the Fabian and Malthusian societies, because they reflect only the most conscious, exceptional, and indeed consciously exceptional, ideas; and institutional records, because they reflect and are shaped as much by institutional regulations and narratives as they are by actual experience.[19] Pornography, of course, follows narrative and social conventions of its own: at the same time reflecting, subverting, and creating dominant cultural narratives about sex, it is extremely hard to read as evidence of sexual practice. Finally, conduct and advice books by

[18] Lesley A. Hall, "Sex in the Archives," *Archives: The Journal of the British Records Association* 93 (1995), 1–12.

[19] The Foundling Hospital, in London, for example, required that the mothers of any babies they accepted to have been sexually pure up until the time of a seduction by the father of their child, and that they not have lived with the father. While some women's sexual experience must surely have taken this particular shape, the requirements of the hospital would produce narratives that concurred with those requirements. Inspectors from the Foundling Hospital would do their best to ferret out the "truth" of the matter, but the very existence of this dominant narrative would influence both inspectors and the women who came to the hospital for help.

definition address themselves to an ideal, although some of these might articulate different and even highly contradictory ideals. Like pornography, conduct books are heavily marked in terms of generic expectations and taboos. Finally, the issue of understanding sexual practice is complicated by its perhaps unusual degree of imbrication in imagination and fantasy. Fantasy can, of course, be thought of as a form of practice: to say that a Victorian subject "only" fantasized about a certain act, or even to say that he or she "lied" about having performed – or not performed – it, is to diminish the close relationship of fantasy, sexuality, and cultural pressures.

Despite the inadequacy of any single source or group of sources, most of them can tell us something about sexual experiences and a great deal about what we might think of as the Victorian sexual imaginary: that set of assumptions – sometimes explicit, sometimes implicit, and sometimes barely conscious – that taken together can begin to define what a particular culture and its many subcultures thought of as possible, right, imaginable. It is also, of course, important to understand that the word "Victorian" is itself in part a product of our own sexual imaginary, serving – perhaps more acutely than parallel terms like "eighteenth-century" or even "Elizabethan" – to tell a story of our own sexual progress, our own sexual knowledge. The books that have been most useful in exposing our own investments in Victorian sexual unity have been those that focus on a particular subculture like working-class men or evangelical Christians; these studies intervene in an all-too-easy and monolithic notion of the "Victorian," exposing contradictions in the culture at large while offering coherent pictures of groups within that culture.

With all this in mind, let me discuss the limits and discoveries of my own sample with regard to sexual knowledge. For the purposes of this project, I want the paucity of the evidence about sex to speak as loudly as any explicit reference to sexuality. In all the papers I could find relating to my 61 couples, and therefore to 122 people, I found only seven references, or series of references, to sex: those by Charles Kingsley in his letters and drawings to Fanny Grenfell, which have been dealt with extensively in Kingsley biographies and need not be revisited here;[20] those by John and Effie Ruskin in their debates over the consummation of their marriage discussed in detail in Chapter 1; those by John Addington Symonds,

---

[20] See, for example, Susan Chitty's *The Beast and the Monk: A Life of Charles Kingsley* (London: Hodder and Stoughton, 1974).

whose thoughts on sexual initiation I discuss in Chapter 2; the one sentence by Eliza Dickinson Wemyss about the honeymoon being the most difficult time in a girl's life from Chapter 1; a quotation by Barbara Caine in her book on the Potter sisters from Rosie Potter Williams's "Confidential Autobiography" that her sister explained the facts of life to her, "fillin[g] her with fear and disgust";[21] two pieces of rather cryptic advice to Margaret Gladstone (later MacDonald) that I take up in the next section of this chapter; and a series of confidences in letters by Maud Sambourne Messel to her mother in 1898, a discussion of which constitutes this chapter's final case study. Of these examples, two came from people whose relation to sexuality was, by their own account, atypical. Not only did John Ruskin seem to feel he was doing something outside the norm in refusing, or being unable, to consummate the marriage, but the records of those refusals and the reasons for them share many of the problems of divorce court papers in general in their double existence as personal confession and public and legal record. Although I have used Symonds to open up a discussion of reorientation for all Victorian men and women, Symonds thought of himself as an exceptional sexual "case" – this in the literal as well as the figurative sense when he consented to become one of Havelock Ellis's case studies. Eliza Wemyss's comment is perhaps more representative of the way many Victorian women at least may have thought about sex, but its very brevity and coyness makes interpretation difficult. Rosie Williams' comment needs to be understood in light of what Caine calls a "brief and bitterly unhappy marriage"; her husband, Dyson died of syphilis only a few years after the honeymoon.[22] The advice offered to Margaret has all the problems associated with advice in general: we do not know whether it was understood, followed, or ignored. Maud's letters to her mother, as we shall see, offer the most extended example of the sex life of an ordinary upper-middle-class woman, although here too the constraints of genre, class, familial relations, and time period make it difficult to generalize from Maud's experience to the experiences of others. With the exception of Maud's and perhaps Margaret's stories, all of the examples are negative to various degrees: Ruskin's refusal of, Symonds's recoil from, and Eliza Wemyss's resignation to sex tell us that something might be wrong with a sex-positive Victorianism, but it is difficult to say how far we should let these examples take us.

[21] Barbara Caine, *Destined to Be Wives: The Sisters of Beatrice Webb* (New York: Oxford University Press, 1988), p. 82.
[22] *Ibid.*, p. 83.

It is the paucity, brevity, and opacity of these examples that have led me to try to provide a fuller context for the sexual experiences of my honeymoon couples through the examples of Margaret MacDonald and Maud Messel. Both women came from the upper reaches of the middle class; both married late in the century: Margaret in 1897 and Maud in 1898. Both were intelligent and articulate, with close relations to their families. Although Margaret was much more educated than Maud, both identified in different ways with the new ideas and movements of their generation: Margaret became a socialist, marrying her colleague and future prime minister Ramsay MacDonald, while Maud's sense of herself as part of a new generation was expressed more through her personal freedoms. Both Margaret and Maud might help us envision the pleasures and limits of sexual knowledge at the end of the century.

TRANSMITTING KNOWLEDGE

In thinking about – to paraphrase the Stopes's informant and the titles of several conduct books – what a young girl ought to have known in the Victorian period, I have chosen in this section to use as a prompt and as an imaginative guide the embodied example of Margaret Gladstone. As we shall see, Margaret's relation to knowledge was probably not representative of that of many Victorian young women: she is, instead, something of a limit case. Exposed to information in a variety of fields, encouraged by her family to think and to travel by herself, relatively experienced with men as friends and colleagues, she stands out from many of the women in my sample. Her relatively late age at marriage (twenty-six) suggests that she might also have known more about the world – and potentially about sex – than women who came to marriage younger. Born in 1870, she had what were presumably her first experiences of sex on the far edges of the Victorian period. Historically, she belongs to the generation of Marie Stopes's earliest informants. With all her presumed advantages of class, chronology, and education, she is a useful figure to contemplate in terms of sexual knowledge. Although we have little direct evidence of what she knew, thought, or felt about sex at the time of her marriage, we can begin to reconstruct a world of personal and professional sexual advice to which she might have had access. "Might," as we shall see, is a key term here as we puzzle out the sources of information theoretically available to her, to those like her, and to those who might not have been so educated, so intelligent, and so open.

Margaret Gladstone was a distant relative of the prime minister and a member of an extended political family; she grew up in a household noted for its emphasis on ideas and education. In his memoir of his wife, Ramsay MacDonald describes her upbringing as having taken place in a home where "wealth, intellectual distinction, and liberality of thought mingled together, and humility reigned over all."[23] Margaret's father was a distinguished scientist and a pioneer in the field of physical chemistry. Twice widowed (Margaret's mother was Margaret King Gladstone of Chapter 1), John Hall Gladstone was the defining intellectual and moral force in the household. Margaret herself loved science; we find her as a young lady attending "a delightful lecture ... with such splendid experiments" on the topic of "quartz fibres."[24] Her education was also cosmopolitan; she records in her early letters another lecture by representatives of different religions, whom she finds "all equally interesting."[25] Margaret apparently considered becoming a doctor and envisioned working among the poor in this capacity. Although it is not clear why she decided against medicine as a profession, her concern for the poor remained central to her sense of purpose; after reading various Fabian essays she became interested in socialism, and it was in this context that she met her future husband and the partner in her life's work, Ramsay MacDonald.

If the fact of Margaret's scientific education makes it possible that she knew more about sex than the average young woman of the period, her age at marriage and her experience with men as friends, comrades, and suitors suggest that she was relatively unsheltered in other ways as well. L. Herbert notes her ease with men in conversation: "She was rather different from girls of her set, because whether she spoke to a man or woman made not the slightest scrap of difference. She was not self conscious during her intercourse with men, and that is why she became a 'man's friend.'"[26] Margaret had had four serious suitors – all cousins – by the time of her engagement to Ramsay. While we do not know exactly what these relations were like, we know from her letters to Ramsay that she was surprised by the intensity of feeling displayed by her favorite among them, Andrew Henderson, after her engagement. Perhaps the best evidence of Margaret's sexual sophistication, or at least her confidence, is that it was she, not Ramsay, who apparently proposed marriage.

---

[23] Jane Cox, ed., *A Singular Marriage: A Labour Love Story in Letters and Diaries, Ramsay and Margaret MacDonald* (London: Harrap, 1988), p. 28.
[24] *Ibid.*, p. 31.   [25] Quoted in *ibid.*, p. 32.   [26] *Ibid.*

I have used the word "unsheltered" to describe Margaret, although Ramsay himself uses precisely the opposite term in describing what he thinks his wife might have been like in her late teens:

The picture which she has left of herself when she was still attending school at the Doreck College, Bayswater (a private school for young ladies) was that of a somewhat serious young person, rich in friends, methodical in habits, clever at work, a shrine of early piety, who was enjoying life. And the photographs of her as she was then are of a bright-eyed, chubby-faced maiden, alert and interested. The garden where she was nourished was very sheltered and very sunny, and she grew up where "falls nor hail nor snow, nor any wind blows loudly."[27]

In thinking of Margaret as a sexual actor, we must keep in mind that this affectionate portrait of his wife by Ramsay is both retrospective and an attempt to reconstruct someone he had not yet known. The twenty-seven-year-old woman of their initial meetings would have been different from the eighteen-year-old girl he imagines her to have been. Nonetheless, the passage suggests a tension between innocence and education; the "maiden" of this passage, despite being "alert," is associated with and defined by the "sheltered" "garden" of her childhood. Certainly, the adult Margaret, writing to Ramsay, makes many apologies about her ignorance of the world, especially in relation to class and to money. Margaret's shelteredness seems itself paradoxical; while she was clearly protected from some experiences, that protection may well have opened up a safe place for the exploration of ideas and feelings. Both implications of the word "sheltered" seem potentially at work here.

So what did Margaret know about sex on the eve of her marriage? And how did she come to that knowledge? We have two pieces of textual evidence: the first is contained in a courtship letter from Ramsay dated 4 September 1896, in which he recommends that Margaret read Edward Carpenter's collection of essays, *Love's Coming-of-Age*. The second is a letter to Margaret from her half-sister Bella, containing advice about Margaret's wedding night. The second letter is part of what we might think of as an informal advice network among female friends and relations. Many scholars posit such a network, although I have discovered very little textual evidence of the conversations and letters that we would logically think would have been a part of women's relations to one another. The first letter – Ramsay's recommendation of Carpenter – is generically more complex. Very little has been written, even in a speculative vein, about what young women learned about sex from their

[27] *Ibid.*, p. 30.

suitors or fiancés. In this case, of course, Ramsay does not himself explicitly discuss the topic of sex; his recommendation triangulates the exchange of knowledge through what I will later be calling expert advice. Taken together, the letters produce a familiar paradox: Ramsay's evokes a version of Margaret that suggests sexual sophistication and at least a theoretical acquaintance with sexual matters; Bella's more concrete recommendations seem addressed to someone far less experienced and in need of practical counsel. While the letters may say as much or more about their writers than about Margaret, read individually and together they highlight important contradictions in the arena of sexual knowledge.

Sandwiched between a joking reference to a promise to take an American wife (Ramsay had dined and apparently flirted with two American girls the previous evening) and a reassurance that Margaret need not hurry with a paper she was writing or reading for the *Progressive Review*, Ramsay's reading recommendation is itself caught between the personal and the intellectual. He says, "I would like you to read Carpenter's 'Loves coming of Age' [*sic*]. I know you will understand it all, & whether you agree with it or not, it is rather appropriate just now."[28] The somewhat imperious tone of the "I would like you" echoes that of his professional and political demands of Margaret in his other courtship letters. Although he is always affectionate, when dealing with books and ideas he tends to write more as a fellow traveler than as a lover. His conviction that Margaret will "understand" Carpenter's difficult – and at the time extremely controversial – critique of marriage as an institution suggests something of intellectual equality between himself and Margaret, as does his implicit interest in her opinion of the essays. Whether his sense of the book's timeliness – "it is rather appropriate just now" – has to do with their upcoming marriage, or with wider political movements, or with both is hard to say.

If Margaret were to have turned to *Love's Coming-of-Age* for advice about her own situation, or for practical information about sex, she would probably have been disappointed or confused. At once intensely celebratory of the physical and committed to the body as allegory, Carpenter oscillates wildly in his essays between a literal and a metaphoric body, and thus between a celebration of physical pleasure and what seems like a real distrust of the merely physical:

Sex is the allegory of Love in the physical world. It is from this fact that it derives its immense power. The aim of Love is non-differentiation – absolute union of

---

[28] *Ibid.*, p. 126.

being; but absolute union can only be found at the centre of existence. Therefore whoever has truly found another has found not only that other, and with that other himself, but has found also a third – who dwells at the centre and holds the plastic material of the universe in the palm of his hand, and is a creator of sensible forms.[29]

It is hard to think of this passage – and the many others like it – as sharing with Bella's letter the status of "sexual information." While Carpenter's book uses the words "sex" and "sex-instinct" in a variety of ways throughout his complicated text, it is hard to imagine *Love's Coming-of-Age* – despite its opening critique of ignorance about sexual matters that, as we shall see, is typical of sex manuals of the period – as a source of practical advice. When I tried to read Carpenter's book as a late-Victorian woman looking for sexual information, I found only one place where Carpenter addresses what might be thought of as practical sexual concerns. This comes in a brief final section entitled "Preventive Checks," which begins, perhaps not entirely encouragingly, "This is no doubt a complex and difficult subject."

Carpenter is fairly clear about the need for contraception. After differentiating between the "animal and plant world," where "nature" seems "careless of the waste of seed," and the realm of the human, Carpenter identifies differently gendered objections to translating nature's plans for animals into the human context: "And not only Man (the male) objects to lower Nature's method of producing superfluous individuals only to kill them off again in the struggle for existence; but Woman objects to being a mere machine for perpetual reproduction."[30] He becomes harder to follow, and less confident, however, when he turns to methods of "prevention." After condemning "artificial checks" for "their uncertainty, their desperate matter-of-factness, so fatal to real feeling," as well as for their potential danger and their diminishment of female satisfaction, he moves more approvingly to what we now call the "rhythm method" and what Carpenter calls the "method ... which consists in selecting, for sexual congress, a certain part of the woman's monthly cycle." Carpenter seems less than fully confident, however, about the results of the method. "Its success truly is not absolutely certain, but is perhaps sufficiently nearly so for the general purposes of regulating the family."[31] More important, however, if we imagine a reader like

---

[29] Edward Carpenter, *Love's Coming-of-Age: A Series of Papers on the Relations of the Sexes* (London, 1902), p. 27.
[30] *Ibid.*, pp. 146–7.   [31] *Ibid.*, p. 177.

Margaret – or Ramsay – eager to apply Carpenter's advice, is the fact that Carpenter never names what he thinks the best period for preventing conception might be.

Finally, and perhaps most problematically, the tone of Carpenter's discussion is reminiscent of the earlier quoted passage. Admitting that the method he advocates would require some – but, to his mind, not excessive – self-control, he speaks approvingly if somewhat mystically about the benefits of controlling one's sexual urges in this limited way. "The effort itself," he concludes, "would lead to that Transmutation of sex-force into the higher emotional elements, of which we have spoken already, and which is such an important factor in Evolution."[32]

I do not know if Margaret followed Ramsay's advice and read *Love's Coming-of-Age* or what she thought of it if she did. She might have read some of it and become bored or indignant; she might never have gotten to the "preventative checks" or she might have started there. If we know anything about the triangulated relation among Margaret, Ramsay, and the text she might or might not have read, it is that Ramsay thought that Margaret would in some way benefit from its reading. Was Ramsay substituting the reading of Carpenter's essays for some more explicit discussion of sex? Did Margaret and Ramsay discuss these things together? Had they experimented with sex, even perhaps with "preventive checks"? Certainly, Margaret's half-sisters and female friends were struck by how physically "cold" to each other Ramsay and Margaret seemed in public; Margaret, however, felt comfortable enough to joke with Ramsay about the subject: "Flo discussed November dates with me & all went smoothly. She thinks I am too cold to you, so you won't mind my sitting with my arms round your neck at breakfast, will you?"[33]

If Ramsay's letter and the text it recommends work within an abstract and theoretical notion about sex in which bodies and ideas are hard to place, Bella's is very concerned with the location of the body, its products, and its accoutrements. In some ways no less euphemistic than *Love's Coming-of-Age*, Bella's wedding night advice addresses very specific concerns about defloration, discomfort, and messiness:

There is one hint I should like to give you before you are married. Auntie Carey gave it me *together with others which there is no advantage in passing on*. It is this. Be sure to provide yourself *at first* with a diaper or something of the kind – *that* is best – for your own personal use – to save soiling the bed clothes. You can pop it

---

[32] *Ibid.*, p. 148.   [33] *Ibid.*, p. 129.

under the pillow till required. And do not overdo yourself at first – don't take long walks etc., but behave as if you were not quite well – which will be the case."[34]

This piece of advice, this rare recorded instance of communication along a female network of sexual informants, raises as many questions as it purports to answer. The epistemological structure of this advice depends on the euphemism "not quite well" for "menstruating." While Margaret would have been more habituated to the euphemism and thus probably less struck by the connection to illness than it might be to us – Lyman B. Sperry, author of the popular late-century conduct book *Confidential Talks to Young Women* notes that this euphemism is so common that in cases of real sickness one should use some other locution – the sentence in which the euphemism occurs might have been as puzzling to Margaret as to a modern reader. The oddly contradictory structure of the last part of the last sentence, "behave as if you were not quite well – which will be the case," points both to a literal fact – "you will be bleeding" – and to a potentially confused relationship between euphemism and literal truth, approximation and reality: behave *as if* you were not quite well, but, in fact, you will not be quite well. In imagining Margaret's reception of this advice, I cannot help thinking that the contradiction between the "as if" and "will be" might reemphasize the language of illness, unanchoring it from the familiar euphemism for menstruation.

The vagueness of the language of diagnosis contrasts sharply with the naming of the paragraph's featured object, the "diaper." The question of where initially to put the diaper is answered very practically; Margaret can "pop it under the pillow till required." Of course the passive "required" takes us back to euphemism and to mystery. Why will it be required? How will she know when to produce it? Is the diaper to be placed on the bed clothes or on the body?

Another mysterious element of this advice is, of course, that it represents a process of selection: Bella has chosen to "pass it on" while remaining silent about other advice Auntie Carey offered *her*. The reason Bella puts forward, that "there is no advantage" in repeating other pieces of her aunt's advice, might well tell us something about Bella's experiences putting that counsel into practice. It also tells us that Bella is taking on the responsibility of editing as she passes advice along the female network. While we do not know whether the original advice from Auntie

---

[34] Isabella Holmes to Margaret Gladstone, 7 November 1896, correspondence of Margaret Ethel MacDonald, PRO 30/69/887.

Carey was in Bella's opinion confusing, useless, or wrong, we do see Bella attempting actively to intervene from her position on the chain of transmission. Something in Auntie Carey's advice did not, in all probability, work out to Bella's "advantage"; it seems that she is protecting her half sister from the consequences of bad advice. Imagining what this might have been is, of course, a useless exercise, although if it was more confusing and joyless than the advice about the diaper, it would indeed have had to be grim.

It is, by some calculations, a long way from the "plastic material" of Carpenter's "universe" to the (presumably cloth) diaper so central to Bella's vision/memory of the wedding night. And yet both pieces of advice have in common an uneasiness with the body and a visible struggle to find a place for its desires, its fluids, and its crises in the language available to the authors. Carpenter's struggles with language might register as more epic; his use of hyperbole, his capitalization of abstract nouns, and his willingness to coin new terms are legible signs of his frustration with the limits of the language he inherits. I would argue, however, that Bella's interventions in language – the compensatory underlining of the "that" of the third sentence to suggest a syntactical reference where there is none and the use and then uncovering of euphemism – are only more subtle and less familiar ways of trying to make language mean the unspeakable. The anxiety over the placement of the diaper becomes, in this reading of Bella's heavily marked prose, a way of both revealing and concealing what the diaper covers – and about what places and acts must be covered by the very language used to describe them. The language of advice, even and perhaps especially advice from close female family members, is no transparent thing.

We do not know, of course, what advice Margaret might have been offered by other family members. Margaret's closest female friends were unmarried; her mother was long dead. She might have received advice directly from Auntie Carey or from another half sister who married only months before Margaret. We must at least consider the possibility, however, that the two pieces of advice that have left their traces in the archive represent the sum total of communication on the subject of sex from her female friends, her fiancé, and her family. What, then, would Margaret likely be feeling about sex as she approached her wedding night and her brief honeymoon? Would she have been thinking about Bella's somewhat pedantic counsel or the euphoric but uneasy proclamations of Carpenter's essays? How would she have brought them together in understanding the sexual dynamics of her own experience?

There would, for Margaret, have been other potential sources of sexual advice. Partly because of her unusual social position, but also because she lived later in the century than the vast majority of my other examples, Margaret Gladstone would have had a wide range of books about sex available to her. As an educated woman and a voracious reader, Margaret might well have come across one or more books on the topic. And here again, we are confronted with a series of questions and possibilities, as these books varied widely in terms of genre, implied audience, explicitness, and attitude toward sexual matters.

Let us begin with what might have been the most obvious source of information – the dictionary. While standard dictionaries did not include sexual terms, some middle-class Victorian libraries might have included popular or even more professionally oriented medical dictionaries. One of the most widely available in the first genre was *Beeton's Medical Dictionary*. Samuel Orchart Beeton, husband of Isabella Beeton, wrote over thirty popular guides to subjects as diverse as gardening and etiquette; his handbooks on various topics made their way into a number of Victorian homes. The subtitle of his *Medical Dictionary* reveals its domestic orientation: "A Safe Guide for Every Family Defining, in the Plainest Language the Symptoms and Treatment of All Ailments, Illnesses and Diseases."[35] The book's alphabetically listed entries are somewhat uneven: it includes such reassuringly domestic terms as "Baking" and "Biscuits" (in their role in diet), as well as more obscure terms like "Caoutchouc" (the solidified milk juice of some tropical plants) and the vaguely alarming "Canine Madness." It has an entry for "Breasts" (they are "globular fleshly protuberances adhering to the anterior and lateral regions of the thorax of the female"),[36] as well as for "Uterus," "Ovary," and, somewhat strangely, "Vulva" (in a non-sexual context), but not for "Clitoris," "Penis," "Hymen," or "Vagina." In displaying a marked preference for internal over external sexual organs, *Beeton's* allies itself, despite the domestic tone of its less fraught entries, with the invisible, the medical, and the expert. Its awkward technical language in, for example, the definition of "Breast" underscores its tone of medical authority. The book's sense of what a reader might or might not know is also contradictory and incoherent. The entry for "Ovary" uses "Uterus" in the definition. "Semen" has no entry, although it is mentioned under "Secretion" and "Anatomy." In other words, Beeton would not provide

---

[35] Samuel Orchart Beeton, *Beeton's Medical Dictionary* (London: Ward, Lock, and Tyler, 1871).
[36] *Ibid.*, p. 71.

very useful information for a reader who had, say, overheard a conversation that included unfamiliar sexual terms, particularly those that might have to do with the appearance or the function of external sexual organs. "Menses" and "Menstruation" are also not present.

A reader like Margaret, frustrated by the silences in Beeton, might turn to another kind of dictionary, presumably less often present in private homes or local libraries: the kind directed toward medical students. These dictionaries ranged in accessibility of language: the most accessible to the lay reader that I was able to find was Joseph Thomas's 1886 *A Complete Pronouncing Medical Dictionary*. I also found the title more hospitable than others of the genre; as I imagined a lay reader scanning a shelf or list of titles, I thought a dictionary that admitted at the outset that pronunciation might be mysterious would be relatively welcoming. Unlike the Beeton's less technical dictionary, Thomas's does include an entry for "Penis," which is described in terms of its anatomical structure and as "the chief organ of generation in man." "Clitoris," also present, would have involved the reader in some cross-referencing: the entry informs the reader that it comes from the Greek "shut up" and that it is an "elongated, glandiform body at the anterior part of the vulva."[37] "Vulva" is the only sign that the clitoris is a specifically female organ. If the reader were confused by the word, she would find under "Vulva" another etymological entry identifying the term as deriving from "that which is wrapped around anything."[38] The entry continues with the observation that the word is "now applied to the fissure in the external parts of generation in the female." The entry for "Orgasm" depends on the understanding of two words my imagined reader might or might not understand: "Eager desire or excitement, especially *venereal; salacity*."[39] It does not include any mention of physical effects. "Masturbation" claims the word "defile" as part of its origin and refers the reader to "Pollution."[40] While these examples from two genres of dictionary might help a lay reader put together pieces of information, and while a very educated reader like Margaret might well get helpful information from Thomas's *Dictionary*, the circumlocutions of both Beeton and Thomas are finally obscurantist and not terribly reassuring about the possibilities of sexual pleasure.

The emphases, asymmetries, omissions, and circular logic of the dictionaries are repeated and fleshed out in the genre I will call the sexual

---

[37] Joseph Thomas, *A Complete Pronouncing Medical Dictionary* (London: J. P. Lippincott, 1886), p. 185.
[38] *Ibid.*, p. 790.　[39] *Ibid.*, p. 412 (italics mine).　[40] *Ibid.*, p. 394.

advice book – to distinguish it from conduct books more generally. In perusing booksellers' and publishers' lists and perhaps her family's library shelves in the 1890s, these are some of the recent and reprinted titles Margaret might have come across: *The Science of a New Life, Esoteric Anthropology, Sexual Physiology, The Elements of Social Science, Confidential Talks with Young Men, Confidential Talks with Young Women, Self-Preservation: A Medical Treatise on Nervous and Physical Debility*, and *Spermatorrhoea, Impotence and Sterility*. Some of these would have been written by doctors, some by laypeople, and at least one (*Self-Preservation*) by a layperson posing as a doctor. Depending on the edition and on what subtitle was used, it might have been hard for Margaret to realize what some of these books were about.[41]

While many of these books enjoyed wide circulation and were re-printed many times, in some cases over a period of a half-century or more, it is hard to know how and by whom these books were used. Havelock Ellis claimed, in a twentieth-century review of the literature of sexology, that *Esoteric Anthropology* was read by respectable Victorian families but kept locked up in a bedroom drawer.[42] He also claimed in another essay that it was "at one period almost the only popularly written manual of sex which reached respectable women."[43] Even if he was right, we cannot know whether unmarried daughters or young women of the household were given access to that drawer or, indeed, to that bedroom. T. L. Nichols's own address in the introduction to *Esoteric Anthropology* confuses the issue further, suggesting a conflict between inclusion and privacy. While expressing ambition to "put [his book] into the hands of every man and every woman – yes, and every child wise enough to profit by its teachings," he stresses the confidentiality, the privacy, even the secrecy of his relation as author to his readers: "As its name imports, it is a *private treatise* on the most interesting and important subjects. It is of the nature of a STRICTLY CONFIDENTIAL PROFESSIONAL CONSULTATION BETWEEN PHYSICIAN AND PATIENT."[44]

I should explain that I am interested here not so much in the different philosophies of the various authors systematically pursued as in the range of

---

[41] One obvious source of information about these books would have been reviews. Based on my searches through journals catalogued through the Wellesley Index, however, none of them – and indeed no book on human sexuality – was reviewed in any of the mainstream journals to which Margaret or her family might have subscribed.

[42] Quoted in Roy Porter and Leslie A. Hall, *The Facts of Life: The Creation of Sexual Knowledge in Britain, 1650–1950* (New Haven: Yale University Press, 1995), p. 140.

[43] Havelock Ellis, *Studies in the Psychology of Sex*. vol. VII (Philadelphia: F. A. Davis, 1928), p. 156.

[44] Thomas Low Nichols, *Esoteric Anthropology* (New York, 1853), p. 4 (full capitals in original).

material available to individual potential readers, especially women. While some readers might consciously turn to books by a particular author from a particular sexological school, I am focusing for the time being on how a woman or a man might look around for information without necessarily understanding the different investments in what we now think of as more radical or more conservative accounts of sex. Thus, George Drysdale's *The Elements of Social Science*, with its more radical sense that sexual organs need exercise, is important for my purposes not because it leads to a pro-birth control position but because it was one of many discourses that individual readers might or might not be able to identify with a particular author. Recent historians of sex, in focusing almost exclusively on birth control, have made sexual politics central to their inquiry. While this is an extremely important project in understanding Victorian culture, I am not sure it is the most useful way to go about understanding real-life relations to books that might have been hard to obtain and difficult – for a host of reasons – to read. In what follows I try to look at these books, not as coherent statements of positions on sex that readers would consume in critical relation to other texts and to ideas in circulation at the time, but as reference books – read perhaps partially, perhaps in haste or in secret – in which readers might look for specific information or browse the table of contents for parts that might sound interesting or useful to their particular situation. This kind of examination on my part is deliberately textual: few sexological accounts of these manuals quote extensively or analyze material from specific texts. In trying to get a feel for what it might be like to read – that is to use – these books, I must work with the effect their words might have on an imaginary reader or readers.

Most of the books in question explicitly utilize the idiom of knowledge to assert the right of the author to touch on sexual topics. The preface to Sperry's *Confidential Talks with Young Men* quotes another "expert," to the effect that "'people are destroyed for lack of knowledge' far more than any natural disposition to go astray,"[45] thus inserting himself into a chain of transmission of expertise. Like the authors of many advice books in both the Victorian period and today, Sperry contrasts the authority of his own advice with the unreliable information garnered by more informal advice networks:

Fathers, mothers, teachers, and physicians, and all others who in any way become the guardians of youth – should early, truthfully, and carefully teach the essential facts regarding sex and reproduction. It is cruelly and culpably wrong to

---

[45] Lyman Beecher Sperry, *Confidential Talks with Young Men* (Edinburgh: Oliphants, 1894), p. 5.

allow children to grope about, picking up half truths and distorted facts and gathering venomous ideas from *corrupt playmates, vile literature, obscene pictures, vulgar stories, and unfortunate personal experience.*[46]

The metaphorical "groping" for information in the first half of the last sentence becomes contaminated by the more literal groping conjured up by the last and presumably most dangerous named source, "unfortunate personal experience." Sperry makes it clear, however, that knowledge is not the same as attention. Unlike later twentieth-century movements in support of sexual knowledge, Sperry's text delegitimizes knowledge of one's individual anatomy. Young men, for instance, "should pay as little attention to the sexual organs and their functions as is compatible with cleanliness and comfort: and then entertain no fears regarding the ultimate perfection of their powers."[47]

R. T. Trall makes even stronger claims for the power of sexual knowledge, as he defines it, to prevent physical and moral catastrophe. Again, the trope of knowledge is a self-authorizing one. He claims in the introduction that, had such a book as his *Sexual Physiology: A Scientific and Popular Exposition of the Fundamental Problems in Sociology* been given to men suffering from the effects of sexual excess, "it would have been their earthly salvation."[48] Such men are carefully portrayed not as naturally debauched but as ignorant:

The majority of young persons unite in matrimony with no education whatever on this subject; and habits, right or wrong, are soon formed which are apt to be continued through life. I have had patients who had for years indulged in sexual intercourse as often as once in twenty-four hours, and some who have indulged still oftener. Of course the result was premature decay, and often permanent invalidism. It was not because these persons were inordinately sensual, or unusually developed in the cerebellum, that they damaged themselves in this way. It was simply because they knew no better. *Many a man who would have been a good husband if he had only known how*, and who would not for his life, much less for the momentary pleasure it afforded, have endangered the health, or hazarded the happiness of a well-beloved wife, has destroyed her health, happiness and life (some men several wives successively) by excessive sexual indulgence.[49]

Trall's account explicitly opposes improper sexuality to knowledge; sexual knowledge in this case involves knowing – and therefore avoiding – the dangers associated with sexual indulgence. Despite the negative valence attached to sex itself, sexual knowledge is expressed not only in

---

[46] *Ibid.*, pp. 9–10 (italics mine).   [47] *Ibid.*, p. 69.   [48] *Ibid.*, p. 245.
[49] Russell Thacher Trall, *Sexual Physiology: A Scientific and Popular Exposition of the Fundamental Problems in Sociology* (New York: Miller, 1866), pp. 243–4 (italics mine).

general affirmative terms but as a set of skills: thus the tragedy of the man who would have been a "good husband if he had only known how." Abstinence becomes, then, not simply a matter of passive restraint but a set of techniques that qualify, finally, *as* sexual knowledge.

Many of the books sound a defensive note when entering into the issue of sexuality, and many exhibit a hyperbolic reliance on the trope of knowledge and truth as they enter this problematic territory. *Esoteric Anthropology*, typical in this respect, introduces the question of anatomy with a plea, indeed a prayer, that its audience will be ready to seek truth: "I beg, therefore, for what I am now about to write, the most earnest attention, and I invoke a spirit of calm, candid inquiry, that seeks simply for the truth. I pray you to clear your mind of cant. 'Put off thy shoes from off thy feet, for the place where thou standest is holy ground.' "[50] And again, as his discussion turns specifically to the "generative organs," Nichols restates the purity of his quest in terms of his commitment to truth and knowledge:

To do justice to a subject of so much scientific interest, and having such important relations to the health and happiness of man, I must treat it with entire freedom. I write for those, and those only, who are ready to accept the truth, and who desire to live it. I must also give more space to its consideration, than to topics which may be found elsewhere satisfactorily elucidated. Let us turn back the pages of the Great Book of Nature, which lies open before us, and earnestly peruse her earlier lessons.[51]

The reader is invited into a community of knowledge seekers, a community defined by the desire not only to pursue, but to "accept" and "live" the truth. The pursuit of sexual knowledge takes on a textual and, indeed, canonical authority as author and reader are invited in the performative cadences of Genesis to read together the "Great Book of Nature."

Like many sex manuals, *Esoteric Anthropology* begins its foray into the sexual with a discussion of plants; and like many of his contemporaries, Nichols insists both on anthropomorphizing and sacralizing his discussion of their reproductive processes:

It is remarkable, that the parts of plants devoted to the sexual function are those that we most prize for their beauty and fragrance. It is the flower of the plant which contains the generative organs. The center [*sic*] of the flower – the home of beauty, and fragrance, and sweetness – is the nuptial couch, the bower of love, sacred to the passionate mysteries of vegetable procreation. In the center of this

[50] Nichols, *Esoteric Anthropology*, p. 73.   [51] *Ibid.*, pp. 127–8.

bridal chamber is the pistil, or female organ; its tube corresponds to the vagina, and below it is the ovary, where the egg is formed and fecundated.[52]

Knowledge of human reproduction, then, gains respectability from its connections to both the vegetable world and to the sacred: these images come together in the rapturous invocation of the "bridal couch" and in the "passionate mysteries of vegetable procreation." The vagina, that first markedly human sexual part to be introduced into Nichols's text, gains verbal entry through its association with the flower, which passes on, as it were, its fragrance and beauty, masking perhaps the odor of scandal.

If we turn from the books' almost univocal assumption that knowledge – whatever its content – is good to the specifics of the information offered by the various authors, we come upon a somewhat contradictory record. Again, it might be helpful to imagine an actual female reader with little or no sexual experience looking for or coming across one or more books on the topic of sex. I assume that such a reader would probably be looking for three kinds of information: the most basic facts about anatomy and sexual difference, including the definition of sex and the words used to describe it; the role of sex in the larger conjugal relationship; and the role of pleasure in sexuality, particularly for women.

Most texts are quite informative about basic anatomical description, and many include anatomical drawings of what are usually referred to in captions as "organs of generation." *Esoteric Anthropology*'s illustrations are particularly detailed; interestingly, they are found, not in the chapters on sex or reproduction, but in a more general chapter entitled "Of the Divisions of the Human Body," which ends with a detailed illustration of the foot and ankle joints. Sperry dispenses with pictures of the external organs, claiming these would be "too familiar" to his readers,"[53] but John Cowan's *Science of a New Life* provides detailed and quite beautiful anatomical drawings in the chapter "Sexual Anatomy and Physiology"; these are especially notable because they compete for visual attention with line drawings of naked cherubs that end every chapter. The precision of the anatomical drawings stands in sharp contrast to the rounded blankness of the cherubs' bodies, whose sweeping lines suggest rather than articulate nudity (see Fig. 3).

Also of interest is how and whether these texts define key sexual terms. The majority, for example, do not offer definitions for "self-abuse" and orgasm. Sperry is the exception here, as he defines male orgasm with unusual directness: "An artificial excitement of the penis sufficient to

---

[52] *Ibid.*, p. 129.　　[53] Sperry, *Confidential Talks*, p. 43.

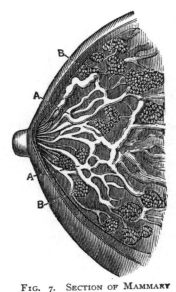

FIG. 7. SECTION OF MAMMARY
GLAND.

AA, Galactophorous Duct; BB,
Lobuli.

Fig. 3 Two illustrations from John Cowen, *The Science of a New Life*
(New York, 1874), pp. 83 and 84.

produce an erection and lustful desires terminating in a spasm of the
sexual organ, which, in those who are sufficiently developed, produces an
emission of semen."[54]

While even the most radical of the books on sexuality agree about the
evils of masturbation, they are divided and indeed often self-contradictory
about the more immediate issue of pleasure in the conjugal context. On
the one hand, many of the books seem interested in the question of
female pleasure and aware of female orgasm. Most include in their
drawings of female anatomy a representation of the clitoris, which George
Drysdale identifies as "probably the chief organ of sexual enjoyment,"[55]
and Nichols as a "miniature, imperfect penis, capable of erection, and, in
the sexual congress, receiving from the friction of the parts where it is

[54] *Ibid.*, p. 65.
[55] George Drysdale, *The Elements of Social Science; or, Physical, Sexual, and Natural Religion* (London, 1867), p. 64.

situated, the most vivid excitement of pleasure."[56] The comparison with
the penis is a common one: Trall notes that the clitoris, "the analogue of
the male penis, is an erectile structure, and the principle organ of sexual
pleasure in the female, for which purpose it is profusely supplied with
nerves."[57] Nichols also notes that "in maturity, women seem to have a
capacity for greater and more frequent enjoyment than men."[58] A reader
of these texts, then, would come away with a sense of anatomy and the
information that female sexual pleasure was built into the structures of
the body. Other books, however, ignore the clitoris and disjoin any
discussion of female pleasure from anatomical description. A careful
reader of Cowan's description of male sexual anatomy could link
emission, semen, and the ejaculatory ducts he identifies in the text and
illustrations, but female "amativeness," covered in a separate chapter, is
not traceable to anatomy as he presents it.

The issue of pleasure gets complicated, however, when even the books
that seem most attuned to and approving of female desire turn from
relatively straightforward anatomical description to a discussion of sex in
marriage. In the context of answering the question of how often married
people should have intercourse – an issue canvassed relentlessly in all the
manuals I have read from this period – Nichols speaks at length about
women's "ardor":

> It seems to be fairly inferable, that once a month is the natural period in which a
> woman requires sexual union; and it may be doubted whether any greater
> frequency is not a violation of natural law. At this period, however, when in a
> healthy condition, she is full of ardor and has a great capacity for enjoyment, and
> is seldom satisfied with a single sexual act. The period of excitement, moreover,
> may last for several days, or all the time the ovum is passing from the ovary to
> the uterus. Once there, it should not be disturbed by any passionate orgasms,
> whose tendency, from that time forward, is to produce abortion.[59]

While this passage seems to assume the probability of female orgasm,
in another place Nichols suggests a less positive version of women's
natural relation to sexual pleasure: "[I]t is by no means certain that this
act is always one of pleasure to animals, while, in our own species, the
sexual congress is often to the woman either entirely indifferent, or
painful. Gestation is to many a long disease, and parturition a death
agony."[60]

---

[56] Nichols, *Esoteric Anthropology*, p. 56.   [57] Trall, *Sexual Physiology*, p. 25.
[58] Nichols, *Esoteric Anthropology*, p. 132.   [59] *Ibid.*, pp. 149–50.   [60] *Ibid.*, p. 149.

These mixed messages about pleasure in the conjugal context take us to the books' understanding of that context for sexual activity and for sexual feelings. Under the conjugal I include the many conflicting opinions offered by these books about the ideal frequency of sex within marriage. While all the books I have read agree that women should not have sex while pregnant, estimates about frequency vary from once a month, in accordance with the menstrual cycle (very common), to as often as desired (Drysdale is again the exception in recommending this). Cowan, taking the once-a-month prescription literally, assuming conception, and adding periods of abstinence for pregnancy and nursing, calculates that married couples should have intercourse once every twenty-one months to be considered truly "continent." He hastens to add that this is a best-case scenario, depending on the wife being "perfectly healthy." Since healthy women are the "exception," he suggests extending the period of abstinence to three years.[61] Perhaps unsurprisingly, no one takes up the question of postmenopausal sex.

For many, although not all, of the authors of these books, the desired frequency of sex is calibrated to reproduction. Trall imagines a future in which scientific knowledge of the female body will prove that sex and reproduction can be brought into perfect alignment:

When the physiology of menstruation is perfectly understood (including the times when the woman is or is not liable to impregnation), a single act of coition will be enough to beget a single child; and that therefore, on the theory that sexual intercourse is intended by Nature merely for the purposes of reproduction, it follows that the acts of intercourse should be "in the good time coming," limited to the number of offspring.[62]

The "good time coming," according to Trall, will be a time of increased sexual knowledge and decreased sexual activity. Scientific research will produce a body that will act as an efficient reproductive machine, spilling neither seed nor blood. Trall also looks forward to a time when healthy women will not "discharge a single drop of blood" during menstruation.[63] Of course, Trall's ideas participate in the familiar paradox of the natural: in order to get back to nature's design one must move forward in time through scientific discovery. What is natural, then, must be learned and taught.

Most of the books admit to some variation among people as to how much sex is consistent with bodily health; almost all present their

---

[61] John Cowan, *The Science of a New Life* (New York: Cowan, 1874), p. 117.
[62] Trall, *Sexual Physiology*, p. 230. [63] *Ibid.*, p. 58.

conclusions in the idiom of moderation, which they define, predictably, in terms of excess. Cowan claims that he has seen many cases of "abnormal amativeness" in marriage that have led to the death of a spouse, going so far as to warn his readers not to marry widows or widowers "the death of whose partners was caused by other than accident or well-understood disease; for when such cases, at the last day, come before the bar of judgement, it will be found that these premature deaths were murders, and that these sensualists were murderers." The honeymoon is a privileged site of warning against excessive sex. Cowan continues:

> The exercise of abnormal amativeness is known in all its positive intensity by those newly married. The honeymoon is one nightly repetition of legalized prostitution, sinking the pure, high and holy into the low, debasing and animal. Think you, oh! New-made husband and wife, that in this you do right? – that in this you elevate your better natures? – that in this you find peace, strength and happiness?[64]

Perhaps more remarkable and more sinister than any purely numerical proscription is a more generalized sense that sex is dangerous unless all conditions for its exercise are ideal. Trall warns, "Sexual intercourse should never, under any circumstances, be indulged when either party is in a condition of great mental excitement or depression, nor when in a condition of great bodily fatigue, nor soon after a full meal, nor when the mind is intensely preoccupied; but always when the whole system is in its best condition, and most free from all disturbing influences."[65] Cowan turns the proscriptions of the Trall passage into a prescription for the perfect conditions for conception: it should be during the day (darkness implies disease), on a sunny morning (vital powers decrease during the course of the day), and preferably in the fall to allow for a spring birth. The husband and wife – lovingly united, in perfect health and strength – mutually desire to

> generate a pure, bright, happy, healthy love-child, having implanted in its organization the qualities of genius, chastity and holiness. They have fixed on the qualities to be transmitted, and the date for conception. They have assiduously, earnestly and lovingly observed the four weeks of preliminary preparation. They have slept during this time in different beds, if not in different rooms. The morning – betokening a clear, bright, beautiful day – arrives. On arising, they take their usual morning bath, and dress in loose, bright, enjoyable costume ... An enjoyable walk and saunter, of an hour or more, into the pleasant morning sunshine. Breakfast at about eight o'clock – a breakfast of

---

[64] Cowan, *Science of a New Life*, p. 104.   [65] Trall, *Sexual Physiology*, p. 246.

plain, unstimulating food. Again into the open air and bright sunshine; and for a couple of hours the husband and wife should lovingly and enthusiastically exchange thoughts, hopes and desires. Keeping their natures as is the bright sun, with not the smallest cloud intervening to darken their joy and happiness they enter their chamber, and in the clear light of day the New Life is conceived and generated – a new soul started into eternity.[66]

While Cowan is extreme in his advocacy of marital abstinence, his sense that the conditions of conception, down to the pictures on the wall in the bedroom, could affect the outcome of the birth, is not unusual. The theory of "maternal impressions," which postulates an intimate connection between parental activity and the character of the offspring, had had quite a long history by the nineteenth century. It is rehearsed, with lesser or greater literalness, in many of the books of the period. Trall, for example, begins *Sexual Physiology* with a justification for his book on the grounds of the effects of its prescriptions on future generations. He couches his argument in the idiom of maternal impressions:

Nothing is clearer than the fact that organization is transmissible, and nothing is better established, if, indeed, it is not self-evident, that the qualities – the bodily and mental states – of both parents at the moment of conception, affect the future being for life, while it is equally demonstrable that the wholesome or unwholesome conditions and surroundings of the mother, her happy or unhappy circumstances, through the periods of gestation and lactation, continually affect and modify the organization of the offspring for good or for evil. Nay, more, the very germ of life – the ovum itself – is affected while in the process of development in its ovarian bed, by whatever disturbs her functions of body or of mind. The renovation of the race, therefore, must begin with the proper training of those who are to develop the germs – in girlhood, yes, in infancy.[67]

Like many contemporary books on pregnancy,[68] *Sexual Physiology* extends the reproductive calendar back to the time before pregnancy; in Trall's case that calendar extends before puberty to "girlhood" and even to the "infancy" of the prospective mother. If we imagine the realization of Trall's ideal, where every act of sex is an act of conception, a girl is unconsciously planning for individual acts of sex from the time of her birth. Trall's account of appropriate sexuality also participates in a more general sense that sex should not be integrated into daily life but should rather take place in a place and time apart.

---

[66] Cowan, *Science of a New Life*, p. 172. [67] Trall, *Sexual Physiology*, p. 1.

[68] See, for example, my discussion of the reproductive calendar in contemporary advice books directed at pregnant women: Helena Michie and Naomi R. Cahn, *Confinements: Fertility and Infertility on Contemporary Cultures* (New Brunswick: Rutgers University Press, 1997), pp. 25–6.

Expert advice like Trall's and Cowan's severely limits intercourse – the only form of sexual behavior imagined with any degree of approval in these books – but perhaps more importantly, it puts an enormous pressure on individual acts of sex and on sexuality in general. If Margaret read Cowan's celebration of the perfect sexual moment, how would she have integrated this fantasy into the structure of the honeymoon? Would she, worried perhaps about pain and bleeding, about the disposition of body and diaper, have also worried about "excess amativeness"? Would she have worried more about the obligation to consummate the marriage or the obligation to prepare for four weeks for this one moment? Would she have worried that the wedding, and even the short journey that constituted her honeymoon travel, would make her too tired to risk sex and reproduction? Would she have worried, if, say, her train got into town after dark, that they should put off sex until the next morning? Would she have been able to rely on the English weather to produce the requisite brightness? Would she have taken Cowan for a fool or a quack and have giggled over his prose with Ramsay? Would she have compared Cowan to other writers on the same subject?

If she had read Trall on the relation between sex and reproduction, how would she have integrated his thoughts with Carpenter's? Would she have found Trall and Cowan retrograde in comparison? Would she, in other words, have identified fully with Carpenter's positions? Even if she did take Carpenter as the authority here, even if she did link his views with her own political ones and consciously take a stand with him, if she had come across Trall or Cowan, would she have had second thoughts?

Our imaginary Victorian woman of the nineties – perhaps Margaret Gladstone – might also have learned about sexual matters from more general sources like conduct books addressed to young women or, sometimes more specifically, to young women or men soon to be married, many of which focus on the honeymoon as a time of discovery. We have seen in Chapter 1 that many of these books get vaguer and more alarming as they approach the topic of the wedding night. If we think of Margaret reading Bogue's *Guide*, for example, and coming to the passage that warns that "even a stray curl" on a wedding night would be an "abomination" and would linger forever in "the future memory of the shuddering husband," should we expect that she would read with that book's sense that what happened on the wedding night could ruin an entire marriage? It is possible, of course, that Margaret would laugh at Bogue's book and others like them, that the genre of the conduct book was repellent or ridiculous to her. But we know that even the most intellectual women are not immune to the effects of popular culture. And what of other women of the time, less confident and less informed than Margaret? After imagining Margaret as our test case, it might be well to remind ourselves of her exceptionality.

KNOWING MORE THAN THE VICTORIANS

As we imagine a more generalized young lady reader who may or may not have access to the locked drawer that may or may not have contained a book purporting to answer her questions, we must also consider how knowledgeable the writers of those books might have been. If, for example, the young lady had unlocked the drawer to find G. H. Napheys's in many ways sensible and empowering *The Physical Life of Woman*, she would have discovered the following advice about the timing of the honeymoon: "[A] time about midway between the monthly recurring periods is best fitted for the consummation of marriage. As this is a season of sterility, it recommends itself on this account, in the interest of both the mother and offspring. The first nuptial relations should be fruitless, in order that the indispositions possibly arising from them shall have time to subside before the appearance of the disturbances incident to pregnancy."[69] Napheys was by no means alone in identifying the middle of the menstrual cycle as a woman's least fertile period; until the discovery of sex hormones in the early twentieth century, most experts believed, by analogy with heat in animals, that women were most fertile during and just after menstruation. While one can applaud Napheys's gradualist concerns here – he is in general an opponent of the continental honeymoon tour because it puts too many new stresses on the couple, especially the bride – this is not exactly good contraceptive advice, at least from the standpoint of twenty-first-century sexual knowledge. What, if anything, can we make of the fact that a certain and crucial percentage of the information our young woman reader received was wrong? If she had followed Napheys's advice and had become pregnant immediately, would she have questioned her sources or herself? If she had read, instead of or in addition to Napheys, Robert Reid Rentoul's *The Dignity of Women's Health*, which also warns against pregnancy on the honeymoon, blaming honeymoon and wedding stress for the fact that "more than three-fourths

---

[69] George H. Napheys, *The Physical Life of Woman: Advice to Maiden, Wife, and Mother* (Philadelphia: Maclean; Cincinnati: Hannaford, 1870), pp. 69–70.

of those children born idiots or imbeciles are first-born children,"[70] would she have worried more than usual during her pregnancy or felt guilty after having given birth to a handicapped child?

The question of misinformation is itself a complicated one and not merely a matter of presentist fact checking. We do not know everything, even in the twenty-first century. Some Victorian scientific ideas about contraception are even beginning to make a comeback – for instance, the idea that female orgasm makes conception more likely. Any epistemology of Victorian sex has to acknowledge the contingency of our own knowledges as well as our especial distrust of and complacency about the "Victorian" when it comes to sexual matters.

AND THEN THERE'S MAUD

The final voice in this chapter on sexual knowledge belongs to Maud Sambourne Messel. It is, in tone as well as content, a knowing voice; Maud assumes her own sexual knowledge and refers to it in letters to her mother. Maud not only "knows," then – or thinks she does – but she also assumes her mother knows she knows certain things about sex. At various moments in their intimate correspondence, Maud can use her knowledge as a form of power over her mother; at other moments, she seems to identify with and to forge a closeness to her mother through the idiom of knowledge.

As the daughter of Linley Sambourne, a respected cartoonist for *Punch*, and his wife, Marion, Maud came from a solid professional family whose connections were often more affluent and of higher social status than they. Maud's young womanhood was quite different from her mother's: while Marion seems by all accounts to have led a sheltered middle-class life before she married Linley, Maud was a young woman of the nineties, enjoying the mobility that loosened class and sexual standards as well as new technologies for travel and communication offered. In the two years before her marriage, Maud visited a long series of country houses, including that of her future husband, Leonard Messel, the son of a wealthy banker. She wrote to her mother of meals and proposals, tennis, bicycle rides, and train schedules – of a world to which her mother had some access, but in which Maud came increasingly to feel at home. A letter from Maud to her mother from Buscot Park, the opulent

---

[70] Robert Reid Rentoul, *The Dignity of Woman's Health and the Nemesis of Its Neglect* (London, 1890), p. 141.

Oxfordshire country house of the Hendersons, suggests both that Maud could still be impressed with signs of wealth and that she assumed herself to be more accustomed to luxury than was her mother: "My own darling Mother. Oh my goodness what a place!!!!!!!! You never saw anything equal to it under the sun – no never because I never have!!!!!!!"[71]

Maud also basked in the luxury of male attention. Shirley Nicholson, the first chronicler of the Sambourne family, describes Maud at seventeen in 1892 as having "not only good looks and a happy temperament, but also that other mysterious and not always welcome gift: sexual attraction." Nicholson quotes Maud as reveling in her power over the "boys" she meets on her visits: she writes from the home of her family friends, the Burnands, that she "is waited on hand and foot by all the boys down here – I have only to express a wish and it is gratified at once – like so many little slaves."[72] By 1897, Maud had received – and refused – two serious proposals, one from a Mr. Blair and one from Leonard Messel. After hesitating for some months, she finally accepted Leonard's offer of marriage. Soon Maud was writing ecstatic letters to her mother that continued throughout the couple's six-week honeymoon to Italy.

Maud's letters to her mother before her marriage are marked by a tone of hyperbolic intimacy and a wide if repetitive vocabulary of endearments that coexist with more traditional forms of period slang like "ripping" and "jolly." The honeymoon letters extend her capacious language of love from her mother and father to her new husband and even to herself. She calls herself her mother's "dear little one," her mother "my dearest darling." With characteristic recourse to the diminutive, she reassures her mother early on in the honeymoon that "I could not possibly have a dearer or kinder or more considerate little being To [*sic*] look after me than your second son [son-in-law]."[73] Leonard, always referred to by the diminutives "Lennie" or "Len" in Maud's letters, seems to share Maud's fondness for "little" as a term of affection. In a brief note to his mother-in-law he assures her that "darling Maudie is very well & happy & looks *so so* pretty in her little brown suit."[74] Maud's enthusiasm extends to place: she tells her mother, "I could write pages and pages about Genoa and of the many happy hours spent in one place & another. The

[71] Shirley Nicholson, *A Victorian Household* (Thrupp, Gloucestershire, UK: Sutton, 1998), p. 141.
[72] *Ibid.*, p. 133.
[73] Maud Sambourne Messel to Marion Sambourne, 29 April 1898, Maud Sambourne Messel letters. (Hereafter all letters from Maud to her mother will be mentioned or cited in text by date.)
[74] Leonard Messel to Marion Sambourne, 30 April 1898, Maud Sambourne Messel letters.

Fig. 4   Photograph of Maud Sambourne Messel at the time of her engagement, in 1897.
Courtesy of Nymans House, Handcroft, West Sussex, National Trust.

afternoon of the day before we left we went out exploring lovely palaces & 2 churches, dinner at a lovely restaurant" (3 May 1998).

Despite her appreciation for sightseeing, Maud's most emphatic honeymoon pleasures take place in the rooms she shares with her husband, which Leonard fills with flowers:

[H]ere am I your dear little one sitting up in her own sitting room by her self [*sic*]. The air is heavy with roses and orange blossom & every vase in the place is crammed with flowers. Len sends me up a huge bunch every morning. The first morning we were here when I was sitting quietly in my room & Len had gone down, a man knocked at the door & handed me a bunch of roses, Zelda roses, pink carnations & orange blossoms so large that the bouquet was quite heavy. It did not strike me that Len had sent them up so I asked who it was from & the man in broken English replied "a very young gentleman." (3 May 1898)

Maud, it seems, is only rarely as she is in this anecdote, "by her self." Maud's ideal honeymoon, so perfectly embodied in her own and in the telling of it, seems centrally to involve Leonard's continual presence. She assures her mother, "I am *never* left for more than an hour in the morning and *that* is *only* because he goes out to see about the lunches" (8 May 1898; italics in original). Later on in the honeymoon, Maud finds time to write her mother from Venice when "Lennie has gone outside for a little stroll" (22 May 1898). The next day she writes again during what she assures her mother is Leonard's brief absence: "Lennie has gone to get some money cashed at Cook's & will be back in a short time. He never leaves me for more than 20 minutes a day if that & that is generally when I drive him out" (23 May 1898).

Leonard's physical presence, a crucial requirement in the "alone together" of conjugality, also involves specifically conjugal care and physical intimacy. On the morning after the wedding, Maud writes her mother from Dover:

I am writing in bed as Lennie won't let me get up & I know my sweet how anxious you will be to have a line from your little own. I did *not sleep very* well last night. I seemed to realize then all that had passed as a dream in the day time & I could not get to sleep. Len was so dear & rubbed my back several times during the night because it ached rather & he did everything he could to make me comfortable and got up three times to get water for me to sip & Eau de Cologne to rub my head with. It does not seem half as strange as I thought it would to have him in and out of my room, partly because he is so natural & [illegible] himself that it takes away any strained feeling one might have. (29 April 1898; italics in original)

This is a rare but not unique piece of written evidence from the morning after; several of my couples wrote from Dover before crossing to

Europe. It is remarkable, however, for what I read as a flirtation with the topic of the sexual. I hear a certain coyness in Maud's voice with her underlining of the fact that she has not slept well, her insistence that she is writing from bed, and her detailing of (always carefully asexual) physical contact during what seems in the telling like a long and intimate wedding night. The letter adheres decorously to the language of illness that enables the daughter to catalogue and indeed to boast about repeated gestures of physical intimacy. This is not to say that Leonard did *not* get up three times to give Maud water, that he did *not* rub her head and back; rather, these acts become rhetorical stand-ins for those other physical acts that might have made the mother – and the daughter – "anxious" about the wedding night. It might even be, of course, that this is "all" Leonard and Maud did that night, and that the gestures themselves substituted for more canonical sexual acts. Whether sex and care were linked for Maud in the telling or the doing, she seems to be taking advantage of a code that substitutes physical care for sex, or, more accurately, that depends on a spectrum of intimacy that includes a variety of expressions of physical affection. What can be read as euphemism or substitution, then, can equally well be read as metonymy: perhaps for Maud, perhaps for Leonard, or perhaps for both of them, the rubbing of Maud's temples and the getting up for drinks of water were profoundly erotic acts. It is, of course, equally possible that Maud with her real, imagined, or exaggerated symptoms was trying to prevent "the" sex act from taking place, and that she was consciously or unconsciously deferring more canonical forms of consummation. Maud's letter is in the first place an act of reassurance; all is well, it is not entirely "strange" to give Leonard access to her room and to her body. In an idiom that might have been borrowed from Francis Wemyss's experience, if not quite from Eliza's, all is "comfortable." "Lennie" has made it so.

The link between illness and sexuality is most acutely expressed in Maud's letters by her continual references to Lennie's special care of her during her period, variously (and often diminutively) described as "ma petite amie" or feeling "seedy" or "not quite well." On 6 or 7 May, a week into the honeymoon, Maud tells her mother, as she has obviously told Leonard, that she is menstruating. The meticulous calendar of her menstrual cycle, as it is embodied in her letters to Marion, comes together with an equally meticulous accounting of Leonard's rubbing: "I am never allowed to put on or take off my boots or to be worried about anything. Since I have been seedy (I have never felt better in my life at such a time) I have been rubbed twice a day for quite a long time. (night and morning)

[*sic*]" (3 May 1898). Soon after, Maud reiterates Lennie's special protec-
tiveness at this time in her cycle: "I am not quite well yet & although I
feel brilliant in myself he won't let me do a thing, I am not allowed to
stand about in Galleries or walk" (8 May 1898; italics in original).

Less than three weeks after the presumed start of her previous period,
on 23 May, Maud senses the approach of another. This time the discourse
of Lennie's care is even more complexly entangled in issues of sexuality as
she raises the possibility of a honeymoon pregnancy:

I am rather near "ma petite amie" & he won't let me walk alone. Lennie is in a
terrible fright in case I shall not look as well when I return home as I did when I
left. I think I may safely say I look flourishing & my pink cheeks are getting
brown with the sun. I feel so so well but for a slight back ache which is the little
sign of a not wished for "amie." Still I would ten Times [*sic*] rather have it than
sail away like most young girls do – & feel horribly ill for a whole year. Which
would you rather darling? Lennie says he would do anything under the sun in his
power to keep me well & strong & he certainly does what he says.

Leonard's anxiety – refracted through Maud – that she be looking
"well" when she returns from the honeymoon might remind us of other
anxious scannings of the honeymoon body by interested relatives in fact
and fiction. According to Maud at least, Leonard sees it as his responsibility that Maud appear to be "well" when he brings her back to her
family. But this idea of wellness is complicated by the state of being "not
quite well," which serves as a euphemism for menstruation; since they
will not be returning from the honeymoon for some time, Leonard, as
Maud sees it, is concerned lest some negligence on his part during this
period of not quite being well will have permanent effects on Maud's
health and will register permanently on the body.

Of course, the alternative to not being well in a temporary sense due to
one's period is, in Maud's corporal economy, not being well for far longer
due to pregnancy. Maud has clearly made her calculations: she does not
wish for her "petite amie," but she is willing to suffer the smaller
unwellness in order to avoid the larger. One might be tempted to see at
work here the limit case of Maud's rhetorical diminutives: the "little
sign" of the "petite amie" is worth bearing in mind at this point because
pregnancy itself cannot be rendered diminutive either on the body or as a
life experience.

This passage might also make us wonder about the limits of Leonard's
caring. What exactly does Maud mean when she claims, after portraying a
potential pregnancy as a long illness, that he "would do anything under
the sun in his power to keep me well & strong & he certainly does what

he says." Does the "well" in this sentence refer to the state of not being too active during one's period or to being pregnant and, thus, to *not* having a period? If the latter, is Leonard doing his best to prevent pregnancy? If so, how much of it "under the sun" is actually "in his power"? Are Maud and Leonard having sex at this point in the honeymoon? Are they only abstaining from sex during her period (again, the supposedly fertile time in a woman's cycle)? Are they using artificial contraception, presumably a condom? Are they practicing withdrawal? If Leonard "certainly does what he says" why are his efforts, whatever they might be, qualified by the phrase "in his power"? Finally, how clear is Maud's meaning to her mother? Could she understand what seems unclear or even contradictory to us?

However unclear Maud is about the means the couple is taking to prevent pregnancy, two things are indisputable: she does not want to get pregnant in the first year of her marriage, and she seems to feel that this outcome is at least to some extent in her power – and in Leonard's. Writing on 31 May in a long missive that begins, "This is to be a strictly private letter darling so I warn you beforehand," Maud tells the story of a prolonged pregnancy scare:

My little amie never came on in Verona, where I waited for it & expected it & it gave me the very worst time in the world because I was in such a terrible fright. Monday arrived & still no little friend & was at my wits [*sic*] end to know what to do, it was perfectly awful. I felt horribly heavy in my head & longed *so, so* much for my darling own to come & tell its little own what to do. Last night Len & I became resigned to our fate ... I got wretched & finally broke down on Lennie's shoulder & wept & he nearly wept too. He was so darling & sweet about it all & I did feel thankful that I was married to him instead of some Lordly personage with an air & an Estate.

Maud and Leonard's mutual grief over the conviction that Maud was indeed pregnant has much to do with the imagined disabilities of the pregnant state and with a sense that pregnancy would interfere with "all the delightful things" the couple had "planned for the season." But the idea of a pregnancy at this time seems also to have endangered Maud's self-image and her sense of control – indeed her sense of difference from "other girls." "[A]bove all," says Maud in the same long letter, "I was so sorry because I always said such a thing should never happen. That comes of turning up my little nose too high ... I pitied all the poor young married girls I had laughed at so unmercifully before – from the very bottom of my heart." Clearly, Maud had felt, before this episode, that she could and would defer pregnancy for a specified time. It is hard to say whether this conviction came from ignorance or knowledge; Maud does not reveal how she planned to avoid the fate of those other married women.

The letter and the story of Maud's scare have a happy ending with the appearance of what is now her "darling little amie," which has "after all taken pity on me." The pity that Maud feels for women who cannot control their reproductive fates is now a property of the embodied friend who signals to Maud that the honeymoon is, in effect, not over. Maud's reaction is to reassert control: "[O]f course," she tells her mother, "we shall never let ourselves have cause to worry about that again" (31 May 1898).

Maud's investment in not being pregnant does indeed seem tied to an ideal of the honeymoon or, more generally, a honeymoon period before what she dismissively and perhaps fearfully calls "that." Throughout her correspondence with her mother, Maud seems both conscious of the high cultural expectations of the honeymoon and eager that her own honeymoon be seen as an embodiment of that ideal. Again, she defines herself against the specter of other young women: "I always used to get enraged when I heard girls talk of being happy when they were first married & here am I, the very worst of them" (23 May 1898). She surprises herself, and imagines that she surprises her mother, with her enthusiasm: "[C]an you believe it darling that it is your daughter's trying little hand writing all this. I can't." Maud's "bliss," a word she uses many times in her letters, is consciously tied to the idea of the honeymoon itself and to the cultural and rhetorical tropes upon which that ideal relies: "I feel that there is a wealth of oil being used for the wheels of our honeymoon & indeed our path has been strewn with flowers" (3 May 1898). In this ecstatic yoking of the honeymoon carriage with the path of flowers, and of the literal with the figurative (this is in the same letter as her description of Leonard's floral offerings), we see the pressures of the honeymoon revealed in the moment of its greatest pleasures. The honeymoon seems here not simply like a carriage but like a machine needing the grease of cultural investment and personal belief.

Maud's reiterations of honeymoon bliss are remarkable not only for their frequency but for the place they make for the sexual. Her letters are the source for another piece of inferred sexual advice. On 8 May, in the same letter in which she describes how Leonard does not let her walk alone during her period, she ends with her most explicit reference to their sexual relations:

One thing darling; you told me *not* to be surprised if Lennie, after he had got all he wanted, seemed a little colder. He is far far far worse & more in love than he ever was [*sic*] He gets worse & worse every day ... There is a newly married couple next door & we are always listening for little squeaks – isn't it naughty of us! ... I am having a delightful holiday which I shall make last as long as I like!

Like Margaret Gladstone's letter from her sister relaying advice from their aunt, this letter is made more difficult to interpret because we do not hear the advice itself. Maud's letter, like Bella's, also references the category of "bad advice" – of sexual knowledge that is understood, after time and experience, as misinformation. It would be easy to read Maud's letter with the grain of a progressivist generational narrative, in which the barely Victorian daughter finds sexual pleasure and confidence in the face of information from her safely Victorian mother. Maud becomes in this narrative a figure of (relative) sexual freedom; with her bicycle and shorter skirts, her money, her slang, and her social mobility, sex becomes just one of many freedoms she enjoys as a New Woman.

No doubt there is something to this narrative, but reading Maud's letters one sees how important it is for her precisely to differentiate herself from other women. We have seen her announce her difference from other married women; the letters are also full of complacent comparisons between herself and Leonard, on the one hand, and the run of honeymooning couples, on the other. (The interest in the "squeaks" of the couple – or the bedsprings – next door, although more overtly sexual in its nature is not unusual for other honeymooners, many of whom, as we saw in Chapter 1, seemed to be fascinated with other couples and eager to differentiate themselves from them.) This particular passage, with its rejection of maternal advice, seems also to be a moment of conscious, and perhaps even somewhat malicious, differentiation. The coyness of "worse and worse" to mean "more and more loving" and thus "better and better" suggests not only a correction of her mother's advice but a comparison with her mother's experience, a comparison made more acute when we realize that Marion, too, took a long honeymoon to Italy, and that Maud more than once asks her mother if she and Linley visited a particular restaurant or touristic site on *their* Italian honeymoon some twenty-four years earlier.

In seeing traces of sexual competitiveness between mother and daughter, I am far from suggesting that the relationship between Marion and Maud was not an intimate or even a loving one. I am arguing instead that the very intimacy of the relationship was based on what I have elsewhere called "sororophobia," or a "negotiation of sameness and difference, identity and separation, desire for and recoil from identification with other women."[75] Although "sororophobia" refers to a relation between women of the same generation, these tensions are also present in matrophobic relationships, which can also exhibit a desire on the part of the daughter not to repeat the experiences of her mother.

Maud ends her discussion of sex with one of her several references to money and to the pleasure and control it brings. In announcing that she will "make" her "delightful holiday" "last as long as I like," Maud can be read as implicitly comparing her financial situation to her mother's, both as it is during Maud's honeymoon and as it was during Marion's own. Although we do not have letters from Marion and Linley's honeymoon, Linley's courtship letters suggest a carefulness about money entirely absent from the feast of flowers and luxuries that constitutes Maud's wedding journey. One example will give a sense of the difference in tone and in attitude toward money. Linley wrote to Marion in 1874: "Very soon darling it will only be one little month & then shorter & shorter until the day. I had a paper from Cook's & have found out the very route we want. Taking all in – available for 2 months – fares 1st class there & back – via Paris £21.8.0 – not too much I think, we'll talk it over."[76] Whether we see Maud as cruel, careless, or simply carried away by love, the discussion of her mother's sexual advice seems to have almost as much to do with her relationship to Marion as it does with her marriage to Leonard. Having marked this letter as one "not to be read aloud only in parts as parts are slightly risky [*sic*]," Maud marks out a complicated intimacy with her mother as her privileged and only reader.

Whatever the underlying motivations of the letter, unless Maud is desperately overcompensating, it is clear that we have finally found a woman who enjoys a physically intimate relationship with her husband on her honeymoon. She seems also to be a person who thinks of herself as possessing sexual knowledge and the control over her body that in her mind comes with that knowledge. As the honeymoon unfolds, however, that sense of control is challenged by an impending pregnancy and by a related feeling that she might ultimately share the fate of other newly married women from whom her knowledge might seem to have differentiated her. Her sense of control and differentiation seems also to be linked to generational difference and to the play of similarity to and

[75] Helena Michie, *Sororophobia: Differences among Women in Literature and Culture* (New York: Oxford University Press, 1992), p. 9.
[76] Linley Sambourne to Marion Sambourne, 8 May 1874, Linley Sambourne letters.

difference from her mother, whose literal honeymoon path she follows but whose sexual advice and financial constraints she rejects.

Maud's letters also display a rich if slippery vocabulary for the sexual. By vocabulary, I do not mean only word-for-word equivalence as in the use of "petite amie" for menstruation. Neither do I want to posit a univocal process of substitution – back rubs for intercourse, for example. I want, instead, to point to multiple strategies that eroticize Maud's letters, making a place for the sexual even if I cannot point to a particular moment or euphemism. Maud's all-encompassing endearments bring mother, lover, and self into an emotional lexicon that heightens the emotional temperature of the letters and creates a feeling of intimacy. This feeling moves metonymically from mother and daughter to daughter and husband and, finally, to mother and husband. The signs of privacy – Maud's declaration in two of her letters that they are for her mother's eyes only – add to this diffuse sense of eroticism at the same time as they carve out a special place for special secrets. The multivalent language of physical care also suggests the primacy of Maud's body. Again this is no simple displacement, but a grid or structuring lexicon of corporeal language that reminds the reader of what is not said even as it dwells on the physicality of what is actually described, enumerated, and categorized. Finally, Maud's persistent interest in the sexual experience of others – her mother, those unnamed women who get pregnant too quickly, the honeymooners next door with their squeaks – suggests a widening of the erotic circle beyond Maud and Leonard, beyond the family to a world of men and women experiencing and making decisions about sexuality. Whether Maud is right about how to control pregnancy, whether she is right in seeing herself as exceptional, her sexual references are wide, her knowledge perhaps generational.

It would be easy to see Maud, coming as she does at the chronologically latest and textually last of my examples, as leading us out of Victorianism into a new set of knowledges and possibilities. Perhaps Maud sees herself in this way. But let us remember Marie Stopes and her admittedly self-selected correspondents; in their articulation of their problems in terms of sexual ignorance, they blur the lines between Victorian and modern, challenging, in some ways, a progressivist history of sexual enlightenment.

CHAPTER 4

Honeymoon gothic

Although I have talked about literary honeymoons in the context of larger cultural imperatives toward transformation and conjugality, I have not yet looked closely at literary representations of the wedding journey on their own generic terms. Despite the prevalence of the Victorian marriage-plot novel and its traditional ending at or soon before the wedding, Victorian novels depict honeymoons with surprising frequency and intensity. I discovered, as I sifted through the (usually grim) honeymoons of the literary canon as well as through the mass of less canonical texts, that most of these depictions have in common three important elements: narrative reliance on honeymoons as extended opportunities for the revelation of character; the imbrication of that revelation in narratives of secrecy, deceit, and violence; and the location of that secrecy, deceit, and violence in the language and landscape of the gothic. Many novels and shorter pieces, in other words, use the honeymoon as a time and place to explore the limits of the ideal of conjugal knowledge. It is no wonder that honeymoons in many works of Victorian fiction feature the insistent sounds, sights, and themes of the gothic, from haunted mansions to portraits, from enclosure to danger and death.

The origin of the gothic honeymoon might well be traced to Évian and to an unnamed house where Mary Shelley's Victor Frankenstein and Elizabeth Lavenza break their wedding journey in the shadow of what was to become one of the landmarks of the Victorian honeymoon: the dome of Mont Blanc. Despite its geographical allegiance to the geography of the Swiss honeymoon, whose lakes and mountains were to be so central to Victorian conjugal fantasies, the Frankensteins' journey also bears an allegiance to a kind of honeymoon more intimately connected with the gothic: the journey to the ancestral home. Victor and Elizabeth are on their way to Villa Lavenza, named after her late father's family and rescued from the financial ruin that precipitated Elizabeth's adoption and the marriage plot of Mary Shelley's novel.

To call the journey to Évian – or even the imagined journey to Villa Lavenza – a honeymoon is to read against fate, the monster, and the plot of the novel. In this rare case the wedding night stands alone, cut off from the honeymoon. We cannot look for clues about the honeymoon's defining act in geographical displacement or the everyday encounters of a couple simultaneously confronting the quotidian and the transformative. This honeymoon *is* in fact a wedding night and only that, painfully short for one member of the couple, interminable for the other.

And yet in some ways the abortive honeymoon of Elizabeth and Victor is only a condensation and an exaggeration of the themes of many a longer and more workaday fictional honeymoon, or at least of a particular kind of fictional honeymoon belonging to the subgenre I am calling the honeymoon gothic. This subgenre is characterized by the presence of a secret, usually associated with money and/or a sexual past, kept by one member of a couple from the other, that is revealed on the honeymoon. Often, although by no means always, the honeymoons belonging to this genre take place in a house associated with the past of one of the protagonists: the vaguely but reiteratively ancestral home in *Tess of the D'Urbervilles*, for example, or, in Mary Elizabeth Braddon's *The Day Will Come*, the mansion haunted by the previous owners after being usurped by the heroine's upwardly mobile father. Fictional honeymoons in ancient and/or ancestral homes are tied, of course, to what I have identified in Chapter 1 as the third, or aristocratic, honeymoon itinerary among real-life couples. Borrowing from traditional gothic novels the mysterious rooms, portraits, and ghosts that signal an uneasy relation to the past, these fictions also specifically place secrecy and therefore knowledge at the center of conjugality.

As we will see, the honeymoon gothic can also attach itself to other journeys, other geographic and class trajectories. Two of the most chilling incidents of honeymoon gothic take on the shape of the two other itineraries I describe in Chapter 1: the honeymoon of *Our Mutual Friend*'s most heartless conspirators, the Lammles, takes place on – and indeed is inscribed upon – the sands of the British seaside, while the horrifyingly revealing honeymoon in Trollope's *The Prime Minister*, which I discuss at the end of this chapter, takes place in the conjugal playground of the upper middle class, the northern Italian lakes.

I want to begin, however, with two pairs of novels whose honeymoons begin and end – sometimes abruptly – in ancestral homes. The first pair, *Frankenstein* and *The Day Will Come*, although written many years apart, have in common an interest in conjugality as a failed protection against the secrets of the birth family. The novels both feature the murder of one member of the honeymoon couple – in each case due to the complicated family history of the spouse that is unknown to the victim. Since both Elizabeth Lavenza and Sir Godfrey Carmichael die before understanding what familial burdens they have taken on with marriage, the novels speak eloquently to the tragic nature of ignorance and turn the honeymoon into an epistemological crisis with fatal consequences. Both novels point out that even the most intimate knowledge of one's spouse – the members of each couple grew up together, Victor and Elizabeth literally in the same household and Juanita and Sir Godfrey on neighboring properties – cannot finally offer protection against the violent return of a family secret. While Shelley's slightly less radical and comprehensive account hints at a "what-if" scenario – a moment where the plot and the characters might have taken a different direction if, for example, Victor had been more forthcoming with Elizabeth or had understood the monster's threats more accurately (in other words, if all concerned had known more) – *The Day Will Come* offers no such hope, since the secret originates in the previous generation, producing a plot of inheritance rather than of creation and a tragic history that must be unveiled and articulated through the detective plot.

The second pair of novels, George Eliot's *Daniel Deronda* and Thomas Hardy's *Tess of the D'Urbervilles*, offers us characters who survive into an education plot. In both novels sexual knowledge and sexual ignorance are very much at issue, and in both, knowledge about sex – and particularly about what we continue to think of as the "opposite" sex – is linked to other more global forms of knowledge: both kinds are figured simultaneously in Eliot's resonant use of the phrase "knowledge of the world." These novels, far more than the previous two, also implicate the reader in the problem of epistemology: neither author chooses to represent the honeymoon except by showing its effects. The reader, then, is left, like the characters, to struggle with the problem of not knowing and of putting together fragmentary pieces of information that might or might not add up to "knowledge of the world." Like *The Day Will Come, Daniel Deronda* and *Tess* are both concerned with history and its impact on the conjugal couple; for Eliot and for Hardy, although in different ways, this is indicatively a racialized history: Gwendolen and Daniel work out the relation of the conjugal to the history of the Jewish people and to their knowledge and ignorance about that history, while Tess and Angel struggle with the impact of the "exhausted race," the ancient and extinct D'Urberville family, on their marriage and on their knowledge about each other. Although there is no murder during the honeymoon in either novel, sexual ignorance sets the condition for murders or equivocal killings later on in the text. The violence of these honeymoons is onto-logical; both use gothic tropes to figure the breakdown of personality and of the object world.

Let us briefly revisit the scene of the Frankensteins' wedding night. It goes without saying that Victor has a secret that he is keeping from his wife: it is literally the secret of life and death. Victor has promised her that he will reveal all on the following day – in other words, after the wedding night. Victor's secret, by definition, involves the problem of knowledge: he is keeping knowledge from Elizabeth. But the secret is also *about* knowledge, about Victor's attempts to gain knowledge: about his attempts to gain knowledge forbidden to human beings. Of course, Victor, as readers all seem to know, does not really know very much. His most relevant piece of ignorance can also be thought of as denial: as he rehearses in his mind the monster's threat to be with him on his wedding night, Victor thinks that it is he and not Elizabeth who is in danger from the monster's attack.

We should be familiar now with how knowledge on and about the honeymoon shifts its ground and is revealed as ignorance and how knowledges brought to and constructed by the honeymoon are partial and competing. Frankenstein is, among other things, a meditation on different kinds and degrees of knowledge, on knowledges that substitute and cover for one another. Feminist critics of the novel have suggested that Victor's scientific researches are in some ways a cover for his reluc-tance to know in the biblical sense; his researches into death distract him from life, from sexuality and reproduction, as the monster's carefully articulated body comes to substitute for the silent body of Elizabeth.[1] Both kinds of knowledge – of the charnel house and of the marriage bed – are part of the novel's investigation of what must be thought of together as carnal knowledge.

The two kinds of carnal knowledge come finally together on what is both a marriage and a death bed, what Victor calls, in a moment of revelation, a "bridal bier":

Great God! Why did I not then expire! Why am I here to relate the destruction of the best hope, and the purest creature of earth? She was there, lifeless and inanimate, thrown across the bed, her head hanging down, and her pale and

[1] See, for example, Sandra M. Gilbert and Susan Gubar, *The Madwoman in the Attic: The Woman Writer and the Nineteenth-Century Literary Imagination* (New Haven: Yale University Press, 1979), p. 232.

distorted features half covered by her hair. Every where [*sic*] I turn I see the same figure – her bloodless arms and relaxed form flung by the murderer on its bridal bier.[2]

Many critics have, of course, pointed out the way the position of Elizabeth's corpse mimics that of a body in the throes of sexual pleasure. The monster then substitutes for Victor as potent lover; it is he who consummates the wedding night, he who has carnal knowledge of Elizabeth. But this climactic scene is also an epistemological one; moments before the discovery of the body we find Victor making another kind of discovery:

She left me, and I continued some time walking up and down the passages of the house, and inspecting every corner that might afford a retreat to my adversary. But I discovered no trace of him, and was beginning to conjecture that some fortunate chance had intervened to prevent the execution of his menaces; when suddenly I heard a shrill and dreadful scream. It came from the room into which Elizabeth had retired. As I heard it, *the whole truth rushed into my mind,* my arms dropped, the motion of every muscle and fibre was suspended; I could feel the blood trickling in my veins, and tingling in the extremities of my limbs.[3]

Before the scream, Victor literally "discovers" nothing; he walks in the mazelike house, like Casaubon on his labyrinthian wedding journey, lost in the "passages" of his own sense of what is real. The scream instantly delivers the "whole truth." But what is Victor's mistake? Narcissism, certainly; denial and avoidance of sexuality, of course. In some ways, however, the error under which he labors is simply grammatical: he has misunderstood the "you" in "I will be with you on your wedding night." For example, if Victor had read the "you" as plural rather than as singular, he might have been with Elizabeth to protect her; if he had read, in other words, *with* the grammar of conjugality, had read according to the paradoxical rules of the "alone together," things might have turned out differently. But Victor, finally, resists the conjugal and spends his wedding night alone and apart. He resists carnal/conjugal knowledge, both by fatally delaying the sexual consummation of his marriage and by delaying the confession of his secret, itself finally indistinguishable, in this novel and others in the genre of the honeymoon gothic, from sex.

In *Frankenstein*, Victor and Elizabeth are stopped on their way to the bride's familial home by the intrusion of the embodied representative of the groom's extended and unacknowledged family. In *The Day Will*

---

[2] Mary Shelley, *Frankenstein* (New York: Oxford University Press, 1969), p. 195.
[3] *Ibid.* (italics mine).

Come, Braddon explores the links between a scandalous and also murderously embodied family history as a honeymoon couple explores the nooks and crannies of the paternal – if not the ancestral – home of the bride. Braddon's novel opens with a honeymoon and with what turns out to be a doomed choice of destination. Juanita Dalbrook, engaged to her childhood sweetheart, Sir Godfrey Carmichael, insists on honeymooning in the house her father bought as a young man and in which she has grown up:

> By a curious fancy Juanita had elected to spend her honeymoon in that one house of which she ought to have been most weary, the good old house in which she had been born, and where all her days of courtship, a ten years' courtship, had been spent. In vain had the fairest scenes of Europe been suggested to her. She had traveled enough to be indifferent to mountains and lakes, glaciers and fjords. "I have seen just enough to know that there is no place like home," she said, with her pretty air of authority. "I won't have a honeymoon at all if I can't have it at Cheriton. I want to feel what it is like to have you all to myself in my own place, Godfrey, among all the things I love."[4]

In rejecting the "fairest scenes of Europe" for a honeymoon at home, Juanita is aligning herself with a more aristocratic model of a honeymoon, and one appropriate for a sophisticated world traveler who has "seen just enough" of the world to ratify her preference for home. Importantly, however, the home in which she consecrates her honeymoon is, despite her attachment to it, not a genuinely ancestral one. Her father, a successful barrister who married an heiress, bought the house before Juanita was born from the Strangeway family, an "exhausted race" who were forced by financial troubles to part with Cheriton, their home for generations. Soon after buying the house the barrister became a judge and then, finally – and to the remaining Strangeways, infuriatingly – Lord Cheriton. Juanita's claim to the property, then, is morally and in terms of class a questionable one: Juanita's tone of ownership and "pretty air of authority," suggest that Juanita has taken up a position inappropriate to one of her class. The plot of the novel challenges Juanita's sense of possession – and ultimately of inheritance – as her husband is shot on his honeymoon through the window of the contested mansion by a descendant of the Strangeways who was also in the distant past the mistress of the present Lord Cheriton.

---

[4] Mary Elizabeth Braddon, *The Day Will Come* (London: Simpkin, 1890), p. 7 (hereafter cited in text and notes as *DWC*).

Juanita's fantasy of a honeymoon, immediately realized as the couple enter Cheriton at the beginning of the novel, is intimately tied to an erotics of place expressed as a desire to "colonize" the house as a couple:

It had been one of her girlish caprices to devise new places for their afternoon tea. Whether it had been as keen a delight for the footmen to carry Japanese tables and bamboo chairs from pillar to post was open to question, but Juanita loved to colonize, as she called it. "I feel that wherever we establish our teapot we invest the spot with the sanctity of home," she said. (*DWC*, pp. 22–3)

Moving from room to room, the couple claim every corner of the house and garden in the name of conjugality – as tea drinking and the rituals of domestic labor that surround it establish sexual, class, and national ownership.

As the honeymoon progresses, however, this occupation of different rooms begins to take on a more sinister – and a more explicitly gothic – cast. Juanita and Godfrey hear disturbing sounds outside the library, and Juanita is convinced that the house is haunted. As a result, the next evening she tells Godfrey that they should drink their after-dinner tea in the drawing room to avoid the "horrors" she would feel in the library. Godfrey responds as though Juanita is merely continuing her erotic "caprices" of the earlier days. He says teasingly: "My capricious one. You will be tired of the drawing-room tomorrow. I should not be surprised if you ordered me to sit on the housetop. We might rig up a tent for afternoon tea between two chimney stacks" (*DWC*, p. 42).

Juanita's horror of the library comes to her only after she has identified it as a safe retreat from another disturbing encounter: in this case, with those touchstones of gothic fiction, old family portraits. The hall at Cheriton is lined with portraits of the Strangeways; when Godfrey asks why Juanita's father chose to keep the portraits when he bought the house, Juanita explains:

He would not part with them for worlds. They are like the peacock's feathers that he *will* bring indoors. I sometimes thinks he has a fancy for unlucky things ... Father's idea is that as we have no ancestors of our own, we may as well keep the Strangeway portraits. The faces are the history of the house, father said, when mother wanted the dismal old pictures taken down to make way for a collection of modern art. So there they are, and I can't help thinking that they *overlook* us. (*DWC*, p. 27; italics in original)

The pictures are identified, through the lovers' banter, as the father's caprice; they have come with the house and produce for the Cheritons an ancestry – and a history – to which they are not entitled. There is, of course, no deception suggested here; the "unlucky" portraits are part of a public myth open to the affectionate ridicule of the next generation. It takes no expert reader of the gothic and of its portraits to understand that the paintings index a deeper, less amusing, and more sinister past, in this case the sexual past of Juanita's father. We find out at the end of the novel that one of the portraits is of a young woman, Evelyn Strangeway, who became Juanita's father's mistress and was abandoned by him in favor of a richer bride, and who should have been, by double rights of marriage and inheritance, the mistress – in the more legitimate sense – of the house.

The history that the new Lord Cheriton appropriates by the purchase of the house and by his ascension to a title that marks his public connection to the place is, one senses from the beginning of the novel, inauthentic. While the novel praises Lord Cheriton for the brilliance and the hard work that help him bring together home, place, and title, ultimately the novel is concerned with his history in a different sense. After the murder, Lord Cheriton's barrister nephew, Theodore, takes on the role, immortalized in *Lady Audley's Secret*, of the family detective; his task becomes the unraveling of the sexual past, first, of his cousin-in-law Godfrey and, then, of his uncle as a motive for the murder.

Godfrey, it seems, has no history of this kind, although both Churton, the professional detective from Scotland Yard, and Lord Cheriton himself consider the possibility:

Young men are apt to be weak. Yes, Lord Cheriton had seen enough of the world to know that this was true. It was just possible that in that young life, which seemed as white as snow to kindred and friends, that there had been one dark secret, one corroding stain ... Such things have been in many lives, in most lives, perhaps, could we know all, Lord Cheriton thought, as he sat meditating on the detective's suggestions. (*DWC*, p. 69)

The novel quickly repudiates the possibility of previous "entanglements" on Godfrey's part. Much of this repudiation depends on the public nature of his love for Juanita, whom he has "adored" from his boyhood on. The vicar who married the couple testifies that he read Godfrey's face on his wedding day, and that there was no trace of another attachment there. Godfrey's love of Juanita, with its long history, is confidently read by the novel as no (sexual) history at all. This lack of sexual history seems, ironically enough, tied to Godfrey's status as an aristocrat; from the moment of his birth, Godfrey has been before the public eye: visibility confers trust; an aristocratic past insures, in the strange historiography of this novel, that he has no past in a sexual sense.

We cannot, of course, have this confidence in the ex-barrister, Lord Cheriton, who never talks about his years of professional advancement before his marriage. Midway through the novel, Theodore realizes that it is these years that hold the clue to the mystery: "A man who marries at forty years of age has generally some kind of history before his marriage; and it was in that history Theodore told himself he must look for the secret of Godfrey Carmichael's death" (*DWC*, p. 231). "Some kind of history" turns out, of course, to mean a familiar kind of sexual history. When, in the course of his investigations, Theodore interviews Lord Cheriton's former charwoman, Mrs. Dugget, at the Inns of Court, she tells him that the then Mr. Dalbrook never slept in his rooms after his first three years as a barrister, and that she suspects him of living under the assumed name of Mr. Danvers at a cottage in the suburbs. She seems to have seen his double life as interesting but certainly unremarkable; in answer to Theodore's question about whether she thought it was "curious" that a "professional man" should behave in this mysterious way, she replies:

It might seem curious to you, sir, but I've seen a good deal of professional gentlemen in my time, and it didn't strike me as very uncommon. Gentlemen have their own reasons for what they do, and the more particular they are from a professional point of view the more convenient they might find it to make a little alteration in their names now and then. (*DWC*, p. 238)

Professional gentlemen, according to the experienced Mrs. Dugget, often have a history. The charwoman was interested enough in Mr. Dalbrook's to have followed him to his suburban home and, like a good historian, to have preserved some of the documents relating to his double life. But a private, and thus secret, history is, it seems, part of belonging to the professional class: that class without a public history or, as Juanita would put it, without ancestors.

If professional men have histories that can coexist with a high social standing and professional respect, women with histories are, predictably, more problematic. Juanita herself, whose youth and public attachment to Godfrey guarantee that she, like her husband, has no secret past, is nonetheless, it seems, characterologically disposed to having one. As she stares at the portrait of the Strangeway daughter, Juanita feels both a recoil and a connection: "[O]h Godfrey," she says, "if I had been married before I saw you – and we had met – and you had cared for me – God knows what kind of woman I should have been. Perhaps I should have been one of those poor souls who have a history, the women mother and her friends stare at and whisper about in the Park" (*DWC*, p. 25).

The young woman in the portrait, Cheriton's discarded mistress turned lodge-keeper of her former home and former lover, is immediately legible as a woman *with* a past at first expressed in the sympathetic idiom of "better days." When Godfrey asks Juanita about Mrs. Porter, Juanita warns him that he "mustn't sneer" at the woman: "She is a very un-assuming person, and very grateful for her comfortable position here, though she has known better days, poor soul." Godfrey understands "better days" as a euphemism, countering with an explicit request for information. "That is always such a vague expression," he says. "What were the better days like?" (*DWC*, p. 40).[5] Her assumed name a rendering of her present function, silent and reserved to all in the village, Mrs. Porter refuses in her very bearing any reference to the past. Conspicuously a woman with a "history," she resists even the most benign attempts to imagine for her a past life.

As the detective plot unfolds, it gives us accounts of both Lord Cheriton's "history" and Mrs. Porter's "better days"; these are, of course, the solution to the mystery, the motive for the murder of Godfrey Carmichael. Importantly, however, Mrs. Porter's double motive – as deserted wife and displaced home owner – is a motive at second hand. She kills, not Lord Cheriton, but the son-in-law who might perpetuate the baronetcy. The fatal honeymoon here, then, is a crisis of knowledge in a sense different from that in *Frankenstein*: neither Godfrey nor Juanita harbors a secret; their lives are open, public, and legible; and their honeymoon is an ideal of conjugal intimacy.

In this case, then, the conjugal ideal as it is embodied in Juanita and Godfrey's honeymoon is insufficient to counter the problem of ignor-ance. And this is what is most radical, most unusual, in Braddon's representation of marriage. She begins with two people who have known each other from childhood, who are deeply bonded to each other and to their community, who have intellectual interests in common, and who exhibit a deep sexual attraction. She deliberately keeps them away from the contested scenery of the conventional honeymoon, bringing together the domestic and the adventurous in their choice of honeymoon locale. Even so, even with these choices, attributes, and histories in their favor, conjugal knowledge is fatally incomplete. One might also sense, in Braddon, a parody of Frankenstein's insistence that it is only conjugality that can keep one safe. Sir Godfrey is killed at the only recorded moment

---

[5] Godfrey's question suggests a Shelley-like moment of "what if." We are, perhaps, being invited to imagine that Godfrey would have made a good family detective had he lived. Had the honeymoon gone on longer, he might have begun to uncover the family secret that endangered his life. In this case the detective function – or the detective function that might have made a difference – dies with Godfrey. Since Godfrey dies, essentially, of conjugality, the conjugal and the detective are set at odds.

when he is out of sight of his bride. Juanita's second marriage, a much more sober and cerebral affair, seems to undercut the conjugal idea of the honeymoon with its monogamy, singularity, and entwinement.

ABSENT HONEYMOONS: *DANIEL DERONDA* AND *TESS*

If the gothic honeymoons of *Frankenstein* and *The Day Will Come* lead directly to murder, *Daniel Deronda* and *Tess of the D'Urbervilles* take a longer and more attenuated journey from the site of the honeymoon to the place of killing. Both *Deronda* and *Tess*, however, make use of gothic elements to dramatize the problem of secrecy and knowledge. Both novels have at their narrative and emotional center a honeymoon, and indeed a wedding night, whose transformative powers are rendered by a stunning orthographic blankness; both wedding nights occur in the ellipses between one volume or named book of the novel and another. In both novels, expected honeymoon transformations of the characters are displaced in two ways: into the chronology of the novel and onto the world of objects that take on a gothic life of their own. In both cases one or more of the honeymoon partners is discovered to have a dubious sexual past; and although the gender dynamics of sexual experience are different in *Daniel Deronda* and *Tess*, both novels focus on the problem of sexual knowledge for women.

Daniel Deronda can be read as a novel of sexual education, not only for its heroine, Gwendolen Harleth, who enters marriage and the marriage plot knowing almost nothing about male sexuality and must learn through her marital experiences about the relation of gender and power, but also for Daniel, who takes the lessons he learns as a child about illegitimacy and applies them in ever widening circles to encompass the largest questions of race, history, and the history of race.[6] That their

---

[6] George Eliot, *Daniel Deronda* (New York: Penguin Books, 1995) (hereafter cited in text and notes as *DD*). There is a recent critical tradition linking *Daniel Deronda* to questions of epistemology. Alexander Welsh, *George Eliot and Blackmail* (Cambridge, MA: Harvard University Press, 1985), chap. 14, takes up the idea that *Daniel Deronda* is "a critique of knowledge" (p. 306); George Levine sees the novel as an investigation of how well one can know another culture or another person ("*Daniel Deronda*: A New Epistemology," in *Knowing the Past: Victorian Literature and Culture*, ed. Suzy Anger [Ithaca, NY: Cornell University Press, 2001]). Susan Tridgell uses Martha Nussbaum's connection between emotion (love) and understanding to posit that Eliot is suggesting that "emotions can create a distorted vision" ("Doubtful Passions: *Love's Knowledge* and *Daniel Deronda*," *Critical Review* 38 [1998], 98). Despite Tridgell's focus on love, none of these critics look at the privileged place of the sexual in the epistemology of *Daniel Deronda*. Those critics who write about Gwendolen's sexuality in the novel tend to see Gwendolen as purposefully denying or refusing sexuality in order to gain power over her body and her future.

respective educations leave them literally and figuratively in different places suggests the limits of sexual knowledge for women and the narrow register in which knowledge and experience can be gained and applied for the heroine of a marriage plot.

We can think of Daniel and Gwendolen's different epistemological trajectories as coinciding with the different meaning of a phrase used several times in *Daniel Deronda*: "knowledge of the world." The phrase links Gwendolen to Daniel, when, on the eve of Gwendolen's marriage to Grandcourt, she learns that Daniel is thought to be the illegitimate son of Sir Hugo Mallinger:

> Gwendolen was silent; but her mother observed so marked an effect in her face that she was angry with herself for having repeated Mrs. Torrington's gossip. It seemed, on reflection, unsuited to the ear of her daughter, for whom Mrs Davidow disliked *what is called knowledge of the world*; and indeed she wished that she herself had not had any of it thrust upon her. (*DD*, p. 333; italics mine)

The tangle of "she"s here makes this one of many moments where Mrs. Davidow's uneasy marital history is paired prophetically with her daughter's. In this time before marriage, Gwendolen can still be protected from what has been "thrust upon her" in a form of carnal knowledge surely not limited to "the" act of sex itself but including, more generally, contact with and placement within complicated sexual histories.

These histories, for Eliot, both contrast with and connect to larger histories and larger fields of knowledge.[7] In the passage quoted above, Eliot seems to distance herself from calling sexual information "knowledge of the world"; compared with other worlds Gwendolen does not know and can never acknowledge – history, the Holy Land, religious persecution, poverty, and prejudice, for example – gossip about one's neighbor seems to narrow the "world" to something quite parochial. Daniel's worlds and the knowledges that are thrust upon him as he explores them seem larger, certainly, and more important. But the novel insists all along that Gwendolen needs knowledge of her own world to make ethical decisions – and at the same time to make her safe within its confines. In resolutely joining Gwendolen's actions to other worlds beyond what the heroine of a marriage plot novel, or a marriage plot

---

[7] Again, while there is much criticism to address the problem of history and historicity in *Daniel Deronda* (and in Eliot's novels in general), there is very little work being done that takes seriously sexual and personal histories as part of the historical project of the novel. See Lyn Pykett on "metahistory" ("Typology and the End[s] of History in *Daniel Deronda*," *Literature and History* 9.1 [Spring 1983], 62–73); and Cynthia Chase on Eliot's historical imagination ("The Decomposition of Elephants: Double-Reading *Daniel Deronda*," *PMLA* 93 [1978], 215–27).

within a novel, might be capable of imagining, Eliot manages both to ironize and to take seriously the "world" of knowledge in which Mrs. Davidow – and Gwendolen – operate.

We can see the insistent connections between small worlds and large in *Daniel Deronda*'s famous "Yea and Nay" passage that situates the consciousness of the heroine in terms of relentlessly global issues:

Could there be a slenderer, more insignificant thread in human history than this consciousness of a girl, busy with her small inferences of the way in which she could make her life pleasant? – in a time, too, when ideas were with fresh vigour making armies of themselves, and the universal kinship was declaring itself fiercely; when women on the other side of the world would not mourn for the husbands and sons who died bravely in a common cause ... a time when the soul of man was waking to pulses which had for centuries been beating in him unfelt, until their full sum made a new life of terror or of joy.

What in the midst of that mighty drama are girls and their blind visions? They are the Yea and Nay of that good for which men are enduring and fighting. In these delicate vessels is borne onward through the ages the treasure of human affections. (*DD*, p. 124)

This passage embodies two movements: one between a girl's closed world of marriage and upper-class society and a larger history of ideas and actions undertaken primarily by men but also by "women," who refuse to mourn, and the other between the singular and indexical "girl" of the first sentence (presumably Gwendolen) and the plural "girls" of the second paragraph. If Eliot had remained with the consciousness of one girl, this passage might have been a parable of egoism like the passage about the pier glass that begins Chapter 27 of *Middlemarch*; but the *Deronda* passage's inexorable movement beyond Gwendolen's individual existence provides her defense as well as her indictment for ignorance. "Girls" have no place in the world of adults and ideas referenced by the passage: it is not so much that they do not as that they cannot know. They cannot possess the knowledge of the world that seems to come with the transformation to womanhood, to having a son or a husband – to come, in other words, with marriage. Mrs. Davidow's intuitive protection of her unmarried daughter from what we might call the facts of life is not, then, a mere gesture of prudery. Marriage is knowledge, carries knowledge with it, and not only because of the euphemism that allows us to read knowledge as sex.

If Gwendolen, then, represents the structural ignorance of the eligible upper-class young lady, she is also a hyperbolic epistemological case. Eliot uses Gwendolen to embody a variety of kinds of ignorance, willful and otherwise. Crucial to Gwendolen's character and to the epistemological structure of the text is Gwendolen's ignorance about her own family, particularly about the two men her mother married. We learn, as she unsentimentally pawns the necklace that once belonged to her father, that "she had never known her father," and we find out soon after that she does not understand how her stepfather's death results in an "establishment of her own" for Mrs. Davidow (*DD*, pp. 19, 23). Mrs. Davidow hides from her daughter the fact that her second husband pawned her jewels. Associated with the circulation of money, value, and jewelry, the two father figures represent for Gwendolen what are for unmarried girls the unknowable links between sexuality, money, and power. Gwendolen's petulant question to her mother, "[W]hy did you marry again?" is both a plea for information and an intuitive objection to women's powerlessness within the system of sexual exchange (*DD*, p. 24). Readings of *Daniel Deronda* that suggest that Gwendolen was herself the object of sexual advances by her stepfather add to the cluster of issues, relationships, and objects that accrue around sexual knowledge.[8] Of course, what Gwendolen does know about her stepfather, whether or not it includes the secret of her sexual abuse, is subject to repression and perhaps also to willed ignorance. The repressive economy hinted at by Gwendolen's horror in the charade scene of the face behind the panel makes it hard to separate knowledge from ignorance, learning from having knowledge thrust upon one. As the novel unfolds it alerts us to the cruel paradox of female sexual knowledge: that knowledge about marriage can only be gained through experience when, by definition, it is too late to make an informed choice.

Whatever Gwendolen knows about her stepfather, she is in daily life almost pitiably ignorant about the meaning of marriage and about what her culture overlooks or condones in terms of male sexual behavior. This is in part because Gwendolen seems to get her information from the narrow spectrum of literature available to her. We are told early on, for instance, that Gwendolen is quite complacent about her education: "[I]n the schoolroom her quick mind had taken readily that strong starch of unexplained rules and disconnected facts which saves ignorance from any painful sense of limpness; and what remained of all things knowable, she was conscious of being sufficiently acquainted with through novels, plays,

---

[8] See Judith Wilt (" 'He Would Come Back': The Fathers of Daughters in *Daniel Deronda*," *Nineteenth-Century Literature* 42.3 [December 1987], 313–38); and Peggy Ruth Fitzhugh Johnstone ("The Pattern of the Myth of Narcissus in *Daniel Deronda*," *University of Hartford Studies in Literature* 19.2/3 [1987], 45–60) for accounts of how family structure affects Gwendolen's sexual development.

and poems" (*DD*, p. 40). The irony of this catalogue of her intellectual achievements gives way to a gentler tone of narrative pity when, in the scene in which Gwendolen meets Lydia Glasher, Grandcourt's mistress and the mother of his children at the Whispering Stones, we are told that

> Gwendolen's uncontrolled reading, though consisting chiefly in what are called pictures of life, had somehow not prepared her for this encounter with reality. Is that surprising? It is to be believed that attendance at the *opéra bouffe* in the present day would not leave men's minds entirely without shock, if the manners observed there with some applause were suddenly to start up in their own families. (*DD*, p. 155)

Again we have the distancing – "*what are called* pictures of life" reminding us of "what is called knowledge." But the narrator refuses the platitude that novels are insufficiently like life to produce valuable knowledge. It seems, in fact, that life is frighteningly like fictional "pictures of life" on the stage and in books, if only we would admit it. Fiction can offer knowledge, but it is a knowledge that must be (sometimes painfully) applied.

This lesson comes to Daniel earlier than it does to Gwendolen, but it takes a crisis of identity to make the connection between text and life:

> [Daniel] had not lived with other boys, and his mind showed the same blending of a child's ignorance with bright knowledge which is oftener seen in bright girls. Having read Shakespeare as well as a great deal of history, he could have talked with the wisdom of a bookish child about men who were born out of wedlock and were held unfortunate in consequence ... But he had never brought such knowledge into any association with his own lot ... The ardour which he had given to the imaginary world in his books suddenly rushed towards his own history and spent its pictorial energy there, explaining what he knew, representing the unknown. (*DD*, p. 167)

The application of knowledge to one's "own lot" is not purely a matter of gender or of genre; Daniel, whose isolated life brings him closer to Gwendolen and to other "bright girl[s]" than to the young men of his class, has nonetheless presumably read more history than has Gwendolen. But both read Shakespeare – Gwendolen makes an ironic reference to *As You Like It* in the lead-up to the woodland scene of the Whispering Stones when she first meets Lydia – and both must go through the process of turning books into their "own history" and of refocusing the "pictorial energy" of their "imaginary world" into the reality that might be called "knowledge of the world."

Unlike many novels of the honeymoon gothic, *Daniel Deronda* allows Gwendolen the opportunity for carnal knowledge *before* the honeymoon, specifically at the site of her encounter with Grandcourt's past in the painfully embodied persons of Lydia Glasher and her children. Before this point she misreads Grandcourt precisely by not imagining for him a history of his own:

> And Grandcourt himself? He seemed as little of a flaw in his fortunes as a lover and a husband could possibly be. Gwendolen wished to mount the chariot and drive the plunging horses herself, with a spouse by her side who would fold his arms and give her his countenance without looking ridiculous. Certainly, with all her perspicacity, and all the reading which seemed to her mamma dangerously instructive, her judgement was consciously a little at fault before Grandcourt ... [H]e was so little suggestive of drama, that it hardly occurred to her to think with any detail how his life of thirty-six years had been passed ... He had hunted the tiger – had he ever been in love or made love? The one experience and the other seemed alike remote in Gwendolen's fancy from the Mr Grandcourt who had come to Diplow apparently to make a chief epoch in her destiny. (*DD*, pp. 137–8)

Gwendolen's failure of imagination is, to some extent, the prototypical failure of egoism: Grandcourt exists for Gwendolen, in the carefully historical language of the Eliot narrator, only to produce an "epoch" in *her* life. But Gwendolen fails as a reader of Grandcourt for other reasons as well: because of her idea – reiterated in her frequent fantasies of her future – that marriage will serve for her as an escape from control and from the need to please others; because of her allegiance to a familiar, locally ambitious but ultimately reiterative marriage plot; because of her refusal of – indeed her contempt for – what at least in this passage is called "detail"; and, finally, because of her limited understanding of the many meanings of "history" and the connections between them. While many critics have noted Gwendolen's mistakes, they have generally attributed them to failings either of character or of a culture organized around a sexual double standard. While these readings help to explain the novel's psychology and, to some extent, its sexual politics, they do not address its epistemology: its insistence on the importance of sexual knowledge for both men and women, its explorations of the culturally determined incapacities of women with a knowledge system tied to the marriage plot, and, finally, its sexualization of most forms of knowledge.

If the encounter with Lydia Glasher begins Gwendolen's sexual education, her honeymoon – fragmented, attenuated, and allusive as is its representation in text – operates as a double, or more accurately as an enlargement, of that scene. Although the marriage follows closely on the heels of the scene with Lydia in the narrative, in terms of the temporality of the story or the action of the novel, the two events are separated by Gwendolen's impulsive journey to Switzerland to escape the temptation of Grandcourt's proposal. Gwendolen's return to England after the collapse of her family's finances returns her ironically from the landscape of the traditional continental honeymoon to the more intimate geography of the gothic wedding journey: from the spas and resorts of Europe to the mansion that embodies her husband's history. It is on her Swiss antihoneymoon, the journey she chooses against marriage, that she meets and becomes fascinated by Daniel through the pawning and redeeming of her father's necklace.

Gwendolen's experience of her wedding day also centers around a necklace – the one she receives along with an unsigned but easily attributable note. Lydia Glasher's parcel, containing the Grandcourt diamonds and an angry note, connects this scene of transmission not only metonymically to the Whispering Stones but also metaphorically to Gwendolen's experience and exchange of knowledge, secrecy, and jewelry with Daniel in the novel's opening moments. Both necklaces are delivered within the idiom of return; while Daniel predictably figures his redemption of the necklace as a return of Gwendolen's property, Lydia also makes use of the term to link it to the idiom of retribution. Her note, while obviously different in tone than Daniel's, is also intended as a lesson: Daniel's *"A stranger who has found Miss Harleth's necklace returns it to her in the hope that she will not again risk the loss of it"* (*DD*, p. 207) articulates the problem of gambling and risk as clearly as Lydia's warning to Gwendolen that "[y]ou took him with your eyes open. The willing wrong you have done me will be your curse" (*DD*, p. 359).

The curse of the diamonds shatters the careful temporal structure of the novel as it shatters Gwendolen's sense of self. The "terror" we have seen in Gwendolen only once before, with the return of the repressed figure in the panel, causes her to "f[a]ll back in her chair." The mirrored panels, which before the receipt of the diamonds reflected Gwendolen's triumph back to herself, become the horrifyingly distorting mirrors of the gothic: "[S]he could not see the reflections of herself then: they were like so many women petrified white" (*DD*, p. 359). Cutting Gwendolen off from the carefully composed self that has throughout her life been her strongest source of comfort, the glass panels simultaneously refuse to reflect Gwendolen to herself and produce endless reiterations of the terrified woman Gwendolen has so long resisted becoming. As in Charlotte Brontë's *Jane Eyre*, this moment of wedding-day revelation collapses the heroine into one of a series of women with whom her husband may have been sexually involved. The jewels that were to announce her as Mrs. Grandcourt ironically destabilize that name and that position by producing a gothic spectacle of many women identical in their fear and helplessness. While in the charade scene, when the panel flies open, Gwendolen is able through her exquisite and instinctive bodily control to convert her terror into a successful pose, here her body takes over and all control over its display disappears.

Grandcourt's entry into this scene of Gwendolen's helplessness suggests a profound scopic violation. By the time he sees her she is not as he expects, "dressed and smiling, ready to be led down," but "pallid, shrieking as it seemed with terror, the jewels scattered around her on the floor. Was it a fit of madness?" (*DD*, p. 359). As in the example from Warne's conduct book in Chapter 1, the emphasis on dressing seems to hint at undress, the displacement from undress to dress connected as it is in the conduct book with a temporal displacement from wedding night to the more speakable rituals of the wedding evening. Reading with these displacements, we might sense with new force Gwendolen's "madness." This more topical reading should not, however, supplant the first: in her current state of terror Gwendolen is undressed, discomposed for the first time in her acquaintance with Grandcourt. If Gwendolen's power comes from her rehearsals of self and costume before the endless flattering mirrors of the text, to be seen in this unflattering light signals a lack of control, itself unspeakable.

And of course, neither the wedding night nor the honeymoon is "spoken" in the text. The depiction of the wedding day ends with Grandcourt's diagnostic gaze and with the connection of Gwendolen and perhaps Lydia to a tradition of women and a language of feeling that suggest both power and lack of control: "In some form or other the Furies had crossed his threshold" (*DD*, p. 359). The language of crossing over, along with the grammatical finality of "had crossed," suggests that a transformation has already occurred, that it is this scene and not the wedding night to follow that constitutes a consummation of the marriage and a consolidation of its power dynamics.

If we initiate another kind of return – to the beginning of the chapter and to the morning of the wedding day – we find an echo of *Middlemarch* and its evocatively awkward use of tenses: "On the day when Gwendolen Harleth was married and became Mrs Grandcourt, the morning was clear and bright, and while the sun was low a slight frost crisped the leaves" (*DD*, p. 353). In contrast to the *Middlemarch* passage, Gwendolen's marriage opens the sentence; there is no building up or moving down to the transformative event. Instead, the marriage seems to be gotten out of the way to prepare for something else – in this case the anticlimax of the weather. Turned inside out, the ghost of the *Middlemarch* sentence lingers in the "while," which suggests that here, too, we will be offered a sense of context, of historical simultaneity. The "while" is, however, deceptive; it means not "at the same time as" but something more like "as long as." This sentence, like its parallel in *Middlemarch*, however, also deals with conflicting temporalities. The phrase "on the day when Gwendolen Harleth was married" suggests a final and definitive act, while the rising sun and the morning suggest a process and a future whose ending will only be known later in the day. Like *Middlemarch*, *Daniel Deronda* suggests that marriage creates a disturbance in time; marriage is simultaneously a transformation accomplished in a finite moment easily identifiable within the ritual, in this case of the Anglican Church, and it is a more gradual process, a series of events – the wedding ceremony, the wedding night, the honeymoon – in which it is made and remade. Gwendolen is married, as it were, three or even four times: in the first sentence of the chapter, which articulates her marriage as a past event; in the scene where Grandcourt crosses the threshold of the room in which Gwendolen discovers the diamonds and in which the Furies cross his; on the wedding night, which happens between chapters; and on the honeymoon, presumably a series of reiterative and consolidating acts of sex and power.

The marriage is framed in the idiom of the visual, not only for the reader but also for the community to which Gwendolen and her husband return. When we next see Gwendolen, it is through the eyes of assembled guests at the Abbey, all of whom are looking there for the kinds of transformation I discuss in Chapters 1 and 2 in the context of the return from the honeymoon. For Daniel, who is a member of the house party, the "prospect" of seeing Gwendolen at dinner

was interesting to him; and when, a little tired and heated with working at amusement, he went to his room before the half-hour bell had rung, he began to think of it with some speculation on the sort of influence her marriage with Grandcourt would have on her, and on the probability that there would be some discernible shades of change in her manner since he saw her at Diplow, just as there had been since his first vision of her at Leubronn. (*DD*, p. 403)

Daniel, who feels free to indulge in this kind of "speculation" despite his recoil from gambling, looks at Gwendolen to trace the history that has made her, in the process of the honeymoon, "Mrs Grandcourt." While Mr. Vandernoot speaks, one assumes, for the house party – "By George, I think she's handsomer, if anything" – Daniel, whose gaze Gwendolen famously seeks out and fears, looks for a deeper change (*DD*, p. 406). He understands, however, that it may be too late for him as a reader, just as it is in the conflicting temporality of the novel both too late and too early for him to act as her suitor:

After what he had seen of her he must have had rather dull feelings not to have looked forward with some interest to her entrance into the room. Still, since the honeymoon was already three weeks in the distance, and Gwendolen had been enthroned not only at Ryelands but at Diplow, she was likely to have composed her countenance with suitable manifestation or concealment, not being one who would indulge the curious by a helpless exposure of her feelings. (*DD*, pp. 404–5)

The honeymoon – or perhaps the three weeks following the honeymoon; we have a fifth temporality at work here – have allowed Gwendolen to regain her "countenance"; in contrast to the earlier scene of hysteria, she is no longer "helpless" but "composed." Composure itself is always an act of return; composing oneself involves regaining one's surface calm, or, as Eliot puts it, one's "countenance."

Let us then ask explicitly what the guests might be thinking and what Daniel must surely be wondering. What happened on the Grandcourt honeymoon? Let us persist in pushing our curiosity further back: what happened on the wedding night? On the wedding evening before supper? Did Gwendolen, whom we left "pallid and shrieking," (re)compose herself, dress herself for dinner? Did she and Grandcourt speak of Lydia? Was the marriage consummated in the usual sense of the term? Although in other places in the novel Eliot makes use of a form of dramatic irony – for example, informing the reader before Gwendolen meets her of Lydia's existence – the reader has no special access to the events of the honeymoon. We become, then, structurally part of the assembly – as Symonds would put it, "alike ignorant" – reaching across the abyss of intervening time and text, across the gap between book 4, "Gwendolen Gets Her Choice," and book 5, "Mordecai," to understand – or to project – "what happened." The reader's position of ignorance exacerbates the problem of carnal knowledge: readerly knowledge, readerly expertise, always insufficient, compounds the problem of Gwendolen's discoveries and her fatal misreadings.

If we think of *Daniel Deronda* as a novel partly about sexual education, access to sexual knowledge within the education plot of the novel is predictably different with regard to gender. Daniel accesses his own history in time to make what the novel defines as a successful marriage – and in time to connect that individual history to larger histories of race, religion, and nation. Gwendolen, for whom belatedness is always an issue, and whose plot is literally disordered in terms of time, can only gain sexual knowledge in any meaningful way after it is too late and after choice has been largely taken from her. If marriage offers only belated knowledge, the honeymoon for women is both a scene of instruction and a breakdown of a self able to learn in the conventional sense. Carnal knowledge is a violent process that leads – in this case in the death of Grandcourt – to further violence.

Tess of the D'Urbervilles, like *Daniel Deronda*, features a horrific wedding-night scene structured around a representational absence; in *Tess* this is an unrepresented narrative – Tess's confession of her sexual history with Alec D'Urberville – that falls between two books whose names are taken from discrete stages of Tess's journey from innocence to experience. And as in *Daniel Deronda*, the breakdown in representation is entangled in psychological and ontological dissolution, itself preceded by a gift of diamonds that throws into question the heroine's status as a wife and her right to the privileges and accoutrements of that position. Both scenes borrow from and comment upon the gothic; the scene in *Tess*, even more than the one in *Daniel Deronda*, unfolds within a gothic topography of familial mansions, mirrors, sinister portraits, empty churches, and coffins, but both novels invoke the affective elements of the gothic: horror, terror, and the dissolution of individual boundaries. Finally, like *Daniel Deronda*, *Tess* is a story of coming to sexual knowledge and of learning to understand the world through an eroticized epistemology. *Tess*, more than *Daniel Deronda*, however, offers a series of sometimes competing and often overlapping gendered epistemologies, all of which break down at the moment of representational crisis that is the wedding night. If *Daniel Deronda* involves a coming to "knowledge of the world" first and more successfully on Daniel's part, and more painfully and belatedly on Gwendolen's, *Tess of the D'Urbervilles* exposes the insufficiency of all of the knowledge systems that shape actions and decisions in everyday life.[9]

[9] In seeing *Tess* as a novel of competing epistemologies, I am in some sense responding to the long tradition of philosophically inspired criticism of *Tess* that aims at untangling Hardy's philosophical assumptions. Most critics, from Lionel Johnson on, seem frustrated by what they see as internal contradictions in Hardy's positions on both sexuality and religion. (See Lionel Johnson, *The Art of Thomas Hardy* [London, 1895]; Bernard J. Paris, "A Confusion of Many Standards: Conflicting Value Systems in *Tess of the D'Urbervilles*," *Nineteenth-Century Fiction* 24.1 [June 1969], 57–79; and Oliver Lovesey, "Reconstructing Tess," *Studies in English Literature* 43.4 [Autumn 2003], 913–38.) In shifting my level of analysis from author to character, and in focusing more closely on epistemology rather than on morality, I hope to suggest one reason for the sense of many readers that *Tess* does not present a unified philosophical system.

Daniel Deronda seems to show both that knowledge of men is essential and that certain men's access to knowledge makes the world a better place; *Tess* suggests that men and women inhabit radically different epistemologies, that male and female versions of knowledge are equally limited, and that their divergence at the moment of possible sexual consummation makes conjugality and the knowledges that surround it an impossible achievement. In other words, *Daniel Deronda*, while exposing the limits of the marriage plot, does seem to believe in something like an education plot and in the intimate if problematic connection between marriage and knowledge; *Tess*'s dysphoric plot does not work with or along the axis of learning.

Tess provides us with evocative detail about the education of both its male and its female protagonist. Tess, who has "passed the sixth standard in the national school under a London-trained mistress," is described as speaking "two languages; the dialect at home, more or less; ordinary English abroad and to persons of quality."[10] The narrator seems to align himself with Angel's assessment of Tess's religious education when, in thinking about whether his family will accept Tess as his wife, he decides that her beliefs do not fit the current taxonomy of "High, Low or Broad." We are told that Angel "himself knew that, in reality, the confused beliefs which she held, apparently imbibed in childhood, were, if anything, Tractarian as to phraseology and pantheistic as to essence" (*T*, p. 174). Caught in her religious ideas as she is in her linguistic affiliations between two worlds, Tess is, in both instances, defined by precisely articulated opposites. While I will discuss Angel's confidence in his diagnosis of Tess and the limits of his own education and knowledge later on, it is clear that the terms used here to define Tess, especially in the second example, come from outside her own vocabulary. It is also clear that the terms are somehow insufficient; the first confident binary between "home" and "abroad," and between "dialect" and "ordinary English," is qualified by the phrase "more or less," while the binary of the second example, between the "Tractarian" and the "pantheistic," is interrupted by "if anything." Diagnostic terms are then invoked and set into motion, only to be qualified and undermined.

Tess's sexual knowledge similarly puts pressure on easy taxonomies, not only because her outward appearance belies her lack of experience, but because Tess is so different at different moments. Hardy embodies

---

[10] Thomas Hardy, *Tess of the D'Urbervilles* (New York: Oxford University Press, 1998), p. 26 (hereafter cited in text and notes as *T*).

this uneasy calculus, for example, in the problem of Tess's age. When Alec first meets Tess during her visit to the Slopes and famously offers her the forced greenhouse strawberries, he looks appraisingly at her as she eats:

She had an attribute which amounted to a disadvantage just now; and it was this that caused Alec D'Urberville's eyes to rivet themselves upon her. It was a luxuriance of aspect, a fulness of growth, which made her appear more of a woman than she really was. She had inherited the feature from her mother without the quality it denoted. (*T*, p. 45)

This somewhat torturous euphemism for, one assumes, developed breasts, puts Tess's body at two removes from readability. She looks older than she is, just as her mother did, but her mother had the quality of sexual precociousness implied by the disjunction between a sexually mature body and relative inexperience. Misread through the body of a mother absent from the scene, as well as through Alec's projections and desires, Tess is written into a narrative of precocity metonymically supported by the early strawberries and roses out of season with which Alec decorates her dress and bonnet. For Tess, time is truly out of joint; not only is she, as many critics have pointed out, a belated D'Urberville, an unfortunate remnant of an old family, but her own body is the highly visible site of contradictions between past, present, and future.

Hardy's representation of his heroine's age is not merely a matter of surface and depth; Tess, as he shows us, is many ages, inhabits many bodies, at the same time. Free of Alec's gaze at the beginning of the novel, and subject only to those of the narrator and the reader, the Tess of the May Day dance is not easily categorized in terms of age: "Phases of her childhood lurked in her aspect still. As she walked along to-day, for all her bouncing handsome womanliness, you could sometimes see her twelfth year in her cheeks, or her ninth sparkling from her eyes; and even her fifth would flit over the curves of her mouth now and then" (*T*, p. 21). The body that contains and gives expression to a series of ages also expresses a contradictory sense of class and the relation of that class to sexual knowledge. When Tess returns after her weeks with Angel to her home in Blackmoor Vale, she accuses her mother of withholding knowledge available to "ladies":

"O mother, my mother," cried the agonized girl, turning upon her parent as if her poor heart would break. "How could I be expected to know? I was a child when I left this house four months ago. Why didn't you warn me that there was danger in men-folk? Why didn't you warn me? Ladies know what to fend hands against, because they read novels that tell them of these tricks; but I never had the chance of learning in that way, and you did not help me." (*T*, p. 87)

On the surface, this is a simple class story, and one that will have much resonance for Angel: ladies know about sexuality through novels, whereas peasant girls are innocent. The novel contradicts itself many times at this point, at once exposing the idea of the untouched village maiden as a fantasy and allowing that fantasy to stand embodied in the other milk-maids and, finally, in Tess's sister, 'Liza Lu. On the other hand, the novel makes it clear that Tess's mother was sexually experienced before mar-rying and that she was knowledgeable enough, in her own terms, to say nothing of her experiences to Tess's father. Even less of a lady than Tess, Joan clearly had access to sexual knowledge. It is also unclear how Tess knows about novels and the kinds of things they represent if she has not read them or learned from talk about them. Was it Alec who told her about novels? Did she begin to read them in her two weeks with him? To know that novels warn against "men-folk" is, after all, all that Tess would have needed to know. While we can attribute some of these contra-dictions to Hardy's own mixed feelings about female sexuality, we also have to see Tess as embodying the class and sexual contradictions of a particular historical period: the teacher who is not quite a lady although she speaks like one or the girl who is not quite a woman although she looks like one. In the crucial matter of sexual knowledge, Tess, as the Victorian proverb goes, falls between two stools: without the experiential knowledge of her mother's class and generation, and without the book learning of a lady, she is uniquely ignorant, uniquely vulnerable.

Tess's physical and mental development fit no easy trajectory. I spoke earlier, however, of her journey from innocence to experience. That journey, signposted by the titles of the novel's books or numbered "phases" – "The Maiden," "Maiden No More," "The Rally," "The Consequence," "The Woman Pays," "The Convert," and "Fulfilment" – is, as many Hardy scholars have pointed out, both teleological and deterministic. The structure of the phases suggests an unhappy accretion of experience. Tess's sexual knowledge, however, cuts across the temporal structure of the novel, appearing as do representations of her body as a series of moments that capture conflicting temporalities. At any moment in the text, even at the end, Tess can be simultaneously the peasant girl of Angel's fatal fantasy, the descendant of the D'Urbervilles who seems to collect in her own body and psyche their historical experience, the aspiring teacher, the student of Angel's philosophy, and the young mother yearning after religious certainty.

Even if we follow the curve of Tess's education plot, then, we are interrupted by knowledge and ignorance from past phases of her life and familial history. But neither the story of her traditional education nor that of her development into womanhood tells the complete story of the novel's competing epistemologies. In Tess's case there are at least two more ways of understanding the world, two more ways she produces and structures knowledge. I will call these the world of signs and analogical thinking. And both these epistemologies come into play not only for Tess but for the reader of the novel.

The world of signs is, on one level, the world of folk wisdom or super-stition. The rural characters in *Tess* are, of course, most obviously embedded in this world: for them, the world and the future are essentially legible; the task is to sort out meaningful from unmeaningful signs in a world filled with objects and actions to be read. Thus, Joan Durbeyfield consults the *Compleat Fortune-Teller* to see if Tess should visit the Slopes; the dairy workers at Talbothays read the afternoon crowing of a cock as a sign of death (although they work to produce less sinister meanings of the sound) and the failure of butter to churn as a sign that two people close to the churn are in love. The rumbling of the D'Urberville coach bodes ill for Tess; the hellfire biblical texts she sees painted on fences she immediately applies to herself. This noisy empire of signs is, however, not merely inhabited by "folk," not merely itself a sign of Tess's historical belatedness. To read the novel *Tess* is to read with the grain of superstition: a careful reader knows that when Tess is splashed with Prince's blood this will figure another scene of violence, and that when Tess parts her lips to take the strawberry from Alec or when she pricks herself on his roses the violence will inevitably take the form of her deflowering. To read symbolically in *Tess* is to read proleptically, and to read proleptically is to read superstitiously.

Symbol and metaphor depend, of course, on similarity and on an underlying kind of thinking that we might call analogical. And Tess is obsessed, it seems, with the analogical as a way to knowledge of herself and the world. When her baby is dying unbaptized, she performs the ceremony herself, not without grave doubts about how valid her private ritual will be in the eyes of God. Her plea to the vicar after the fact is a plea for successful analogy: "And now sir," she asks him, "can you tell me this – will it be just the same for him as if you had baptized him?" The vicar, despite his own professional misgivings, assures her "it will be just the same." It is quite "another matter," however, when Tess asks if, given that she has baptized her child, the parson will give him a "Christian burial." Tess counters the vicar's refusal with another even more despe-rate analogical supplication: "Perhaps it will be just the same to him if you don't ... Will it be just the same? Don't for God's sake speak as saint to sinner, but as you to me myself." The vicar struggles again, but his answer is an echo both of his former statement and of Tess's analogical idiom: "How the Vicar reconciled his answer with the strict notions he supposed himself to hold on these subjects is beyond a layman's power to tell, though not to excuse. Somewhat moved, he said in this case also – 'It will be just the same'" (*T*, p. 101). This plea for sameness, for identity between different acts, will, of course, become the burden of Tess's brief marital experience.

So far we have spoken only of how Tess thinks about the world, how she acquires and sometimes refuses knowledge. Angel, too, has an education plot, one that is in some ways similar to Daniel Deronda's, but which ultimately does not align itself with the authority or the epistemology of the novel in which he is educated. The novel is quite specific about Angel's intellectual development, especially as it contrasts with that of his father and brothers. Chapter 18, devoted to Angel's conflicts with the religion of his family, begins with a formative debate with his father over the matter of Angel's taking orders:

> I fear that I could not conscientiously do so. I love the church as one loves a parent. I shall always have the warmest affection for her. There is no institution for whose history I have a deeper admiration, but I cannot honestly be ordained as her minister, as my brothers are, while she refuses to liberate her mind from an untenable redemptive theolatry. (*T*, p. 120)

We might read in Angel's separation of himself from the church, with his somewhat unconvincing protestations of affection, a prefiguration of his separation from Tess; this kind of analogical thinking on the part of the reader might be supported by his recourse at the end of the passage to a language that was probably almost as incomprehensible to his evangelical father as it would have been to Tess. The invocation of an "untenable redemptive theolatry" strikes at the very heart of the Christian narrative; if redemption was particularly central to evangelicals, it was nonetheless crucial to almost all Christians. Angel's objection to his literal and metaphoric "parent" is no mere quibble. I stress both the comprehensiveness of Angel's objections and the obscurity of their expression to emphasize the role of specialized discourse in Angel's education. Feminist critics have long noted that Angel often speaks to Tess in words that he must know she cannot understand;[11] I would add that Angel uses the

[11] For analysis of Tess's linguistic negotiations with Angel, see especially Adrian Poole, "Men's Words and Hardy's Women," *Texas Studies in Language and Literature* 31.4 (October 1981), 342; and Rosemarie Morgan, *Women and Sexuality in the Novels of Thomas Hardy* (New York: Routledge, 1988), pp. 91–103. For the "figuration" of Tess into a masculine scopic economy, see

discourse of the intellectual agnostic not so much to consciously appropriate others' experiences but to frame unfamiliar and potentially threatening events in the safer idiom of his own set of knowledges. Again, one kind of knowledge comes into play at the expense of others.

Angel, like Tess, relies on analogy, in this case between Tess and the world she represents, on the one hand, and a lexicon of figures, ideas, and events to which she has no access, on the other. The most infamous example involves his literal renaming of Tess: "She was no longer the milkmaid, but a visionary essence of women – a whole sex condensed into one typical form. He called her Artemis, Demeter, and other fanciful names, half-teasingly – which she did not like because she did not understand them. 'Call me Tess,' she would say askance; and he did" (*T*, p. 135). In this relatively rare example of Tess talking back to the discourse of upper-middle-class education in which he frames her,[12] we see once again that the conflict is not quite as simple as it looks. The "half" in "half-teasingly" suggests here, as it does in George Meredith's *Modern Love*, a consciousness – perhaps on Angel's part, and certainly on Hardy's – that Angel has only half the story: that he is speaking from his lexicon and not from hers. While the words Angel speaks might be incomprehensible to Tess, the underlying structure of analogy is crucially similar. Not only does Angel routinely compare Tess to figures from Greek mythology and from history, not only does he invoke literary similes like the Elizabethan "roses filled with snow" to describe her mouth, but he has a sense of essential womanhood that depends on the idiom of sameness.

Despite Angel's sophistication, he is also no stranger to the empire of signs. While he balks at predicting the future through a legible object world, he works with and from an almost archaic faith in the identity of sign and substance. For him, Tess's innocence is embodied in her face and form as well as in what she "principally lives on," those pure (and

Kaja Silverman, "History, Figuration and Female Subjectivity in *Tess of the D'Urbervilles*," *Novel: A Forum on Fiction* 18.1 (1984), 5–28; and Susan David Bernstein, *Confessional Subjects: Revelations of Gender and Power in Victorian Literature and Culture* (Chapel Hill: University of North Carolina Press, 1997), Chap. 5. For an analysis of the different kinds of knowledge systems in the novel, where Tess represents nature and Angel reason, see Penny Boumelha, *Sexual Ideology and Narrative Form* (Totowa, NJ: Barnes & Noble Books, 1982), pp. 121–4. In Margaret Higonnet, "A Woman's Story: Tess and the Problem of Voice," in *The Sense of Sex: Feminist Perspectives on Hardy*, ed. Higonnet (Chicago: University of Illinois Press, 1993), the opposition is between word and heart (pp. 17–18).

[12] This moment is made much of in a feminist critical tradition that challenges notions of Tess's passivity. See for example Morgan, *Women and Sexuality*, p. 103; and Higonnet, "Woman's Story," p. 18.

purely metonymic) dairy products produced by Talbothays. Angel is, in fact, quite bitter when the physiognomical system upon which his assumptions about Tess depend breaks down after her confession: "My position – is this . . . I thought – any man would have thought – that by giving up all ambition to win a wife with social standing, with fortune, with knowledge of the world, I should secure rustic innocence, as surely as I should secure pink cheeks; but – However, I am no man to reproach you, and I will not" (*T*, p. 234). Like Eliot's Adam Bede, Angel makes the mistake of reading his beloved according to physiognomical codes. But in this novel, unlike Eliot's, there is more than a gentle critique of the hero's hermeneutic failure: the pink cheeks serve not only as, to use Saussurean terms, an index of rustic innocence; they also participate in an economy where they can be exchanged for and can "secure" it. In giving up larger economic ambitions, Angel understands himself to have entered a simpler and perhaps more archaic language of local exchange. Of course, the key mistake on Angel's part is embodied in the phrase we also saw in circulation in *Daniel Deronda*, "knowledge of the world." Here one meaning of the phrase, perhaps something like "education" or "sophistication," elides another, something like "sexual experience." Angel is clearly trading on Tess's ignorance, on her lack of knowledge of *his* world of literary and historical allusion.

If Angel assumes and desires an erotic economy in which his giving up of ambition can buy innocence of the world, a woman, as it were, not only ignorant of history but without one, he does not see that his own knowledge interferes with understanding or in the deepest sense acknowledging Tess. This is clearer if we think about history as a term crucial to both Tess and Angel. To Tess "history" means her own experience, the story that she wants but is afraid to tell about her sexual past. To Angel the term signifies more largely: he speaks of the "history" of old families, the "history" of the church, the "history" of Greece. He can only receive Tess's use of "history," then, ironically. In her penultimate effort to tell her story before their wedding day, Tess insists on telling Angel "about my life before I came here":

"But my history. I want you to know it – you must let me tell – you will not like me so well!"
"Tell it if you wish to, dearest. This precious history then. Yes: I was born at so and so, Anno Domini –" (*T*, p. 189)

This example of what might be called Angel's "half-teasing" actually inhibits the telling of the "precious history" for which he has seemed to give permission. Like his answer to a previous attempt to tell about her experiences – he teases that she must have had as many experiences as a "wild convolvulus that has just opened that morning" – his ironic treatment of Tess's history betrays the fact that there is no room for her story in his mental landscape, that a mind ever ready to analogize from woman to flower, a mind filled if not encumbered by canonical historical forms, has no place for what Tess so pathetically refers to as "history." It is no accident, then, that Tess quickly changes her confession to accommodate the kind of history that makes sense to Angel: she substitutes the confession that she comes from the kind of "old family" that he "hates." Tess is, of course, quicker at understanding Angel's idiom than he is at understanding hers; after all, he promises early on to teach her all she needs to know "in the way of history, or any line of reading [she] would like to take up" and, according to her fellow milkmaids at least, she seems to be learning from him (*T*, p. 130).

But even Tess's quick acquiescence to her lover's idiom is incomplete because of what Hardy presents as the impossibility of their knowledge of each other. In a crucially symmetrical scene of misunderstanding, Hardy shows us that while Angel sees that Tess is somehow different from many of the young women around her, he cannot imagine the cause of that difference:

> He was surprised to find this young woman – who though but a milkmaid had just that touch of rarity about her which might make her the envied of her housemates – shaping such sad imaginings. She was expressing in her own native phrases – assisted a little by her sixth-standard training – feelings which might almost have been called those of the age – the ache of modernism ... [I]t was strange that they should have come to her while yet so young; more than strange; it was impressive, interesting, pathetic. Not guessing the cause, there was nothing to remind him that experience is as to intensity, and not as to duration. Tess's passing corporeal blight had been her mental harvest. (*T*, p. 129)

Tess is equally mystified by Angel, sensing perhaps even more acutely his difference from those around him:

> Tess, on her part, could not understand why a man of clerical family and good education, and above physical want, should look upon it as a mishap to be alive. For the unhappy pilgrim Herself [*sic*] there was very good reason. But how could this admirable and poetic man ever have descended into the Valley of Humiliation ... It was true that he was at present out of his class. But she knew that was only because, like Peter the Great in a shipwright's yard, he was studying what he wanted to know. (*T*, p. 129)

Tess's pieces of sixth-standard knowledge, which include the widely disseminated tale of Peter the Great, allow her to use scraps of history, biblical and other, to frame the questions about Angel to which she can find no ultimately satisfactory answer. Although Tess again is more supple with Angel's discourse than he with hers, it is clear that neither understands the other: "Thus, neither having the clue to the other's secret, they were respectively puzzled at what each revealed, and awaited new knowledge of each other's character, and moods, without attempting to pry into each other's history" (*T*, p. 129). This crucial scene of parallel ignorance, although relatively early in their relationship, is never replaced in the depiction of their relatively long courtship with one of mutual understanding. The "pry[ing] into each other's history" is left to the wedding night and to its system of asymmetrical exchanges.

Tess and Angel's wedding night is famously surrounded by the trappings of the gothic. *Tess* echoes *The Day Will Come* with its use of a problematically ancestral home and ancestral portraits as the gothic background for the honeymoon. In this case, of course, Tess is a member, not of a usurping family and a narrative of capitalist progress, but of an extinct original family whose decline is figured in the carving up of the estate into, among other buildings, the farmhouse in which Tess and Angel spend their abortive honeymoon. Despite his initial identification of the house – based on the actual Wool house in Dorset – as a farmhouse, Hardy often uses the word "mansion" to describe it. The house, then, as Hardy represents it, brings together in an uncomfortable and ultimately painful way the past and present of the D'Urberville family.

This sense of colliding temporalities is also at work in Hardy's depiction of the family portraits, which like their relatives in other gothic novels immediately register as sinister:

"What's the matter?" said [Angel].
"Those horrid women!" she answered, with a smile. "How they frightened me."
He looked up and perceived two life-sized portraits on panels built into the masonry. As all visitors to the mansion are aware, these paintings represent women of middle age, of a date some two hundred years ago, whose lineaments once seen can never be forgotten. The long pointed features, narrow eye, and smirk of the one, so suggestive of merciless treachery; the bill-hook nose, large teeth, and bold eye of the other, suggesting arrogance to the point of ferocity, haunt the beholder afterwards in his dreams. "Whose portraits are those?" asked Clare of the charwoman. "I've been told by old folk that they were ladies of the D'Urberville family, the ancient lords of this manor," she said. "Owing to their being builded into the wall they can't be moved away." (*T*, pp. 214–15)

The ("life") size of the portraits, the "smirk" of one, and the fact that they are "builded" into the masonry suggest that the D'Urbervilles are lingering beyond their extinction to haunt the visitor to their home. Even Hardy's putative tourist – and Hardy assumes a touristic familiarity with the portraits or perhaps a literary familiarity with others like them – is "haunt[ed]" by their sinister faces. How much more frightening, how much more "horrid" when the portraits are literally brought home to Tess as her ancestors, and when Angel traces Tess's "fine features" in their "exaggerated forms" (*T*, p. 215). The one dichotomy that seems so far to have remained stable – that Tess gets her face and figure from her mother and her name from her father – begins to collapse in her visual juxta-position to her ancestors.

Despite Tess and Angel's attempt to reframe the D'Urberville mansion as their own and to achieve, in the absence of the charwoman, "an absoluteness of possession"; despite their performance of a conjugality that leads them, for example, to share one cup and to eat from each other's lips; despite their mixing of their fingers in the wash basin and Tess's "pretty" announcement that "they are all yours," the honeymoon is increasingly vulnerable to forces from outside. If one of the most powerful of these is the D'Urberville past, others come in the shape of visitors to the honeymoon house. First comes the packet of diamonds from Angel's family and then Jonathan from Talbothays with the luggage and tragic news of how the other milkmaids have fared in the few hours since the wedding: Retty has attempted suicide and Marian has been found drunk. It is this second visit that takes Tess out of the immediate context of her wedding night to think about the other potential marriages hers has made impossible:

This incident had turned the scale for her. They were simple and innocent girls on whom the unhappiness of unrequited love had fallen: they had deserved better at the hands of fate. She had deserved worse; yet she was the chosen one. It was wicked of her to take all without paying. She would pay to the uttermost farthing: she would tell, there and then. (*T*, p. 220)

Competing with the intimacy and isolation of conjugal withdrawal are the specters of other women: those in the portraits and those flesh-and-blood fellow workers with whom Tess has shared so many secrets. It is not finally enough to have kept their secrets; she must, according to the exigencies of her moral economy, pay for her privileges by telling her own. Honeymoon intimacy is shattered, then, not so much by knocks on the door or by actual visits as by visitations of spectral other women multiplying, if not endlessly, as in the case of Gwendolen, then certainly with a bewildering intensity experienced by Tess as the pressure to tell the story that in Angel's mind will turn her into "another woman" herself.

This transformation is, of course, hinted at before the confession in the scene with the diamonds, which come to Angel – or rather to his wife – through a bequest from his godmother. Although the letter from Angel's family suggests that the diamonds will be "somewhat incongruous" given Tess's class status, Angel is caught between an instinctive agreement with this assessment and a sense that the diamonds are well suited to Tess:

> He remembered how, when he was a lad of fifteen, his Godmother the Squire's wife – the only rich person with whom he had ever come in contact – had pinned her faith to his success; had prophesied a wondrous career for him. There had seemed nothing at all out of keeping with such a conjectured career in the storing up of these showy ornaments for his wife and the wives of her descendants. They gleamed somewhat ironically now. "Yet why?" he asked himself. It was but a question of vanity throughout: and if that were admitted into one side of the equation it should be admitted into the other. His wife was a D'Urberville: whom could they become better than her? (*T*, p. 217)

Angel has his own silent calculus, his own train of numbers and "equations," as he ponders Tess's relations to other women – in this case the imaginary woman he might have married and her "descendants." The diamonds' ironic gleam is the penultimate sign in a world of readable signs: the gleam is hard to read but nonetheless portends a distance between Angel and Tess – and perhaps more to the point, a distance between Tess and the women he could have married, for whom the gift of the diamonds would have been less "incongruous." At this point in the novel, poised before the twinned confessions, Angel's calculations are based on calibrations of class; Tess's on moral worth: both predicate their accounts and their accounting on an economy of exchange.

For Tess – for a moment – exchange is in fact analogy. When Angel finishes his confession about his sexual experiences with an older woman, she tells him she is "almost glad – because now *you* can forgive *me*" (*T*, p. 221; italics in original). Their subsequent verbal exchange takes up a closer comparative calculus:

> "Perhaps, although you smile, it is as serious as yours, or more so."
> "It can hardly be more serious, dearest."
> "It cannot – O no, it cannot!" She jumped up joyfully at the hope. "No, it cannot be more serious, certainly," she cried, "because 'tis just the same! I will tell you now." (*T*, p. 222)

Critics have, of course, focused from the beginning on the double standard embodied in what will be Angel's rejection of Tess. But Tess's ignorance of the double standard and her conviction that her experiences and her story are equivalent to Angel's betray a fundamental strategy of apprehension on Tess's part: the same cognitive and emotional strategy that makes her insist to the vicar that the two forms of baptism of her baby must also be "the same." Angel, although also in some ways committed to analogy in this emergency, bases his calculations on difference: after her confession Tess is no longer the woman she was before but "another woman in [her] shape" (*T*, p. 226). The emergency is, of course, sexual difference itself. Most analyses of the honeymoon in *Tess* begin and end with what we now call the sexual double standard and the breakdown of an assumed gender equality. Of the many things that break down as a result of Tess's confession, however, we must also number a particular epistemology, a particular way of understanding and experiencing the world through analogy.

Even more sinister, perhaps, is the breakdown of the second epistemological system of which I have spoken: the connection between signs and events. Seconds before the beginning of Tess's story, the diamonds, whose ironic gleam has led Angel to try to interpret the results of his conjugal choice, give one last flickering sign: "[Tess] bent forward, at which each diamond on her neck gave a sinister wink like a toad's; and pressing her forehead against his temple she entered on her story of her acquaintance with Alec D'Urberville and its results, murmuring the words without flinching, and with her eyelids drooping down" (*T*, p. 222). These are the last words of "Phase the Fourth: The Consequence." "Phase the Fifth: The Woman Pays" begins, famously, with the phrase "her narrative ended." Somewhere between consequence and payment, in the blank pages between books, are the ghostly forms of what Tess might have said. What we have instead of narrative is, ironically, *only* consequence. In a doubled strangeness, that consequence is first minutely registered in the object world:

> But the complexion even of external things seemed to suffer transmutation as her announcement progressed. The fire in the grate looked impish, demonically funny, as if it did not care in the least about her strait. The fender grinned idly, as if it too did not care. The light from the water bottle was merely engaged in a chromatic problem. All material objects around announced their responsibility with terrible iteration. (*T*, p. 225)

This is one of the oddest passages in Tess, defamiliarizing in both structure and content. The objects in the room register an important change, losing the ability to embody or at least to register human emotion. Perhaps most importantly, the domestic objects that surround Angel and Tess on their honeymoon, those temporary household gods of an all-too-temporary home, refuse to signify in the way upon which Tess has come to depend: as portents of her future, intimately involved in her progress. Neither the fire nor the fender "care[s]" about Tess; the light from the water bottle does not wink or blink or take on human characteristics: it "merely engage[s] in a chromatic problem" separate from human agency or fate. We tend to think of the gothic as in part embodied in objects or dead beings that come alive: portraits that speak, tables that move, the dead who live again. But here the gothic takes the inverse journey, as objects previously personified – however sinisterly – refuse to reflect or indeed to affect the human condition. The objects in the room, in other words, are no longer signs but things. In this setting, the rumbling of the D'Urberville coach might almost be a comforting sound.

The abortive wedding night in *Tess* is, like the wedding day in *Daniel Deronda*, a time for the revelation, or at least the realization, of what one might immediately think of as carnal knowledge: Tess and Angel reveal the secrets of their sexual pasts; Grandcourt's history becomes real to Gwendolen in a new and terrifying way. But in each case, the coming of the protagonist to a more fully realized sexual knowledge threatens older epistemologies – ways of knowledge that have brought the heroes and heroines of the text to this point in the marriage plot. Gwendolen is forced to remove herself from the center of the world: this is as much an epistemological problem as it is a moral one. Angel and Tess must confront in their different ways, and with asymmetrical results, the inadequacy of previous forms of knowledge. It is not only, then, new information that must be absorbed but new ways of categorizing that information. Both novels offer a parody of the gentle and accretive acquisition of carnal knowledge at the center of the ideal honeymoon: both focus on one extended moment, on the wedding night rather than on the honeymoon more generally, as the time and place for a terrifyingly accelerated paradigm shift.

It is, of course, interesting that the forms of carnal knowledge painfully gained during the Clare and Grandcourt honeymoons do not involve and seem, at least in the case of *Tess*, to exclude the possibility of carnal knowledge in the usual sense. The honeymoon in *Tess* does have its gothic parody of a consummation in the sleepwalking scene, where Angel carries Tess across the bridge to a coffin, but despite Tess's hope that their proximity will induce desire, the marriage remains unconsummated until, after Alec's murder, the two spend the night in another empty mansion as fugitives. The locations of these honeymoons in private homes associated with – indeed deeply tied to – the past of one or the other of the protagonists is crucial not only to the gothic flavor of these wedding journeys but to their idiom of epistemological crisis. Put another way, these journeys to ancestral homes are depicted not so much as honeymoons but as wedding nights, as condensations of what might on an extended honeymoon be weeks or months of accretive change. Writers such as Hardy, Eliot, and even Shelley employ these locations to embody (emplace) tensions between birth family and the conjugal, sexual past and marital present.

If *Tess* and *Daniel Deronda* take up the question of knowledge of the world partially in terms of the heroines' knowledge of men, Anthony Trollope's *The Prime Minister* in some ways narrows the issue to knowledge of two specific men: the titular (and titled) prime minister, Plantagenet Palliser, and his double in the novel's dysphoric marriage plot, Ferdinand Lopez. The Plantagenet plot, which, of course, features characters well known to the reader from the four previous novels in the Palliser series, takes up in a very serious way the problem of conjugal knowledge in an ongoing and evolving marriage. Palliser and Lady Glencora – now a duchess – have to readjust their sense of each other as they fashion together a more public and more overtly political life. The fact of the reader's knowledge of – and indeed intimacy with – the couple gives to new revelations about the characters a sense of characterological surprise that calls into question readerly as well as conjugal knowledge. The Lopez plot takes up the problem of conjugal knowledge at an earlier and somewhat more characteristic point; although the courtship between him and the novel's heroine, Emily Wharton, is elided in the text, Trollope represents the honeymoon and the early discoveries of marriage in compelling detail. The compression of time and opportunities for knowledge of Lopez for both readers and characters turns characterological knowledge into an epistemological emergency.

The depiction of the Lopez marriage in *The Prime Minister* makes a strong contrast with those in the novels I discuss earlier in this chapter, for two linked reasons: first, because the Trollope novel makes no general epistemological claims, focusing with relentless minuteness on the level of the interpersonal; and second, because the problem of conjugal or carnal knowledge, although equally fatal in how it plays out, is represented accretively. If we work backward from the violence of Lopez's suicide, as he is "knocked into bloody atoms" by the morning express train from

Euston to Inverness,[13] we see a persistent refusal on Trollope's part of the climactic encounter. The wedding night is itself not gothic: there are no coffins, portraits, or confessions. What we do see, even before the Lopezes' arrival in Dover, however, through Lopez's interior monologue, is that Lopez, despite himself, is beginning a slow journey toward marital ruin. And "journey" is clearly the operative term here: the Lopezes' is strung out across the landscape of the classic continental honeymoon, taking in Dover, France, and northern Italy. If the coming to carnal knowledge is reduced in scope, the honeymoon itself is attenuated to give context to and thus to de-emphasize the wedding night.

The eschewal of larger epistemologies does not mean, however, that *The Prime Minister* is not deeply concerned with knowledge systems, particularly as they are embodied in what we might think of as a homosocial culture of male relatives who are expected in their daily encounters – in their houses, clubs, and places of work – to find out all there is to be known about potential suitors for their daughters, sisters, and nieces. It is the breakdown in this masculine knowledge system that produces the crisis of conjugal knowledge in *The Prime Minister* and the failure of individual men to do the work of knowing that creates the tragedy at the center – or should I say at the end – of the Lopez plot.

The Prime Minister opens with and continues to be preoccupied by the question of interpersonal knowledge. The first sentence is proverbial on the subject: "It is certainly of service to a man to know who were his grandfathers and who were his grandmothers if he entertains an ambition to move in the upper circles of society, and also of service to be able to speak of them as persons who were themselves somebodies in their time" (*PM*, vol. 1, p. 1). With a movement both ruthlessly efficient and unre-marked, this sentence moves from knowing to speaking, from knowing, in other words, to being known. The "somebodies" with which the sentence ends suggests a further link between class and ontology: to be somebody one must have had relatives who can be spoken of as some-bodies.

Trollope becomes more explicit about class in a hypothetical (and hyperbolic) example:

No doubt we all entertain great respect for those who by their own energies have raised themselves in the world; and when we hear that the son of a washerwoman has become Lord Chancellor or Archbishop of Canterbury we do, theoretically

---

[13] Anthony Trollope, *The Prime Minister* (New York: Oxford University Press, 1991), vol. II, p. 194 (hereafter cited in text and notes as *PM*).

and abstractedly, feel a higher reverence for such [a] self-made magnate than for one who has been as it were born into forensic or ecclesiastical purple. But not the less must the offspring of the washerwoman have had very much trouble on the subject of his birth ... After the goal has been absolutely won, a man may talk with some humour, even with some affection, of the maternal tub;– but while the struggle is going on ... not to conceal the old family circumstances, not at any rate to be silent, is difficult. (*PM*, vol. 1, p. 2)

The "somebodies" of the first passage undergo a negative embodiment in the figure of the washerwoman. The womblike "maternal tub" becomes not only a class signifier and a metonymy for labor but also an image of a bodily origin about which, until "the goal has been absolutely won," a man might find it difficult to speak.

By the second paragraph, the proverbial and the general are themselves embodied as we are introduced – the term is a equivocal one here – to Ferdinand Lopez, the novel's antihero and love interest:

Ferdinand Lopez, who in other respects had much in his circumstances on which to congratulate himself, suffered trouble in his mind respecting his ancestors such as I have endeavoured to describe. He did not know very much himself, but what little he did know he kept altogether to himself. He had no father or mother, no uncle, aunt, brother or sister, no cousin even whom he could mention in a cursory way to his dearest friend. He suffered, no doubt; – but with Spartan consistency he so hid his trouble from the world that no one knew that he suffered. (*PM*, vol. 1, p. 2)

Knowledge here is explicitly conflated with origin and with family; to know one's family is to be known and, indeed, knowable. The litany of missing family members – "no father or mother, no uncle, aunt, brother or sister, no cousin" – produces Lopez as an epistemological as well as a social orphan. Lack of knowledge is contagious, within and even across narrative levels: Lopez's friends know nothing about him; Lopez himself knows "little"; the reader is not told here or in the course of the novel what it is that Lopez does – or does not – know about his family. The narrator can be said to know only one thing for sure: that his lack of family (to speak of) causes Lopez to suffer. His suffering is not known to those around him, of course, but the reader and the narrative forge an intimacy with each other and with Lopez through a shared knowledge of what lies behind his "Spartan" exterior.

While the general ignorance about Lopez is a given from the first mention of him in the novel, the Trollope narrator does not hesitate to give us more – or less – of the same thing by a persistent repetition of how little is known about the man. Trollope offers us a sort of counter-biography or counter-résumé structured by ignorance, rumor, and speculation:

> At the time with which we are now concerned Ferdinand Lopez was thirty-three years old, and as he had begun life early he had been long before the world. It was known of him that he had been at a good English private school, and it was reported, on the solitary evidence of one who had there been his schoolfellow, that a rumour was current in the school that his school bills were paid by an old gentleman who was not related to him. Thence at the age of seventeen, he had been sent to a German University, and at the age of twenty-one had appeared in London, in a stockbroker's office, where he was soon known as an accomplished linguist, and as a very clever fellow ... Then it was known that he had left his regular business, and it was supposed that he had lost all he had ever made or had ever possessed. But nobody, not even his own bankers or his own lawyer, – not even the old woman who looked after his linen – ever really knew the state of his affairs. (*PM*, vol. 1, p. 4)

Occurring as it does on the fourth page of the novel and proceeding chronologically from the protagonist's childhood to the present, this paragraph displays many of the genre markers of the character introduction. But the list – the professional résumé – that would normally provide background is structured so that readerly knowledge and even narrative omniscience are called radically into question. Only one sentence, "Thence at the age of seventeen, he had been sent to a German University," is not prefaced either by "it was known" or an even more equivocal form of explanation – "it was reported" or "it was supposed." By the end of the paragraph, the more confident "it was known" loses epistemological authority through repetition; finally, "it was known," stripped similarly of agency, becomes a form of "it was supposed." The final sentence takes us back, if not to the true origin of Lopez's life, to the origin of the problem of family and knowledge in the novel: the washerwoman resurfaces not as a mother but as a final guarantee that there will be no story of maternal – or paternal – origin. Lopez, like his clothing, will remain unmarked by signs of his history.

If at the beginning of the novel lack of family knowledge is expressed as a problem among male friends and coworkers – a problem, as the proverbial opening insists, of professional reputation – the rest of the novel investigates the problem of knowledge within the marriage plot. We learn almost parenthetically that Lopez is a suitor for the hand of Emily Wharton. This is first hinted at in a conversation between Lopez and Emily's brother, Everett, in which Everett complains about the "closeness" of his wealthy father. Lopez responds by wishing he had a father like Everett's, boasting that if he did he would "succeed in ascertaining the extent of his capabilities, and in making some use of them too." The expression of this wish – Lopez's mere mention of a hypothetical father – provides Everett with an opportunity for learning more about Lopez's history:

> Wharton nearly asked his friend – almost summoned courage to ask him, – whether his father had done much for him. They were very intimate; and on one subject, in which Lopez was very much interested, their confidence had been very close. But the younger and weaker man of the two could not bring himself to the point of making an inquiry which he thought would be disagreeable. Lopez had never, in all their intercourse, hinted at the possibility of having or having had filial aspirations. He had been as though he had been created self-sufficient, independent of mother's milk or father's money. Now the question might have been asked almost naturally. But it was not asked. (*PM*, vol. 1, p. 13)

The question that was not quite asked would have been a question between men: one young man asking another about his father in the context of considerable if unspecified intimacy. Like the exchanges between men of which Eve Kosofsky Sedgwick speaks, however, this one happens across the body and the future of a woman.[14] The "one" also unspecified "subject" in which intimacy seems to have shaded into confidence is soon revealed, of course, to be Lopez and Emily's mutual love. This one exception to Lopez's silence on personal matters turns out, as the story progresses, to turn ignorance into an emergency as, despite a series of opportunities, none of Emily's male relatives succeed in asking Lopez the questions on which Emily's happiness will depend.

If Emily's brother chooses not to ask and not to know about Lopez's family for fear of offending his friend, Emily's father asks those questions, but for complex reasons he declines to ask about the more crucial topic of Lopez's financial situation. When Lopez visits Mr. Wharton's chambers to ask permission to court his daughter, Wharton's first reaction is to use his ignorance of Lopez's parentage as an objection:

> Well – to tell you the truth I know nothing about you. I don't know who your father was – whether he was an Englishman, whether he was a Christian, whether he was a Protestant, – not even whether he was a gentleman. These are questions which I should not dream of asking under any other circumstances ... But when you talk to a man about his daughter_____!

---

[14] Eve Kosofsky Sedgwick, *Between Men: English Literature and Male Homosocial Desire* (New York: Columbia University Press, 1985).

Lopez acknowledges Wharton's "right of inquiry" and proceeds to tell his prospective father-in-law something – we are given to understand by the narrator that it is not entirely accurate or complete – about his parents: "My mother was an English lady . . . but my father was certainly not an Englishman. I never had the common happiness of knowing either of them. I was an orphan before I knew what it was to have a parent" (*PM*, vol. I, p. 27).

The "melancholy" nature of Lopez's parental narrative stops the conversation both because Wharton feels he cannot pursue the issue of parentage without rudeness and because Lopez's revelation that his father was not in fact English allows Wharton not to ask financial questions; Wharton's strategic thinking depends on the issue of family trumping any financial considerations:

[Wharton] felt . . . that as he had luckily landed himself on a positive and undeniable objection to a match that was distasteful to him, it would be unwise for him to go to other matters in which he might be less successful. By doing so, he would seem to abandon the ground which he had already made good. He thought it probable that the man might have an adequate income, and yet he did not want to welcome him as a son-in-law . . . The foreign blood was proved, and that would suffice. (*PM*, vol. I, p. 28)

Wharton does not ask about finances because he is afraid that the answer would – or should – satisfy him. Ironically, this conjecture is based on probability, on an epistemological version of the "sort of gambling" of which Wharton accuses Lopez when Lopez, describing his business in the most general terms, says that he is "engaged in foreign loans" (*PM*, vol. I, p. 29). The foreignness of the loans, and indeed of the speculative culture, to a man like Wharton, who has written a treatise on mortgages and has his money safely in the 3 percents, is for this father "ground" enough to deny Lopez access to his daughter.

Wharton's failure to ask Lopez the kind of questions about money one would expect from a loving father with considerable financial resources of his own is, of course, fatal. Trollope is masterful at depicting the process of attrition by which parents give in to children when love is at stake.[15] After Lopez takes advantage of an attack on Everett in the park to present himself as Everett's rescuer, and after Emily and Lopez meet at Everett's bedside, Mr. Wharton feels he has no choice, although even as he gives in

---

[15] Trollope is perennially interested in the moment in which parents know that they must give into a child's choice of marriage partner. Often, the parents continue to perform refusal long after they acknowledge the hopelessness of their position to themselves. Trollope parodies this moment in Chap. 58 of *Orley Farm*, entitled "Miss Staveley Declines to Eat Minced Veal."

to the marriage he tells Lopez that he has "reasons on my mind ... as strong now as ever" against it (*PM*, vol. 1, p. 220).

Emily's doom – her marriage to a penniless speculator completely devoid of ethics – points to a failure of the system of upper-class courtship that relies on male relatives to protect women by the careful evaluation of potential suitors. The breakdown of this system in the case of Lopez is overdetermined: the problem results in part in and is blamed on – at least by the larger Wharton family and connections – the blurring of class lines. What we see in the case of Emily's marriage, however, is a linked epistemological breakdown; Wharton's questioning of Lopez involves a system of class codes so delicately calibrated that they result in the loss of crucial information. Part of the problem is, of course, characterological as well: Emily's father, as we remember Everett complaining, is himself mysterious about money; his son accuses him of "closeness," by which he means that he finds his father to be both stingy and secretive. Lopez articulates this feeling about Wharton's reserve in a bodily metaphor that will resonate later in the novel in his marriage to Emily and in his political and sexual rivalry with Emily's old suitor, Arthur Fletcher. Lopez complains to Everett, "I never seem to get beyond the skin with him" (*PM*, vol. 1, p. 17).

It is, of course, the conjugal relationship that in the nineteenth century makes it possible to get – indeed requires getting – "under the skin." And it is the process of increasing conjugal intimacy that Trollope details with excruciating precision. Ferdinand and Emily's honeymoon is the first stage in a slow and painful process of conjugal knowledge. Unlike those in the novels I discuss earlier in this chapter, the epistemology of the honeymoon in *The Prime Minister* depends less on sudden and climactic revelation than on a creeping awareness that something is wrong; there is no single moment when Emily discovers the secret to Lopez's past. Instead, Trollope frames the honeymoon as a series of moments of partial discovery in which Lopez manipulates the ideal of conjugality toward his own financial ends.

In their different ways, both Lopez and Emily begin the honeymoon in ignorance of their financial prospects. Lopez, despite repeated "resolutions" not to think about money for the first two weeks of his honeymoon, is nonetheless obsessed with, as he puts it, what his father-in-law "means to do for" him (*PM*, vol. 1, pp. 231, 235). Wharton's silence on this matter arises partly from a hostility to his son-in-law and more generally from the uneasy choreography of silence, power, and vulnerability that defines his relationship with the next generation. Desperate for money to pay a bill he has forced his partner to sign for him, and frustrated by the silence on the part of his father-in-law, Lopez, like Emily, seeks information from a "closed" and powerful man:

Up to the last moment he had hoped, – had almost expected, – that a sum of money would have been paid to him. Even a couple of thousand pounds for the time would have been of great use to him; – but no tender of any kind had been made. Not a word had been said. Things could not of course go on in that way. He was not going to play the coward with his father-in-law.

Lopez's resolution not to think about money comes of course from his understanding of the honeymoon as a time of leisure, of "freedom from all carking cares"; it conflicts however, with another understanding of the honeymoon as work – in this case the work of instruction embodied in other of Lopez's "resolutions":

[H]is third resolution had reference to his wife. She must be instructed in his ways. She must learn to look at the world with his eyes. She must be taught the great importance of money, – not in a gripping, hard-fisted, prosaic spirit; but that she might participate in that feeling of his own which had in it so much that was grand, so much that was delightful, so much that was picturesque. (*PM*, vol. 1, p. 231)

In Lopez's insistence that Emily be made on the wedding journey to "look ... with his eyes," we have a sinister version – one hesitates to say parody – of the conjugal gaze that I argue, in Chapter 2, is one of the privileged productions of the ideal honeymoon. This honeymoon shares with many others its status as a scene of instruction; the lesson to be taught is harsher, but the gendered pedagogical structure remains intact. Lopez even turns his financial vision into a form of touristic sight; like the art and architecture of the prototypical European honeymoon, it is "grand," "delightful," even "picturesque." The subsuming of the visual and the pedagogical under the rubric of conjugality links Lopez's honeymoon ambitions to those of less overtly gothic couples in fiction and in history: Emily Jowitt Birchall, for instance, or Dorothea Brooke.

Lopez clearly understands marriage, and in particular the lessons of the honeymoon, as producing an almost literal version of Blackwell's legal formulation whereby husband and wife become one flesh – that of the husband. In Lopez's vision this idea leads to the wife's obligation to act as a part of the body represented by the husband. In demanding that Emily write to her father demanding money, Lopez treats Emily as his amanuensis, as the hand that carries out the desires of the conjugal body. When Emily protests that the letter might be better "coming from" Lopez because, as she reminds him, "I never have even spoken to him about money, and of course he would know that you had dictated what I said" (*PM*, vol. I, p. 237), Lopez appears to see nothing wrong either with his request or with the fact that Mr. Wharton will immediately perceive that he has dictated the crucial paragraph. Wharton, of course, sees through, or rather reads along with, the conjugal metonymy. Although his reply is addressed to Emily, Wharton's letter begins, "What you have said under your husband's instruction about money, I find upon consideration to be fair enough" (*PM*, vol. I, p. 241). Wharton leaves intact the structure of address, writing to his daughter in the second person, while at the same time writing within the larger legal structure of the conjugal. This is another exchange between husband and father-in-law mediated by the woman who will, for much of the rest of the novel, struggle with the competing identifications of daughter and wife. The letter, like Jacques Derrida's postcard, and like the many pieces of mail in the postal system in which Trollope was so personally and professionally invested, does find its way to the right address. It is Lopez who first reads Wharton's letter; Emily hands it over to her husband because she is too "nervous" to read it (*PM*, vol. I, p. 24).

For the next three hundred pages of the novel – for the rest of Lopez's life – Lopez will insist on increasingly, to Emily, repulsive versions of the conjugal metonymy. Early in the second volume, when Wharton is actually considering remaking his will in favor of Emily and thus of Lopez, Ferdinand accuses Emily and her father of making "cabals" "behind [his] back," explicitly comparing his rights in Emily to Wharton's: "Why don't you act as my friend rather than his? Why don't you take my part? It seems to me that you are much more his daughter than my wife" (*PM*, vol. II, p. 34). Later, after the impoverished Lopez moves himself and his wife into Wharton's house and Wharton asks his son-in-law to leave, Lopez threatens to take Emily with him. When Wharton responds, "[T]hat must be as she pleases," Lopez produces the most violent and explicit rendition of the conjugal metonymy to date: "She belongs to me, – not to you or to herself. Under your influence she has forgotten much of what belongs to the duty of a wife" (*PM*, vol. II, p. 115). In moving among the three meanings of "part" – from an Adamic notion that a woman is a piece of her husband, to a sense that she should be partial to him, to the idea that marriage is a performance involving playing certain roles – Lopez himself enacts an ideal of a conjugality that is both theatrical and, of course, deeply misogynistic. Although the connection between conjugal identification and sex is less obvious than it is in the preceding Palliser novels, *Phineas Finn* and *Phineas Redux*, where the villainous husband tries to sue for the restitution of his conjugal rights, we sense an erotic component to the language of duty.

It would be easy to read backward from the end of the novel – and from Lopez's suicide – to an interpretation of his character in which he uses the conjugal consciously and strategically. This, however, is only part of the picture. Lopez, Trollope assures us, really loves Emily; I would add that he truly believes in conjugality. When, as a prelude to what he thinks of as Emily's first "lesson," he tells her to "[s]it down, dear, till we have a real domestic talk," he is, I maintain, not being cynical about domesticity or about conjugal conversation. Emily responds in the appropriate idiom of mutual understanding and knowledge: "'Tell me everything,' she said, as she nestled herself close to his side" (*PM*, vol. 1, p. 234). At this early stage in the honeymoon, both husband and wife believe in the possibility and the promise of a psychological intimacy reflected in physical closeness. While later in the novel, as we shall see, physical closeness becomes a way for Emily to record her separateness from her husband, at this point in the honeymoon both are searching for what in Chapter 3 I have called carnal knowledge – a complete and eroticized closeness.

If we take seriously Lopez's investment in the conjugal, we can read *The Prime Minister* as a sustained interrogation of the conjugal ideal, and we can read the Lopez plot more intimately with the novel's other exploration of the gendered limits of self in the marriage through the figures of Plantagenet and Glencora Palliser. We can read Glencora's struggles to find a public footing in her husband's political world and Plantagenet's insistence that she not "separate" herself from him as an argument about how closely marriage depends on the ontological absorption of the wife into the husband. The novel repeats with a difference across plots and from sentence to sentence the central problem of identity in marriage. Lopez's case becomes, then, not so much an exception as a slight twist that reveals the problem endemic to the marital relation.

If the relationship between Lopez and Emily reveals the problems in the conjugal metonymy on which the Victorian legal and ontological understanding of marriage was based, it also calls into question the issue of conjugal knowledge. And it is here that the novel comes closest to the honeymoon gothic. At the chronological and narrative center of the honeymoon comes a moment that in other hands, in other novels, would immediately erupt into the gothic.

It is part of the Lopezes' "domestic talk," when Lopez is instructing Emily on their need for her father's money:

"To tell you the truth, this is quite essential to me at present, – very much more than I thought it would be when I fixed the day for our marriage." Her mind within her recoiled at this, though she was very careful that he should not feel any such motion in her body. "My business is precarious."

"What is your business, Ferdinand?" Poor girl! That she should have been allowed to marry a man, and then to ask such a question! (*PM*, vol. 1, p. 235)

While Emily's "mind" begins the long work of untangling itself from her husband's, and while, despite their physical closeness, she does not allow her body to betray the beginnings of what Trollope will refer to in both plots of the novel as a "separation," she reveals her utter ignorance of her husband's past, present, and future. The narrative interjection that follows her question puts the blame not so much on Lopez but on Wharton's – and also perhaps Everett's – inability to protect Emily through their refusal to know.

In other novels, this epistemological crisis would have immediately resulted in a little separation, in enmity, perhaps, or violence. But it is a long way still to Lopez's violent end. Separation is betrayed here not by even a movement but by Emily's checked recoil from her husband. Likewise, this is not a moment of revelation, where Emily comes immediately to know not only what Lopez does but what it means for her future. When Lopez explains his "business" – "[I]t is generally commercial. I buy and sell on speculation. The world, which is shy of new words, has not yet given it a name. I am a good deal at present in South American trade" – Emily does not begin to understand. We are told that "[s]he listened, but received no glimmering of an idea from his words" (*PM*, vol. 1, pp. 235–6). Emily has passed from one kind of ignorance to another, from an ignorance based on silence to one based on words. This episode is also, of course, a verbal echo of Lopez's encounter with Wharton, discussed above, in which he claims to be in foreign trade, a euphemism Wharton immediately translates into "gambling." Emily has no such powers of translation; she has no verbal idiom into which to appropriate and absorb her husband's words.

Trollope's depiction of the Lopez honeymoon borrows in many ways from the structure of the honeymoon gothic with its reliance on an epistemological crisis that points to the necessary – and spectacular – failure of the marriage. As Trollope writes the honeymoon, however, it is a more complicated journey in which motives are mixed and revelations are gradual. In a sense, Trollope is truer to the motif of journey and to the dailiness of travel. He uses the canonical landmarks of the honeymoon itinerary – Dover, Florence, the northern Italian lakes – to signify a slow process of resolution, counterresolution, and instruction mapped out across the terrain of the ideal honeymoon. In the case of Lopez, Dover signals not so much the wedding night and a sexual and epistemological crisis as it does a sign of his failure to match the ideal honeymoon, in which business cannot be thought of, to the journey he is actually undertaking. By the time the train has reached Dover, Lopez has made and unmade several resolutions; the work of the honeymoon is both anticlimactically short and necessarily repetitive. It is simultaneously over before it has begun and a long slow process that fades imperceptibly into marriage.

Trollope is also able to show that the ideal honeymoon has, as it were, a life, even a daily life of its own. Even at the honeymoon's midpoint in Florence, as they await the fateful reply from Wharton, the business of the honeymoon proceeds:

> They went on from day to day inspecting buildings, looking at pictures, making for themselves a taste in marble and bronze, visiting the lovely villages which cluster on the hills round the city, – doing precisely in this respect as do all young married couples who devote a part of their honeymoon to Florence; – but in all their little journeyings and in all their work of pleasure the inky devil sat not only behind him but behind her also. (*PM*, vol. 1, p. 240)

It would be easy to read this passage as mere negative – indeed gothic – juxtaposition as husband and wife, each with his or her separate inky devil, go through the form of the honeymoon without affection, interest, or desire. But such is the power of form – whether of social ritual or of historic buildings – and such the efficiency of the "work of pleasure" that, despite everything, Emily and Lopez do in some sense enjoy themselves, creating for themselves in the conjugal singular "*a* taste in marble and bronze" (italics mine). Despite his sinister plans for Emily's reeducation into conjugality, Lopez is "an eager lover," "tender" and thoughtful in the daily tasks and pleasures of the honeymoon (*PM*, vol. 1, p. 240). The fact that Trollope gives us a gothic honeymoon that *works*, despite the presence of the inky devil, makes the critique of conjugality all the more devastating, the gothic honeymoon not the exception but perilously close to the ideal.

We can think, then, of *The Prime Minister* as activating elements of the gothic honeymoon for realism, as moving the honeymoon out of the ancestral home and onto the Continent in part to attenuate both the geography and the psychology of the honeymoon. There is no doubt, however, that the marriage that begins with a refusal of the gothic ends with a terrible moment of disintegration that translates into bodily terms the dissolution of personality of the wedding nights in *Daniel Deronda* and *Tess*.

As a coda to this chapter, I will turn now to a brief consideration of a Hardy short story written six years before *Tess*, which also takes up the question of a mutual marital confession and a gothic wedding night. On the surface, nothing could be more gothic than "A Mere Interlude," whose improbable plot involves, in a strangely prescient figuration of the burial of Hardy's heart between his two wives, a young woman who spends her wedding night in the best bedroom of an inn with her groom on one side and the corpse of her unacknowledged late husband on the other side of the wall. In the Hardy story, the heroine, Baptista, is on her way to her island home to marry – reluctantly – a much older man. On the mainland, while waiting for the boat that will take her home and to her wedding, she meets an old, that is to say, a young, flame. When the boat is delayed for a few days, they decide to marry and to arrive at home as a couple, confessing their position minutes before the wedding. Fate intervenes, as it tends to do in Hardy: in this instance, Charley, the young husband, drowns on a short swim he takes before the boat leaves. Baptista decides to say nothing of her brief marriage and to proceed with her original wedding. She is shocked, after the ceremony takes place, to find that Heddegan, her second husband, has planned a honeymoon in the very town in which her first husband has so recently drowned. They end up passing their wedding night in the room next door to where the corpse of her first husband is laid out, or, as Hardy puts it, "in hideous contiguity to the dead husband and the living."[16]

Secrets never, of course, stay secrets in the genre of honeymoon gothic. After being blackmailed by a witness after her return from the fatal honeymoon, Baptista decides to confess. To her surprise, Heddegan is gleeful: he, too, has a secret – he is a widower with four grown and ignorant daughters and has married Baptista, who is a teacher, so that she can educate them. For Heddegan, Baptista's secret gives him the freedom to confess his own: "[T]he balance of our secrets, mine against yours, will comfort your heart with a sense of justice," he says, knowing that in this choreography of confession and withholding his secret will have more permanent effect on his wife than hers will have on him. "How very well matched we be" (*MI*, p. 131), he gloats as he confesses. This particular

---

[16] Thomas Hardy, "A Mere Interlude," in *"The Distracted Preacher" and Other Tales*, ed. Susan Hill (New York: Penguin Books, 1979), p. 122 (hereafter cited in text and notes as *MI*).

story ends happily for a Hardy tale of marriage and betrayal. Baptista learns to love the hulking daughters, and through their shared secrets husband and wife grow to be friends: the daughters generate "a sterling friendship, at least, between a pair in whose existence there threatened to be neither friendship nor love" (*MI*, p. 133). The ending of the tale offers a twist on the issue of knowledge and secrecy; by implication, the "balance" of the secrets provides a "balance" in the relationship, which becomes, in the carefully nonhyperbolic language that challenges the excesses of conjugality, "friendship, at least" (*MI*, p. 131). Thus tragedy (and this is a term Heddegan insists on to describe both secrets) becomes comedy in all senses.

The mutual confessions of "A Mere Interlude" offer an economy of exchange powerfully different from those in *Tess*. The acts confessed by the two members of the couple, although widely different as to detail, become, as Tess might have put it, "the same": in this story analogy and conjugality triumph together as Baptista's history, unlike Tess's, becomes "a mere interlude" in an ongoing marriage. The honeymoon in "A Mere Interlude" functions, then, neither as metonymy nor synecdoche: the gothic honeymoon and the memory of it coexist with what is in many ways a successful marriage.

CHAPTER 5

Capturing Martha

THE TWO MARTHAS

This final attempt at reconstructing a Victorian honeymoon returns to Martha Rolls Macready, to her honeymoon diary, and to the moment I discuss in Chapter 3 where reading archival sources gives way to speculation. Although in that chapter I frame the problem of interpreting Martha's diary in terms of a climactic moment of epistemological refusal – Martha does not tells us the cause of her new husband Edward's "low spirits" that have so shaped her experience of the honeymoon – Martha's diary also presents more quotidian mysteries: references to books, to medical procedures, to people who write to or visit her. These mysteries of the everyday are, of course, usually "resolved" by scholars through research and, for the reader, by annotation. This chapter consists of two parts: extended annotated excerpts from Martha's diary, in which I provide as literally and as conscientiously as I can "solutions" to the small referential mysteries, and a speculative ending free (at last) from annotation or other scholarly apparatus. The first part lingers in and only rarely strays from the imperatives of historical research. If there is something wrong about or missing from my account of the context for Martha's diary, it is because I have made a mistake, because I have not used the archive sufficiently well, or because the reference books, histories, biographies, images, newspapers, or other primary sources on which I depend do not have the information I need. When I speculate I do so cautiously, explicitly, and sometimes apologetically. In the second section, when I turn openly to speculation and to fiction, the limits are different. I have certainly tried in my speculations not directly to contradict anything I know to be true; I have tried to avoid the anachronistic and the truly improbable. I have enjoyed and been relieved by the freedom to invent thoughts, words, and ideas for the two central people – now characters – in this tantalizing honeymoon story. The freedom of speculation is, of course, by no means complete: as Martha and Edward become characters, they become subject to other generic restraints associated with fiction, from the identification of perspective, to the limits of dialogue, to the limited vocabulary of a narrator focalized through characters from the early nineteenth century.

The Martha of my speculations responds to my two experiences with her diary that are separated by seven years and two trips to the archive. My encounter with Martha's papers – and thus my first sense of her – came on a trip in 1997 to the Rolls papers in the Gwent Record Office in the Cwmbran, Wales, Town Hall, a square gray building visually linked, through a series of traffic circles, to the area's geometric postwar landscape. The sterility of the building, and even the efficiency of the Record Office, made the actual encounter with Martha's diary surprisingly intimate. The small fat book with the embossed word "Album" on its brown leather cover signaled, of course, the kind of encounter with the personal I discuss in the first chapter, but the diary's most remarkable characteristic was its thoroughness: unlike other diarists whose words I had read for this project, this one seemed to be characterized by an uneasy persistence, as if the writer imagined herself held accountable, even and especially at this crisis in her life, to the diary form. I could not help interpreting her meticulous diary entries, as well as the many letters she reports having written, as somehow compensatory. Where was Edward when Martha wrote in her diary and when she wrote the letters that Edward often took to the post? Where was he when she read the many books with which she passed her honeymoon time? Where was he when she wrote over and over again how much she loved him? Although there is no direct evidence that she wrote only when Edward was out, Martha never recorded his physical presence at the moment of writing, and she only rarely mentions shared reading. The diary, for all its many words, gave me a sense of something missing, a something that was not, for me, completely satisfied by her repeated declarations of love and need.

Although Martha's was clearly, even at that first reading, the most interesting of the diaries I had found, part of that interest lay in my negative judgment of Martha. If anything, Martha seemed too clearly to support my arguments about the conjugal: clingy, hypochondriacal, and almost desperate in her attachment to Edward and to her identification with him. My first readings of the diary produced in me a slight feeling of recoil. Grateful to Martha for helping to prove my case, but pathologizing her for the characteristics that made her so useful to it, I found Martha to be a source of both fascination and unease. After returning to Texas to write up my research, I found myself returning repeatedly to Martha: passages from the diary would surface as I wrote about other honeymooners. The Martha of my quotations became familiar to me; she became over time fixed in my mind as a woman clinging desperately to her husband and to a particular historical ideal of conjugal intimacy, a woman struggling to bring her feelings for her mother in line with her feelings for her new husband, to create a world centered around the capacious but not always manageable fact of her marriage. If familiarity breeds (slight) contempt, it can also over time begin to question its own premises. I could not quote Martha without thinking about her and without hearing in her words an intelligence and energy – and moral and intellectual determination – that made her more than an illustration of an argument, however nuanced that argument might be made to be. I had already read Martha's mother's diary – in an entirely different genre – and the conflict between the rambling journal of the daughter and the precise logistical notations of the mother made me want to read more. My return to the Rolls papers, although part of a fact-checking trip, became much more. I hoped it would inspire a new way of writing about Martha, a way to speculate about her and simultaneously to acknowledge and to move beyond the limits of the archive.

Before I even made the second trip to the Gwent Record Office in 2004, Martha began to come alive to me through the Internet, where I learned that the grounds of her childhood home, the Hendre, were the site of local protests against corporate ownership. It was unclear from the account whether the actual house was still standing. I had seen pictures of it as a background to the activities of Martha's most famous descendant, Charles Stewart Rolls, aviator, sportsman, and founder of the Rolls-Royce company – there is a wonderful photograph of a balloon launch on the lawn of the Hendre, whose many turrets serve as a solid but somehow fantastical background to the swelling white balloon – but these photos take us only to the end of the nineteenth century. I learned from the Internet that the extensive grounds of the house are now a golf course.

With Martha's childhood home very much in mind, I made reservations at a bed-and-breakfast named after the Hendre, assuming (rightly, as it turned out) that the farmhouse would once have formed part of the Rolls estate. I also made plans for a return to the archives in Cwmbran, about an hour away, to visit, also for the second time, the scene of Martha's honeymoon in Littlehampton, and to look at papers and photographs in the Littlehampton Museum. The order in which I made my arrangement meant that I began with Martha's home and with her birth

Fig. 5 Sketch of Littlehampton, site of the Macready honeymoon. Rolls Family Papers F/P 6.35. Courtesy of the Gwent Record Office, Cwmbran, Wales.

family – like Martha, I was to move away, through the journey from the Hendre to Littlehampton, from a family that dominated and defined a particular place to a far more isolated scene of conjugality.

The bed-and-breakfast was run by Pamela Baker, whose family had worked, I think for generations, on the Rolls estate. Her brother Colin Cowles, who appeared to visit often from a neighboring farm and to help with breakfasts, was especially knowledgeable about the Rolls family. The day after I mentioned my project, he appeared with a copy of the Rolls family tree that was slightly different from the one I had copied from the Rolls papers in the Record Office: from then on, throughout my stay, along with my eggs and English bacon, would come documents and scraps of information. Pamela told me about an exhibit in Monmouth on the Rolls family, and introduced me to the curators. She drove me to the house of the current John Rolls, who was living in what had been the woodsman's cottage on the former estate. (Mr. Rolls and his wife were, unfortunately, away.) Pamela also told me the history of the golf course, originally started by the last John Rolls, but after financial troubles sold to a Japanese corporation who were also turning the original house – now a clubhouse – into a hotel. As we drove I began to understand how closely the family was linked to place, this place; Pamela noted, with some regret, that the town had only recently been put on the map of the area, presumably as a guide to golfers. Until recently the old estate and the town had been one and the same, occupying a place mapped only by family history.

None of the people at the Hendre Farmhouse had heard specifically of Martha. Their stories began with the generation after Martha's, with the John Allan Rolls who became the first baron Llangattock. They had heard of Martha's brother, John Etherington Welch Rolls, who had been a magistrate and sheriff and who had presided at the trial of Chartists in Monmouthshire. Until the eruption into fame of Charles, that splendid second son who was to put the family on the national and international map, the received history of the Rolls family was a litany of Johns, whose fortunes were made as landlords in poverty-stricken suburbs of London and whose identities were forged in and through Wales, Monmouthshire, the Hendre. The origin of the Rolls story with the baronetcy also assured that a still older John – Martha's father – was not part of the picture. This John had almost gambled the family into oblivion, but his decision, when Martha was in her twenties, to recoup his fortunes on the Continent, allowed the rebuilding of the Hendre and the consolidation of the Rolls into place and history.

The stay at the Hendre Farmhouse, despite the absence of Martha from family narratives, made her come alive to me in a new way. The kind of research experience I was having was new to me; I had never worked with a specific family (although it is relatively easy and fun because most archives in England are organized around families), and I had certainly never used living informants. The Rolls family, even and perhaps especially with its D'Urberville-like story of decline, was in fact a living thing, and Martha, dead to direct memory, lived differently for me over my eggs and coffee.

And Martha's childhood home had also had a life of its own. Neither museum nor archive, it was part of a living present as a golf course – complete with signs for nongolfers to keep out. While I have often experienced nervousness at records offices, libraries, and other places where archives are housed, preserved, and protected, I had never felt less that my position of researcher qualified me to visit. But visit I did, with my family in a rented car. After taking pictures for about twenty minutes, I screwed up my courage to enter the golf shop, thinking perhaps that someone there might know something, however vague, about the history of the house. In the shop I spotted a woman behind the counter, busy with tee times and golf balls. In this setting, which seemed to have no connection with Martha, I waited my turn and hesitantly asked the most general of questions. The woman, who later told me her name was

Barbara Shelton, looked at me with polite impatience. It was a Saturday morning, she told me, the busiest time at the golf course. She would only be able to give me an hour's tour of the house.

And it was a fascinating tour. Ms. Shelton, as it turned out, knew everything there was to know about the history of the Hendre. She was able to guide me to and through a series of renovations – those restorations made by the current owners to turn the house into a hotel, those made by the two barons as they consolidated enormous fortunes derived from properties they held in the slums of London, and those made by Martha's father in the 1830s when he moved to Europe to recoup his fortunes. The parts of the house Martha would have known were almost all changed, although there was a beautiful stained-glass window dated 1837 which might have marked the end of the first renovations. Once again, the house precipitated me into the future of the family, putting Martha into the context of a series of inheritances, events, and inventions she could hardly have foreseen. It is, of course, a given when doing historical research that one not read back from the future; this means, in reality, paying almost no attention to events that happen after the time in which one is specifically interested. But what I was experiencing was a different kind of retrospective history that moved Martha toward the present as surely as I was imaginatively sent back, first, toward 1840, the time of her honeymoon, and, then, to a Martha in her twenties, exiled to Europe because of a family crisis. Martha's attachment to her family became suddenly more complicated: how, at this interesting age had she understood her time in France? Had she enjoyed it, recoiled from it, blamed her father for the gambling that sent the family abroad? Was her father's reason for the journey to France made known to her or was it part of what would become a tradition of secrets culminating in Martha's own diary with its strange mixture of confidence and reserve?

If Martha's story widened and deepened in the living history of the golf course and the bed-and-breakfast, my return trips to the Records Office, during my stay near the Hendre, suggested a family story infinitely more complex than I had at first imagined. A dependent clause in a history of Monmouth revealed to me that Edward, Martha's husband, was the brother of William Macready, the Victorian actor-manager, a celebrity. This brought me back to Martha's mother's diary and to her obvious passion (shared by her daughter?) for theater. When I looked at letters to Martha's father from his land agent, John Searles, who I thought might well be (or be related to) the "Mr. S" who played such havoc with Martha's feelings and made her feel so guilty, I found a propensity to

Fig. 6 Postcard, Beach Hotel. Courtesy of the Littlehampton Museum.

interlace information about various properties with theatrical gossip. I also found playbills – some with parodic cast lists – from a home theater at the Hendre, indicating that Martha's brothers and friends were avid amateur actors; books of word games suggested a more diffuse and playful theatricality. The fact that Martha was not mentioned in any of the contexts put her, to my mind, at a tangent to the family with whom I had imagined she identified completely. Other papers in the Rolls archive suggested a complicated relation to money: the marriage settlement of Martha's sister showed her to be quite comfortable (I could not find Martha's marriage settlement), but Edward's pocket book, accounting for every penny he and Martha spent on the honeymoon, suggests that Martha might well have had to be as "economical" as she boasts she is in the diary.

And the diary itself took on a new life. When I went back to the diary and copied out what had previously seemed too dull and repetitive to note, I realized that I was reading the words, not of a woman isolated from the rest of the world, but of someone who participated fully, if somewhat mysteriously and unevenly, in it: a woman who in the five months of her honeymoon read systematically through at least thirty novels and histories; a woman who had traveled in France and who probably read long books in medieval French; a woman who could recognize a misattributed Van Dyck painting; a woman who related effects of light and shade in the dull coastal town of Littlehampton to the most advanced painters of the day; a woman who thought of herself – through her husband – as part of a military community with something to say about military scandals; a woman who was part of a rich and ambitious family with strong connections to the theater. Edward, it soon became clear, was not the anonymous officer of my first reading but someone with access to culturally central figures – from his brother William Macready to Charles Dickens. This new Edward bumped up against the most canonical of my understandings of the Victorian period: William's memoirs regularly place his brother in the same room with the famous. We see him walking and dining with and calling on that familiar parade of famous Victorian dinner-goers, that set of people who make one wonder if everyone one has heard of in the Victorian period dined with everyone else. We see him sharing jokes with William about John Forster's foibles; we see him entering history. Edward himself is no more famous, no more successful, than the Edward I first imagined, but he is infinitely more connected to worlds beyond Littlehampton and beyond the conjugal: nowhere did this become clearer than when I saw, in Martha's handwriting, a copy of a letter the sixteen-year-old Edward wrote to his father from Waterloo two days after the famous battle.

Much about Martha and Edward, however, remains a mystery, and part of that mystery seems to have something to do with a withdrawal from the world signaled perhaps by but not limited to the honeymoon. William Macready's memoirs mention Martha, his future sister-in-law, only as a "Miss Rolls" with whom he dines before his brother marries her. There is no mention of the wedding or of Martha as Edward's wife, although the two brothers were, at least until the period just before the marriage, exceptionally close. Edward is mentioned only a few times after the wedding. Martha more than hints that there is something wrong between her and William's wife and sister, but we do not know what it is. Although we see from Martha's mother's diaries that Martha, like her mother, was an avid theatergoer before her marriage (she first met Edward at the Haymarket almost a year before the marriage), there is no mention in the diaries of the kind of theatrical gossip so enjoyed by the rest of the Rolls family. It seems, then, that, for Martha, crucial to the reorientations of the honeymoon whose structuring movement was from the birth family to Edward was, in some sense, a movement away from the theater and toward the military. This is complicated by the fact that theater was important – albeit in different ways – to both sides of the

family and by the fact that Martha certainly did not move to join
Edward's family after her marriage. And this leaves us perhaps in the same
place: in Littlehampton and with the couple. The pull of the theater, of
Ceylon where Edward was stationed, and of Waterloo makes more
remarkable the work of reorientation that Martha, at least, undertook on
the honeymoon. The Martha of my second journey, finally, had much in
common with the Martha of my first.

No account of the two Marthas would be complete without my
mention of a central and, to me, strangely disturbing revelation. Even in
the first version of my diary reading, I was constantly confronted with the
problem of Martha's name. I had encountered her, according to the
archival index, as a member of the Rolls family: she was "Martha Rolls"
to me – even though by the time of the diary her last name was, of course,
Macready. As I mention in Chapter 1, naming was a frequent problem
with my female honeymooners – a problem that thematized both the
problem of reorientation in their own lives and my investment in the
women as independent subjects. My problem was solved, if not entirely
to my satisfaction, by technology: for each woman I did a "search and
replace," substituting the birth name plus the husband's name for the
woman's "maiden" name. In a sense, then, my female honeymooners
married again in the pages of my manuscript as, one after the other, they
assumed a new nominal identity. But Martha was – as she was to be so
often – a more complicated case. I do not remember the moment when it
became clear to me that everyone who knew her well – from her mother
to Edward to William – called her Patty. By the time of the second trip, I
knew this was her mother's name for her, but I continued, despite the
clumsy distinction that this made necessary between herself and her
mother, to call her Martha. On the second trip to the archives, when I
found Edward's account book, I learned through his tiny notations about
the price of her boots or cakes that he too knew her as Patty, and realized,
with some sense of disorientation, that the woman who wore the boots
and ate the cakes probably thought of herself (when she was not "Mrs
Edward" or the "Major's wife") as Patty Macready.

"Martha Rolls," then, does not, in some sense, exist. The name
belongs to the mother, not to the daughter and the bride. To put it
another way, "Martha Rolls" is my own invention, something like the
working title of a book that enables one to talk about it and apply for
grants before it is written and hardened into a name. "Martha Rolls" is,
in effect, a *nom d'archive*, the official trace of a life lived under many
names. The name became for me a stand-in for the many different

women my various encounters with "Martha Rolls" brought together. And it is to mark this process of archival investment and reorientation that I let "Martha Rolls" stand. Besides, I cannot bring myself to call her Patty.

II. MARTHA'S DIARY

[The following entries are from Martha's journal, Beach Cottage, Littlehampton, 1840]

September

TUESDAY, 1 [SEPTEMBER]

I have been now married one month. How very singular it is the feeling which possesses me – it appears as if we had always been as we now are – all the past seems to have faded – to have gone for nothing and I cannot imagine it possible that I have ever loved anyone but my dear Edward – I don't think, in point of fact I ever did – I fancied I did – but I am convinced that he is the only man with whom I could have been happy – and happy I am to the very utmost. Thank God for it. Bathed this morning and walked – after dinner sat on the beach expecting Mama, who arrived about six. They are both looking very well & we were enchanted to meet. Poor Miss Sherrats was very much affected. Mama walked on the beach with us and we drank tea with her.[1]

WEDNESDAY, 2 [SEPTEMBER]

Bathed. After breakfast went to the Hotel and had a long chat. Walked into the town. They [Mrs. Rolls and Miss Sherrats] drank tea with us.

THURSDAY, 3 [SEPTEMBER]

Very late: did not bathe – Mama came in after breakfast and showed us a foolish letter from Jessy[2] – it is really provoking. Edward went to bathe – we walked on the beach – on his return walked to Rustington – what

---

[1] Mrs. Rolls appears to be staying at Beach Hotel, where Martha and Edward moved from more inexpensive and modest lodgings at Beach Cottage on 8 October. The Beach Hotel was built in 1775 by Peter le Cocq, a London tavern owner. Receipts found in the walls of the hotel indicate that le Cocq was a smuggler, or at least a receiver of smuggled goods. The hotel was one of the first purpose-built holiday hotels – as opposed to a tavern with rooms to let. Originally the Beach Coffee House, the hotel was extensively remodeled several times during the Victorian period and was a feature in accounts and images of Littlehampton. The hotel stood behind the esplanade, between a grove of cottages – including perhaps the one Martha and Edward rented – and the town of Littlehampton.

[2] Martha's youngest sister (1810–42).

The Hendre, seat of John E.W. Rolls Esqʳᵉ Monmouthshire.

Fig. 7 Printed copy of a sketch of the Hendre. Rolls Family papers F/P misc. 5. Courtesy of the Gwent Record Office, Cwmbran, Wales.

happy walks these are – how I love him! – He can't know how much – but it seems to be more and more every day. After dinner, went down the Arundel road, across some nice fields, home by Rustington again.[3] Called in at the Hotel and sat a little while with them. Stormy looking evening – very fine moonlight effect.

FRIDAY, 4 [SEPTEMBER]

Bathed: temperature [80? {illegible}] which made me jump – had some warm water put in. Did not get dressed till past 12. Laughed considerably at breakfast at the United Service Journal[4] – I don't think dear Edward is quite well Today – and he won't take any thing – which vexes me – he does not attend to him self [*sic*] enough.[5] Today – Thank heaven, I

---

[3] Martha was inconsistent in her spelling of "Rustington," a town about two miles from Littlehampton. Rustington seems to have had few attractions in the way of shops or tourist sights.

[4] *The United Service Journal* is the journal of the British Army and Navy, published under this title from 1828. Martha's reading of the journal indicates her identification with Edward's military career, perhaps more clearly revealed in her careful copying of a letter from the then seventeen-year-old Edward to his father a few days after the British victory at Waterloo (Rolls Family Papers, F/P 6.33)

[5] The reference to "troubles" is mysterious, although it is perhaps typical of Martha's sense of the conjugal that her "troubles" should not only be imagined primarily in terms of their effect on Edward but that the word "trouble" itself should slip, unmarked except for the terminal *s* from wife to husband, changing perhaps in meaning but keeping its essential emotional freight.

believe I am really getting over my troubles, which I rejoice at more on his account than my own – for I give him too much trouble and he is so kind, so very kind. God bless him. Went over to the Hotel after dinner & sat an hour. Read Bulwer and one of Crabbe's tales after tea.

SATURDAY, 5 [SEPTEMBER]

Tried the plunge – rather an annoyance than not.[6] Letter from Smith announcing the arrival of my seal. Walked on the beach with Mama. After dinner went down the Arundel road and through some fields home. Drank tea with Mama.

SUNDAY, 6 [SEPTEMBER]

Called to take Mama to church returned to the hotel & saw Miss Sheratts arriving from Arundel.[7] Walked to evening prayers at Russington [*sic*] – the old gentleman who performed the service, a regular father Paul – read the lessons particularly well – sermon by another gent – terribly composing [?] – singing awful – walked home by the beach where we found Mama & Miss S – sat with them on the pier till dinner time. They drank tea with us. This fortnight has passed with a rapidity that is quite astonishing – we cannot believe we have been here so long – and what a happy time it has been – My dear, dear husband! How devotedly I love him – my whole world is centered in him – I hope he knows how perfectly he is beloved.

MONDAY, 7 [SEPTEMBER]

Bathed – Went to the Hotel – and then into the town [Littlehampton] – a shower coming home. Walked after dinner on the beach till 7 then went to tea at the Hotel.

TUESDAY, 8 [SEPTEMBER]

Donagan retrimmed my bonnet with grey ribbon. Read Bulwer which is at length coming to a close.[8]

---

[6] Martha seems to be undergoing a process, perhaps a treatment, of slow immersion, whereby she would for a period of time have taken warm baths in seawater and then moved on, first, to cold baths and, finally, into the sea via horse-drawn bathing machine.

[7] Arundel, the main tourist attraction in the area, is about four miles from Littlehampton. Touristic sights would have been Arundel Castle, home of the Dukes of Norfolk, purchased in the eighteenth century, and Arundel Cathedral. Miss Sheratts's being at Arundel on a Sunday may suggest that she was attending Catholic services at the castle; the family at Arundel was Catholic during this period. Miss Sheratts may even have been French, perhaps a family friend from the period during Martha's childhood when her father was forced to live in France.

[8] Although it is unclear if Martha and Edward are reading Edward Bulwer-Lytton's collection of tales, *The Student* (1835), which she mentions the next day, or some other text by the same author, the two seem to be working their way through the Bulwer-Lytton canon. Later, on 8 October, Martha will object to Bulwer-Lytton's "wit" in *Devereux*. Reading aloud to each other is mentioned as a central activity for several honeymoons.

WEDNESDAY, 9 [SEPTEMBER]

Bad day – not very well – walked to the Hotel and staid [*sic*] there while Edward went into the town . . . read the Student [*sic*], and thought it poor – Drank tea at the Hotel.

THURSDAY, 10 [SEPTEMBER]

Edward walked to Arundel before breakfast. Took my first bath in the sea which was not so disagreeable as I expected. Walked through the fields home by the windmill – in the evening had a delightful walk on the beach by moonlight, tide coming in. Fetched Mama & Miss S. to tea. A letter from Louisa [Martha's sister] today enclosing Miss Creed's [?] critique.

FRIDAY, 11 [SEPTEMBER]

Gloomy morning – Went to the Hotel – crossed the ferry and walked on the Bognor road – very flat and uninteresting. Drank tea at the Hotel.[9]

SATURDAY, 12 [SEPTEMBER]

Very fine day – walked to Rustington – it is impossible to manage a walk without falling upon this village – They came to tea.

SUNDAY, 13 [SEPTEMBER]

Letter from Eliza.[10] Heard a sermon which for absurdity and foolery cannot be equalled.[11] Walked on the beach – tea at the Hotel.

TUESDAY, 15 [SEPTEMBER]

Very fine – bathed – sea very rough – came out ornamented with seaweed. Walked to Rustington drank tea at the Hotel.

WEDNESDAY, 16 [SEPTEMBER]

Letter from Louisa – a terrible day – sea in a passion. Went out to look at it. They came to tea.

THURSDAY, 17 [SEPTEMBER]

Sat with Mama while Edward took a long walk. Wrote to Louisa – walked after dinner – tea at the Hotel.

---

[9] The ferry crossing the river Arun was a "chain ferry," a platform drawn across the water by a chain and a crank.

[10] Martha's sister, Louisa Elizabeth (?-1853), married to John Francis Vaughan. Eliza became a devout Catholic; six of John and Eliza's sons became priests. Martha alludes to Eliza's religious differences with the family later in the diary. Names are confusing in the Rolls family. The family tree in the Rolls papers has Eliza listed as "Louisa Elizabeth," but Martha (Patty!) clearly called her sister Eliza. The "Louisa" of the diary, then, is quite another person – a friend or a cousin. To make things more confusing, the wife of Martha's eldest brother, John Etherington Welch, was also named Elizabeth. Martha's generation, then, contained two couples consisting of a John and an Elizabeth. I do not know what she called her sister-in-law, but the diary reveals that she sometimes calls her brother-in-law "Vaughan."

[11] This is the first of Martha's extremely negative comments on the preaching of the Reverend William Gilkes. Although listed in contemporary directories as living in Littlehampton, he apparently preached at Rustington, at least for the evening services. He was not listed as the vicar of Littlehampton's St. Mary's church; this would have been the Reverend J. Atkyns.

FRIDAY, 18 [SEPTEMBER]

Letter from Kitty – bathed – the sea beautifully smooth. Mrs Wackford [the Macready's landlady] confined. Walked on the beach – they came to tea.

SATURDAY, 19 [SEPTEMBER]

Wrote to Kitty.

SUNDAY, 20 [SEPTEMBER]

Letter from Melina [?] Unwell in Church – obliged to come home. They came to tea.

TUESDAY, 22 [SEPTEMBER]

A miserable stormy day – at home reading the water witch [*sic*].[12]

WEDNESDAY, 23 [SEPTEMBER]

Letter from John Vaughan [married to Martha's sister Eliza] to say they are coming to see us. Answered him.

THURSDAY, 24 [SEPTEMBER]

Bad weather – letter from Jessy [Martha's youngest sister (1810–1842)].

FRIDAY, 25 [SEPTEMBER]

Letter from Jane Williams – had a fire for the first time which caused such smoke that we were obliged to escape to the Hotel. Fine evening, walked through Rustington home by the shore – the sands are quite spoilt by the banks of seaweed washed up. Read the Phantom Ship a most stupid affair.[13] Tea at the Hotel.

SATURDAY, 26 [SEPTEMBER]

Very ill which prevented Mama from coming to tea. * [Martha's mark. This is the only mark of this kind in the diary, and may indicate the beginning of Martha's period. Martha's mother's diary includes several such marks, about three to four weeks apart.]

SUNDAY, 27 [SEPTEMBER]

Did not go to church being unwell. Went to evening prayers – Mr Gilkes more [illegible] than ever – a singularly stupid person.

MONDAY, 28 [SEPTEMBER]

Very bad weather. Edward will not do anything for his eye which fidgets me very much. Went on with the Disowned[14] which at present is no great thing. At home all day. [Change of ink] Dearest Edward was in very bad spirits all the evening – he says he was quite well – but evidently something was the matter – which made me very unhappy.

---

[12] James Fenimore Cooper, *The Water Witch* (1830).
[13] Captain Frederick Marryat, *The Phantom Ship* (1838–9).
[14] Edward Bulwer-Lytton, *The Disowned* (1828).

TUESDAY, 29 [SEPTEMBER]

Edward still low spirited and so unlike himself it made me quite uneasy – He says it was caused by a fancy – what he will not say. I feared I had inadvertently done or said something to annoy him – but no – he said not – I cannot bear to see him out of spirits – he is my whole world, and as he is, so must I be too. Went into the town – caught in a hail storm – quite wet through & obliged to go to bed.

WEDNESDAY, 30 [SEPTEMBER]

Edward seems quite himself today thank God [no punctuation]

October

THURSDAY, I [OCTOBER]

I do not feel well at all – at home all day – wrote to Vaughan. Drank tea at the Hotel.

FRIDAY, 2nd [OCTOBER]

Not well; very faint after breakfast. Better after dinner. Took a walk. They came to tea.

SATURDAY, 3RD [OCTOBER]

Letters from Louisa and [illegible] – the latter a most extraordinary one, concerning the procuring of a house for an interesting invalid lady – thirteen stone – and to ride hard! Drank tea at the Hotel.

SUNDAY, 4 [OCTOBER]

Put 8 leeches on Edward's temples for the inflammation in his eyes – my first attempt at doctoring. A terrible sermon from the Revd Gilkes – soporific [illegible]!

MONDAY, 5 [OCTOBER]

At home all day – dear Edward's eyes better – read and thank the Gods! Finished the Disowned – a most complete failure. Mama unwell & could not come to tea.

TUESDAY, 6 [OCTOBER]

Edward told the people last night we should leave on Thursday – Master Wackford becomes a nuisance [the infant son of the landlady confined in September]. Donagan washed my hair. Mama sat with me, and we talked of my unbounded happiness – Indeed – I am most blest in the love of one whom I love with the whole strength of my being – and he – dearest love – how truly does he love me – and how fond am I of his affection. God bless him! The newspapers are rather alarming this morning – and my heart sickened when I heard Edward say if there were

a war he would seek to be employed – God forbid there should [be] a
war – it would kill me to part from him.[15] Took a walk on the sands – a
lovely day – Drank tea with them at the Hotel – they go tomorrow I am
sorry to say.

WEDNESDAY, 7 [OCTOBER]

Were going to see them off when Robert met us with a note saying
they would rather not say adieu – Edward went over to them. Walked. A
lovely day too warm for a bath. Wrote to Mama. Read Devereux in the
evening – very dull affair – the wit worse than ever. It is very odd, but
certainly I liked the book when it first came out.[16]

THURSDAY, 8 [OCTOBER]

Eliza's birthday. I wonder we do not hear from her – [crossed out
"Letters from Mama"] Wrote to Mama. Packed up and came to the
Beach Hotel where we are to be lodged and boarded for three guineas a
week – wine exclusive. It is cheap for what it is – every thing being
excellent – but as we could do it for two guineas – one grudges what really
are superfluities – I am desperately economical and would save every
farthing possible. Walked to Post Office & Smarts' – Took a dose of
Devereux, sweetened by a sketch or two from Boz who is always the
thing.[17]

---

[15] Martha is referring here and in later entries to a threatened war with France over the rights of
French protégé Mehemet Ali to add all of Syria to his Egyptian possessions. In this complex set of
moves and countermoves, England had allied itself on 15 July with Russia, Austria, and Prussia
against the French over the Egyptian issue. The treaty signed that day issued Mehemet Ali an
ultimatum allowing him to remain a hereditary ruler of Egypt, but granting him only Southern
Syria, and that only for life. The French were incensed by this, and for the next two months there
was a serious possibility that France might declare war on England. For more on this issue see John
M. Knapp, *Behind the Democratic Curtain: Adolphe de Bourqueney and French Foreign Policy
1816–1869* (Akron, OH: University of Akron Press, 2001).

[16] *Devereux* (1829) is another novel by Edward Bulwer-Lytton. It is interesting to try to account for
Martha's change of heart about the novel. Given her identification with her husband, is she
influenced in this by Edward? Why did they choose to read so much Bulwer-Lyttton if, as it seems,
she at least was not enthusiastic?

[17] It is hard not to read Martha's substitution of "Wrote to Mama" for "Letters from Mama" as a
moment of boundary confusion. It is of course interesting that Martha and Edward should move
to the Beach Hotel only after Martha's mother had left. Perhaps this shows a desire on Martha's
part to maintain some distance – but perhaps the choice to delay the move was Edward's or
Martha senior's. Martha's resolve to be "desperately economical" brings up the question of the
couple's finances. Certainly, Martha came from a well-to-do family, even if at this point it was not
nearly as wealthy as it would become toward the end of the century, when it is estimated that
family properties in Bermondsey, Surrey – an impoverished suburb of London – brought in rents
from 600,000 working-class tenants. Since Martha's father's retrenchment in 1825, when he moved
his family to France for six years to recoup gambling debts, the Hendre, the family home in Wales,
had been remodeled into an impressive estate. Although I could not find Martha's marriage
settlement, the marriage settlement of her sister Louisa Elizabeth (Eliza), shows Eliza's father
settling £8000 on her in 1830. This would have produced an income of over £300 a year – no

FRIDAY, 9 [OCTOBER]

Letter from Mama. Wrote to her & Jane Williams. Magnificent weather – "*splendid*" as my darling pet, Johnny, says – [Probably Martha's nephew, John Allan Rolls, son of John Etherington Welch (1807–70) and Elizabeth Mary Long (1813-?). He would have been three at the time of this entry.]

SATURDAY, 10 [OCTOBER]

Wrote to Mama as usual and Ellen [Edward's sister] whom Edward has invited to come and see us. Letter from Mama giving a curious account of her visit in Clarence Terrace[18] – neither lady enquired after us – they might have asked after their brother, tho' I am to be excommunicated. Strange people – to understand them is beyond my ability – therefore they must e'en take their own way.

SUNDAY, 11 [OCTOBER]

A most distressing account by Today's post of dear Miss Sherrats' alarming illness – It has quite upset me, and I feel fit for nothing – She was much better when the post left but Dr Nevinson's [?] opinion is very melancholy – No post too Tomorrow! Wrote to Mama a short letter – but I am quite unhinged by the news and have a bad headache. Went to evening church and heard a very stupid charity sermon.

MONDAY, 12 [OCTOBER]

No post – what a bore that is! – weather delicious – parcel from Mrs Bushell – Miss Sherrats is better thank heaven.

---

extravagant amount, certainly, but a good supplementary income in 1840. The terms of John Rolls's will, as described in the marriage settlement, show him dividing £19,500 among his younger children (Rolls Family Papers, E/1 116 1–8).

Edward's expenditures for the year of his marriage are meticulously recorded in a pocket book, where we see that Edward, like her mother, calls Martha "Patty," and that he duly pays for a bathing machine (1s.) about very two days. Other items are $4\frac{1}{2}$ weeks of lodging at the inexpensive Mrs. Wackford's (£6 15s); wine (3s.); Patty's stockings (5s.), and many Eccles cakes (1s. apiece). Edward also allowed $7\frac{1}{2}$d. for beggars on 29 August, as well as larger contributions to charity (see 20 December). An approximate total cost for the five-month honeymoon was £189 (Rolls Family Papers, F/P 6.17).

"Boz" was the pen name of the young Charles Dickens. *Sketches by Boz*, written as a series of magazine pieces beginning in 1833, was published as a collection in 1834.

[18] Clarence Terrace was the home of Edward's brother, the illustrious actor and theater manager William Macready, his wife, Catherine, and his sister Letitia. It is unclear why the "ladies" of the Macready family would have disapproved of Martha. Letitia initially disapproved of William's marriage to Catherine, apparently on the grounds that Catherine was insufficiently educated. Letitia's objections delayed the marriage, while Catherine, as Macready puts it in his *Reminiscences*, "continued" her "studies" (p. 288). Although Letitia eventually accepted Catherine, she may have similarly tried to control the marriage of her younger brother. Certainly no one, not even Letitia, could have accused Martha of not reading enough.

Fig. 8 Sketch of the theater at the Hendre. Rolls Family papers F/P54. Courtesy of the Gwent Record Office, Cwmbran, Wales.

TUESDAY, 13 [OCTOBER]

A most unsatisfactory and extraordinary letter from Mr S. This matter has bothered me more than I can describe because I have been the cause by my thoughtlessness, of annoying the two persons dearest to me – I have been quite ill about it. Wrote to Mama.[19]

WEDNESDAY, 14 [OCTOBER]

Miss Sherrats is going on favorably [*sic*] – I cannot get over my vexation – and dear Edward is so good and kind [illegible] a terrible headache all day.

THURSDAY, 15 [OCTOBER]

Satisfactory letters from Mama – as for Mr S. I think he is gone mad. Letter from Ellen – declining to come at present. Wrote to Mama & Eliza. Read Castle Rackrent – clever but not interesting – I cannot care either for Sir Kit or for Sir Condy.[20]

FRIDAY, 16 [OCTOBER]

This is a memorable day – on the evening of this day last year I first met Edward – I can't say I *saw* him – for he was in the back of the dark little box at the Haymarket – who would have thought then of all that has happened since? Went out before breakfast to the bath – no hot water ready, so put off till 12 o'clock. Letters from Mama – very satisfactory – that Mr Searles is perfectly unaccountable – wrote to her [illegible] Jack Brag a great bore – I wonder when we shall succeed in getting a bearable book?[21]

SATURDAY, 17 [OCTOBER]

Only Edward had a letter from Mama – I am so vexed she has been so annoyed and all through my fault . . . The war question keeps me in a

---

[19] The two people are presumably Edward and her mother. See Chapter 1 for a discussion of this triangulated relationship. See 16 October for discussion of the identity of Mr. S.

[20] Maria Edgeworth, *Castle Rackrent* (1800); this was her first novel.

[21] Is Mr. Searles the "Mr S." of the previous entries? Robert Searles was, since the early 1800s, the land agent for the Rolls family. He lived not near the Hendre but in Surrey, near the Rollses' other properties. Could this Mr. Searles – or his son – have claimed some sort of romantic relationship with Martha? It is difficult to tell if the Robert Searles listed as land agent until about 1828 and the R. T. Searles listed after are the same person or near relations. The class position of land agent would certainly have been below Martha's, but the Rollses seemed to treat the Searles family with some intimacy. Letters from R. T. Searles to John Rolls in France include discussions of and gossip about the theater. Martha senior's diary for 1840 records several occasions on which "the Searles" came to dine with her – always on Sunday nights – in London. (Sunday night dinners tended during the period in question, to be less formal. This might indicate either that the Searleses were being treated as family or that they were considered to be less important than other, more socially prominent, guests.) Edward's brother William notes on 20 September 1845, five years after Martha's marriage, that he dined with "[John?] Rolls and Searles." There is also a letter from Martha's brother Aleck, on holiday in Brighton when he was a young child, to Mr. Searles. In other words, there does seem to have been considerable intimacy between the two families.

Jack Brag (1837), by popular novelist Theodore Hook, features a vulgar braggart for a hero. It is not surprising that Martha, given her feelings about "wit," would not have liked the book.

ferment – and makes me feel quite sick. Had a very nice walk within a mile of Angmering – went on with Jack – faute de mieux –[22]

SUNDAY, 18 [OCTOBER]

This day was such a disagreeable one that I won't write about it.

MONDAY, 19 [OCTOBER]

Wrote to Mama & Jacko – it grows so dark now that we have altered our dinner hour to six and walk before dinner – Had a very nice walk to Angmering a very nice village and regretted having lunched at home – the little Inn looked so very tempting. Finished Jack Brag.

TUESDAY, 20 [OCTOBER]

Letters from Mama & Eliza, walked on the Arundel road as far as the Six Bells and round by some fields home – some disagreeable looking cows in the fields – Began Paul Clifford.[23]

WEDNESDAY, 21 [OCTOBER]

Read Paul Clifford which is very superior to his predecessors, but the jokes and *wit* detestable.

THURSDAY, 22 [OCTOBER]

At home all day with Paul Clifford. [illegible]

FRIDAY, 23 [OCTOBER]

. . . At home all day again – and finished Paul Clifford which is very superior to Disowned or Devereux – but the wit is awful and the character of Brandon . . . absurdly unnatural and impossible.

SATURDAY, 24 [OCTOBER]

Wrote to Louisa. At home again all day – read parts of Mrs Jameson's Loves of the Poets – her chapter on the French poets & their [illegible] might as well have been left unwritten – it is so indelicate and not at all necessary to the subject indeed has nothing to do with it.[24]

SUNDAY, 25 [OCTOBER]

Louis Philippe is a dear creature.[25] Went to church and had a sermon on the *Personality* [emphasis in original] of the Holy Ghost!! Oh Gilkes, Gilkes!!

---

[22] Martha clearly felt left out of her mother's correspondence with Edward. Martha senior's diary for the same day notes, "Wrote to the Major on business" (Rolls Family Papers, F/P 3.5).

[23] Again, a Bulwer-Lytton novel. *Paul Clifford* (1830) was one of the first Newgate novels, a subgenre associated with the depiction of criminal life. It famously begins, "It was a dark and stormy night." Martha's aversion to wit suggests her fundamental earnestness.

[24] Anna Jameson's second book, *Loves of the Poets* (1829), consists of a series of biographical sketches of poets and the women who inspired them.

[25] Although the immediate catalyst for this statement is unclear, articles appeared in the *Times* of this week noting that British foreign minister, Viscount Palmerston, seemed to believe that Louis Philippe would not risk war. Four days later, on 29 October, the appointment of a new minister less hostile to the English would have been further good news for Martha. See

MONDAY, 26 [OCTOBER]

Read two tales of Crabbe, "The family of Love" – and "equal marriage" [*sic*] – both good – but a good deal of the *Crab* in them – as there is in all he wrote – he certainly had no very great idea of human nature.[26] I have prevailed upon dear Edward who has complained of headache lately, to try Mr Bushnell's dinner [?] pills – I think they will do him good.

WEDNESDAY, 28 [OCTOBER]

Letters from Mama and Miss [illegible]. Edward had a face ache again last night – I think it is occasioned by a tooth which requires stopping – I shall try to prevail upon him to go to Paterson Clarke – The dear creature is gone to take a walk, and I am here thinking of him – how deeply, how entirely I love him! Read part of the Surgeon's daughter [*sic*][27] while he was gone – it is very interesting. Edward came back about half past three and we walked along the sands a short way . . . it is very muddy which makes walking rather hard work and takes the starch out of one – Read Crabbe in the evening with great pleasure.

THURSDAY, 29 [OCTOBER]

Very gloomy day. Last night I had the family dream for the first time in my life. [This seems to mean not a dream about family but an inherited dream, perhaps prophetic in nature.] Took a walk on the shore in the afternoon – sky and clouds very fine – quite a Bonington effect.[28]

November

MONDAY, 2ND [NOVEMBER]

Very fine day – walked along the shore and home by the spire church – read Reynolds life and then walked again till dinner time. Found the United Service Journal arrived – a dull number – but some good remarks on Lord Cardigan and rather interesting articles by [illegible] and Cameron.[29]

T. E. B. Howarth, *Citizen-King: The Life of Louis-Philippe, King of the French* (London: Eyre & Spottiswoode, 1961).

[26] George Crabbe, *Posthumous Tales* (1834).   [27] Sir Walter Scott, *The Surgeon's Daughter* (1827).

[28] Richard Bonington (1802–28) was a painter known for his landscapes and light effects. Often thought to provide a link between English and French romantic painting of the period, Bonington was a close friend of Delacroix in the last years of his short life. Martha might have seen his paintings in person in London in 1826 and 1828, or perhaps earlier in France.

[29] Martha's comment on Lord Cardigan is part of a series of reactions by her to the infamous "black bottle" affair which led to the court-martial of Captain J. W. Reynolds of the 11th Hussars. Captain Reynolds had ordered a bottle of Moselle for the end of a dinner in mess hall; Lord Cardigan, the colonel of the regiment had objected to the black bottle, claiming that it reminded him of something from a tavern. Captain Reynold's reply was determined by Lord Cardigan to be insubordinate. Both Martha and her brother-in-law, William Charles Macready, noted their

TUESDAY, 3 [NOVEMBER]

A very mild day – last night quite suffocating – walked on the shore – sky very fine – lurid red, and stormy grey with a mixed tint of both over the sea. Read the new number of Humphrey[30] – dull and heavy – too much inclination towards fine writing – stars, flowers, angels &c &c After dinner read Reynolds.

WEDNESDAY, 4 [NOVEMBER]

A very good letter from poor Captain Reynolds requesting the idea of subscription and petition may be given up – hope he will be restored, and then Lord Cardigan may "grind his teeth and look supercilious" in vain. Read Sir Joshua ... Finished Sir Joshua's life – he was far too much the courtier – and began Monstrelet.[31] Since I have become acquainted with him and Froissart, and considered the case a little, I begin to see that the preux chevaliers were very great [illegible], and that though the middle ages may be the age of gold for poetry and painting, we should find them rather an annoyance than not, if we could return to them. They are a famous possession for the novelist and the painter et voilà tout.

THURSDAY, 5 [NOVEMBER]

... An evening visit from Guy Fawkes.

FRIDAY, 6 [NOVEMBER]

Most stormy – the angriest sea we have yet had. Wrote Mama to say we will leave this place on the 17th of next month. No chance of getting out and except that it is better for our health to do so, c'est egal we are perfectly happy at home and wish for no other company than ourselves. Monstrelet's [illegible] get tiresome ... A terrible hail storm with thunder & lightning about eight o'clock. It really makes one nervous.

disgust for the army's high-handedness in dismissing Reynolds, although Macready found Reynold's letter to the queen "abject" (William Toynbee, ed., *Diaries of William Macready, 1833–1851* [New York: G. P. Putnam's Sons, 1912,] vol. II, p. 92, 3 November 1840). It is interesting to see William and Martha reacting to the same articles when William's diaries do not mention Edward and Martha's marriage or honeymoon. Articles and letters about the scandal appeared regularly in the *United Service Journal* from October through December of 1840.

    Somewhat confusingly, as Martha is reading in the *United Service Journal* about Captain Reynolds, she is also reading what is presumably James Northcote's *Life of Sir Joshua Reynolds* (1819).

30   *Master Humphrey's Clock* was a serial begun by Charles Dickens in April 1840 to contain monthly parts of his novels. The first novel he published in *Master Humphrey* was *The Old Curiosity Shop*; Martha is probably reading the November part issue of the novel when it is becoming clear, to the distress of many readers, that the heroine, Little Nell, is going to die. *OCS* ran until February 1841.

31   Martha would have been reading Enguerrand de Monstrelet's (d. 1453) *Chronicles*, a history of France from 1400–7. Jean Froissart's (1338?-1410?) *Chronicles* end in 1400. Martha might well have been reading them in the original French. Although Froissart's *Chronicles* were translated by Sir John Bourchier (Lord Berners) from 1523 to 1525, they would have had available to them only one modern English translation, by Thomas Johnes (1803–10).

SUNDAY, 8 [NOVEMBER]

Louis Philippe speech very satisfactory – dear old man. I am quite fond of him.[32]

MONDAY, 9 [NOVEMBER]

A fierce sea dashing over the pier in grand style. Contrived to get a walk in the afternoon – found Neptune had been committing terrible havoc along the beach, washing all over the walk. The lightening at sea very vivid – sky particularly fine – I have never seen so great a variety in the sky since we have been here – it is quite an amusement in itself. Dear Edward has not been well today – which makes me very uncomfortable – I cannot bear to see him unwell. Read Monstrelet & Sir Joshua.

TUESDAY, 10 [NOVEMBER]

Dear Edward had a bad night and seems very unwell. I wish I could be unwell instead of him! Heard that my lay figure has been sold to [illegible] for 28 guineas – which being the original price and independent of duty is very well. Aleck & Kate [Martha's brother and sister-in-law] were to arrive there yesterday. A finer day. Walked into the town and ordered a pair of strong boots [duly noted in Edward's pocket account book.] Edward is better this evening thank God – the *noire doré* has certainly been successful.

WEDNESDAY, 11 [NOVEMBER]

A very wet morning. Dear Edward *much much* better – I am so glad – rain all day – worked very hard at Monstrelet.

FRIDAY, 13 [NOVEMBER]

A treacherous gale – the tide unusually high – and Neptune breaking over the beach, walked up even unto our door forming foaming rivers all over the green – the waves dashed gloriously over the bath house and a brig came into harbour in grand style – the river too ... has overflowed and got into the houses – the bath people have decamped furniture and all, fearing the bath would be carried off in the night – It has been an interesting morning. Read a whole book of Monstrelet – a much more interesting one than usual. Henry of Monmouth does not shine in these pages, indeed a plain tale like this destroys the prestige of chivalry and shows the "preux" as they really were – steel clad barbarians.

---

[32] Louis-Philippe made a speech opening the session of the Chambers on 6 November, in which he indicated in guarded and general, but legible, terms a desire for peace with England. Martha could have read the speech in the second edition of the London *Times* on 6 November or, with positive commentary, in the morning edition of 7 November.

SATURDAY, 14 [NOVEMBER]

Walked out to see the havoc of yesterday – alas! The poor walk! All gone – benches posts &tc. washed down and the solid embankment broken to pieces – two or three more such tides would destroy Little Hampton. Edward was not himself this afternoon – I know not why – but when he is thus it makes me feel so utterly depressed I can scarcely contain my tears. My spirits depend entirely on his, and rise and fall with them.

SUNDAY, 15 [NOVEMBER]

The cause of Edward's depression which I have now learnt has made me still more uncomfortable – indeed truly unhappy – I must do all in my power to remedy it and think I shall succeed – God grant it – Church evening – awful lesson from Gilkes.

MONDAY, 16 [NOVEMBER]

... Edward went down to Smart's[33] and got a paper containing an account of the hurricane and damage along the coast.

TUESDAY, 17 [NOVEMBER]

Sad news in Mama's letter this morning – Poor dear Miss Sheratts has had a violent attack of spasms on Sunday – so much so that Bushell [obviously the Rolls family physician – see Martha's comment on his pills on 26 October] feared at one time they were fatal – she was a little better when Mama wrote – This account has made me very unhappy and I now live in constant fear of anything happening before we get to town – she is a friend who never can be replaced – God preserve her yet awhile is my earnest prayer ...[34] Mama's letters also contained another subject of uneasiness – the mischief which religious interference is likely to do in Aleck's marriage.[35] I think Eliza exceedingly wrong and would not hesitate to tell her so if she said anything to me on the subject. The rest of today's occurrences were of so painful a nature, that I make no further record of them.

WEDNESDAY, 18 [NOVEMBER]

Miss S. better. But I cannot cease being in a state of uneasiness till we get to town. Rain – at home all day & very unwell – quite bouleversée.

---

[33] The *Littlehampton Directory* for 1839 lists Nevil Smart as a "chemist, stationer, news agent and sub-distributor of stamps."

[34] According to Martha's date book from 1865, in which she records important anniversaries, Miss Sheratts died in 1843 (Rolls Family Papers, F/P 6.6).

[35] Martha's younger brother, Alexander (1818–82), married Kate Steward in 1839. I do not know how the Catholic convert Eliza "interfered" in her brother-in-law's new marriage.

THURSDAY, 19 [NOVEMBER]

Letter from Louisa – Miss S. continues better. Edward took a walk and smoked another cigar. Wrote to Louisa. The parcel Mama said would come this evening is not arrived – which has made me very sick and nervous. I wish I could get over this turning of the stomach when anything annoys me.

FRIDAY, 20 [NOVEMBER]

Very indifferent account of Miss Sheratts. This keeps me in a constant state of worry. Bought ribbon to retrim my bonnet – the parcel arrived this evening – I like the work much – read Major MacNamara's pamphlet on the Army which was very interesting.

SATURDAY, 21 [NOVEMBER]

A terrible day – My bonnet came home – at home all day working on Monstrelet – wrote to Eliza.

SUNDAY, 22 [NOVEMBER]

Today Edward has been a Major a year. The provoking Queen has a daughter it seems so there is an end of the brevet.[36]

MONDAY, 23 [NOVEMBER]

Poor dear Edward has had the toothache all night – I wish I could have it instead of him. Staid at home all day reading & working – a parcel per coach with the bag, a capital account thank God of dear Miss Sheratts.

TUESDAY, 24 [NOVEMBER]

Letter from Vaughan to say they will be here on the first – still a good bulletin of Miss Sheratts. A most lovely springlike day – Walked inland – was too warmly dressed. Edward rehearsed the part of Clown by stuffing his pockets with my boa and shawl. Read Monstrelet – and Edward tried Peregrine Pickle, but found it too coarse.[37] Sent the bag to Ellen.

WEDNESDAY, 25 [NOVEMBER]

Find by the papers that Wright's bank has stopped – I fear this will affect the Vaughans.

THURSDAY, 26 [NOVEMBER]

Both of us felt very unwell Today – sick and back achy, for which we cannot account . . .

---

[36] On 22 November, Queen Victoria gave birth to her first child and namesake daughter, Victoria Adelaide Mary Louise, the Princess Royal. A brevet is an honorary commission, usually with no raise in pay. The expectation was that if the queen had given birth to a boy that she would have handed out such honors. The queen herself recorded her disappointment – and that of her husband, Albert – that the baby was a girl.

[37] Tobias Smollett, *The Adventures of Peregrine Pickle* (1751).

FRIDAY, 27 [NOVEMBER]

Took a long walk to Poleing [*sic*] church through some fields whose stickiness was very fatiguing.[38]

SATURDAY, 28 [NOVEMBER]

Melancholy news ... of the death of my poor little goddaughter Joan and of the dangerous state of little Henry. This will be a sad blow to poor William. I grieve for him most truly. I scarcely know if it is wise to wish for children – the loss of them is so fearful a trial. Dear Edward was very much distressed and wrote the most beautiful letter I ever read to William ... Began Anne of Geierstein.[39]

MONDAY, 30 [NOVEMBER]

The last day of our fourth month. It seems to me as if it must always have been as it is now – I can't imagine having existed without my beloved Edward. I am afraid the weather is changing. We did not go out – but very cozy all day working & reading Anne of Geierstein which is very tedious.

December

TUESDAY, 1ST [DECEMBER]

Rain this morning – a better account of poor little Henry. Took a walk on the pier during which the Vaughans arrived. Eliza looks very well and John immensely fat – Gladys [?] is a little beauty & very sociable. Herbert very handsome.[40]

WEDNESDAY, 2ND [DECEMBER]

Letter from Jacko inviting us to go there for their wedding day – I answered in the affirmative. Vaughans drove us to Arundel.

---

[38] The Saxon church of St. Nicholas, in the nearby town of Poling.

[39] William's own diary mentions several letters he received about Joan's death – most notably Foster's – but there is no mention of Edward's letter. This continues the odd absence of references in William's diaries to his beloved brother during the latter's honeymoon. It is also worthy of note that Martha does not mention William's wife (and Joan's and Henry's mother), Catherine, in her sympathetic reference to William's grief. If we are to imagine that Martha was literally Joan's godmother, there must at one time have been warmth between the couples. (It is more probable, however, given the recent date of Edward and Martha's marriage, that Edward was the child's godfather and that Martha claimed a kind of conjugal right in her.) Although Henry was to get sicker and sicker to the point where William despaired of his life, he did in fact recover from the consumption that claimed his little sister and, eventually, other siblings and his mother. It was understood that Catherine was the source of this tendency toward consumption; biographers make much of her "Fatal Dowry" to William, punning on the title of the first play they were in together.
   The book mentioned by Martha is by Sir Walter Scott, *Anne of Geierstein, or The Maiden of the Mist* (1829).

[40] Herbert Vaughn (1832–1903) became, like five of his brothers, a Catholic priest. He succeeded Cardinal Manning as archbishop of Westminster in 1892.

THURSDAY, 3 [DECEMBER]

Got up at seven to breakfast with the Vaughans who left for East End at eight. Took a walk – matched some merino for Mama and went on the sands – Read Humphrey's Clock not a good number, and finished Anne of Geierstein – which we do not like – there is not a single interesting character in the whole book. Wrote to Louisa about the earrings.

FRIDAY, 4 [DECEMBER]

Terribly cold, walked on the sands – fog – read the U.S. Journal which is a particularly stupid one and began Cooper's Spy – which amused us much.[41]

MONDAY, 7 [DECEMBER]

At home all day – Mr Lee [unidentified] arrived by the evening coach which also brought a parcel from Mama – we had a very lively evening talking and laughing sans cesse. And for the first time since our marriage did not get to bed till twelve o'clock.

TUESDAY, 8 [DECEMBER]

A wretched day – lots of talking – gave Mr Lee a set of etchings with which he seemed very much pleased . . .

WEDNESDAY, 9 [DECEMBER]

Drove over to Arundel to see Mr Lee on to Portsmouth by the coach – went over to the castle which was in rather more decent order than our first visit, the pictures having been hung up, which were tumbling about the floor. Among them is a capital Charles 1st by Vandyck – quite one of his good ones – the hands very elegant . . . also a Cromwell, very good, said to be also by him, but is not in the Vandyck manner according to my humble opinion.[42] [Mr Lee] is certainly a very amusing person and I like him because he appears to like Edward so much. He has two or three little peculiarities that might make a large dose of him tiresome, but we found him very agreeable and could have been content with another day's visit.

TUESDAY, 13 [DECEMBER]

[ellipses across page]

I have omitted any memorandum since Wednesday and can only say that happiness seems to increase with every hour – how can I ever be

---

[41] James Fenimore Cooper, *The Spy: A Tale of the Neutral Ground* (1821).

[42] Apparently Martha's instincts were correct. Cromwell portraits once thought to be by Van Dyck are now thought to be misattributions. The Arundel Castle Collection includes a number of Van Dycks, includ ng the Charles I portrait and portraits of the Arundel family. (Thanks to the curatorial staff at Arundel castle for this information.)

sufficiently grateful to God for having given me such an inestimable blessing in my dear Edward. The cold today is excruciating!

MONDAY, DECEMBER 14

Alarmingly Cold – wished ourselves at Naples all the time we were dressing.

TUESDAY, DECEMBER 15

My 36ᵗʰ birthday – and what a happy one. Edward wrote Mama such a dear dear letter!

WEDNESDAY, DECEMBER 16

Our last day at Little Hampton – dear Little Hampton! Where we have spent four as blessed months as mortals can deserve, and sufficiently proved that we are all in all to eachother [*sic*] and independent of the world.

THURSDAY, DECEMBER 17

[to London]

FRIDAY, DECEMBER 19

Called in Clarence Terrace.

[Does not note Xmas]

THURSDAY, DECEMBER 31

And so ends the year 1840 – the most eventful of my life and the most blessed. Although in its commencement I suffered perhaps more than anyone can imagine – and from the conduct of women – it is a certain and most unpleasant fact that women are capable of the most cruel behaviour towards eachother and seem often to delight in marring each other's happiness – but *finis coronat opus* – I am happy in spite of all the attempts to blast my hopes – am blessed, and I hope I am the cause of happiness to the best of husbands.

III. LITTLEHAMPTON

Martha Waits

A curve in the Sussex coast protects the beach, protects Martha. Littlehampton, the advertisements say, is warmer than the towns that jut out on England's channel coast to the north and to the south of it. Martha and Edward chose this location for its shelter and safety: one can stay in Littlehampton through November, although some guides do warn of southwesterly gales. Martha's sister Jessy honeymooned on the Continent, but this was before the troubles over there. Martha's friends do not think that Littlehampton is a glamorous place to honeymoon, but Martha has chosen – will always resolutely and, indeed, bravely choose – safety over glamour. Littlehampton is famous – if one can use that word for so quiet a spot – as a family destination. Martha knows one story about the place that might suggest danger; it was where the river Arun meets the sea that Lord Byron was almost drowned. To Martha, this simply validates Littlehampton's familial claims; it is as if the very waters of the place worked to expel the man who for Martha and many in her generation represents above all others a threat to domestic peace. The waters also have the power to heal. Martha knows vaguely that another, more acceptable, Romantic poet, Samuel Taylor Coleridge, came to Littlehampton for a cure. She does not know that his disease was suicidal depression and an anxiety so great he could not write a word until, deep into his holiday, he walked along the coast and said aloud to himself the first few lines of his sonnet of reintegration, "Fancy in Nubibus, or The Poet in the Clouds." Of course Martha cannot know that twenty-two years after the end of her honeymoon, fourteen years after Edward's early death, George Eliot would come to Littlehampton and to the hotel in which Martha is staying in search of words for *Romola*, and that she, like Martha, would rejoice in the emptiness of Littlehampton's "delightful" sands.

On clear days Martha looks over across the channel, as Matthew Arnold, that other seaside honeymooner, would do eleven years later. She feels before he will the tidal pull of France. For Martha there are two Frances – Edward's and her father's – and it is hard to think of them together. Today, and almost every day, she thinks first of that long six-year period in her early twenties, when her father, all but bankrupt from years of gambling, took his family to the Continent to retrench. Those, for Martha, were the years of almost paralyzing shame. She knows now, as she knew then, that France is beautiful; if she closes her eyes she can see its landscape of strong lights and shadows, a landscape that flits too quickly past her eyes, leaving only interior scenes: people coming to visit, people leaving, bantering with her father and mother as if nothing were wrong. And such people too! Her mother and father had always kept an open house; at the Hendre, this had seemed natural. There in France, the gaiety, the wit, and the parties seemed forced, her mother in particular unnaturally gay. It was in those years that Martha, who had been as lighthearted and as frivolous as her sisters, began, under the pressure of her shame, to read. It was reading – and sometimes the picture galleries – that saved her, that took her out of the glare of the French sun and the glances of men she could not marry. Eliza and Jessy were younger, of course; it was not so important that they be settled. Martha sometimes blames her father that she spent so many years unmarried.

In some ways, Martha admits, the journey to France was all for the best. Martha does not understand what made it possible for her father to return to Wales a richer man with a house so splendid that it frightened Martha just at first. She knows that while he was in France business went well for her father. "Business," Martha has come to know, means her father's properties in London. It has come to her slowly that the Hendre is not everything to her father – in the way of money, that is. She has only a vague sense of how her father makes his money, but she knows he would rather lose the Hendre than the houses along the Old Kent Road. This is what Mr. Searles told her. Now she feels disloyal for having listened. She prefers to think of the Hendre as the center of her family life. Mr. Searles's connection to London is part of what made him so vulgar. How could she not have seen it when he first started talking specially to her? Mr. Searles is the one who has made Martha feel ill when she thinks of anything to do with London life – he with his love of the theater and his pride in coming to dinner at their house in London.

After the return from France the family was different; Papa, Mama, John, and especially Aleck were just as devoted to wit, word games, charades, and theater, but it made all the difference that these things happened at home. Every few weeks the family would put on a play in the new theater; although people from the town came to watch, they were coming because John Rolls – and later his namesake son – had an unmistakable position. They could – in all senses – afford the theater. Martha herself did not act. Often she did not join in the evening entertainments. She was safe at the Hendre but still dreamed many nights uneasily of France and of the pretending, the talking, and the bright lights.

It was not until she met Edward that Martha could think of France in a new way. It was odd, thinks Martha for the hundredth time, that she who so hated play-acting, should have met her husband at the theater. And, odder of course, that the man she married was brother to the most famous actor-manager of the day. But Edward, of course, was serious in a way his family was not. Even Letitia and Catherine, with their studies, were really too gay for Martha. She had not known, until she met Edward, anything about the real world – not the fashionable world of London theater and parties, but the one where soldiers fought and sometimes died for the crown. Martha still trembles when she thinks how many times Edward might have died in the service of his country.

She keeps his letter to his father from the battle of Waterloo in her workbox and stops, sometimes in her work of reading and sewing, to think about the sixteen-year-old boy who walked unknowingly into Paris and to the most famous battle of what Martha knows as history.

She would have gone for her honeymoon to that France, Edward's France. She wishes she could have been at Waterloo, not as a soldier of course, but in some other role – as Edward's sister, perhaps, or as one of the many women who, she heard, drove in their carriages from Paris to watch the fighting. Of course, Martha would only have been eleven at the time of the battle, but it is one of Martha's principles that if she thinks of something that would have changed the past, she can do so completely, without regard to the limitations of time. Now, in the summer of 1840, it looks once again as if there will be war. Martha is more than old enough to join Edward, but she cannot. He may perhaps have to return to France and to the fighting that seemed for so long to be over. For Martha, as for many of the military men who write articles in the *United Service Journal*, which she and Edward read together, it is as if this war, which might happen at any minute, is part of the older war that Waterloo should have ended. Although she knows the figure of Louis Philippe from cartoons and drawings, she always seems to superimpose upon him the figure of Napoleon. Her greatest fear is that Providence has ordained that Edward will return to France only to be killed: that a severe God will only delay his death until He knows how much that death will cost her. Surely she has done nothing to deserve this. Except, perhaps, to think, even for a minute, that God is cruel. Martha takes comfort in something she holds deeply to be true: that God understands the love of married people for one another.

Martha has what she calls a little prayer, which she invokes whenever she thinks of the possibility that Edward might go to France. Under her breath she murmurs five times the word "Littlehampton." Although Martha knows the town name is spelled as two separate words – and it will be until some time in the early twentieth century – in the prayer she is prescient. By bringing 'Little" and "Hampton" together, she keeps Edward by her side. There is something else she can do. As she prays, Martha counts on her fingers the people who did not want her to marry: Mama (the thumb), Eliza (the index finger), Edward's sisters (together, the ungainly middle finger), Mr. Searle (the ring finger). None of these has the power to put an end to the honeymoon. When she gets to the fifth and smallest finger, to Louis Philippe, she closes her hand. If Louis Philippe does not declare war, she – they – will stay until December invades the beach. To keep Louis at bay, Martha invokes the magic of place.

Although Martha is superstitious, she is not literal minded. In invoking the name "Littlehampton" she does not do what Maud Sambourne might well have done in her place – but why would Maud have chosen this place over Italy? – fifty years later. She does not identify herself with "Little" and Edward with "Hampton." Martha is, after all, quite the largest of her female friends and relatives. She is thankful that Edward is so large, even for a gentleman. Martha's head comes up only to his shoulder; she actually has to stand on tiptoe to rest her head where, if Edward were in uniform, you would find his epaulets. Martha blushes to think how much easier it was to reach Mr. Searles's shoulder. "Littlehampton," she says to herself, and Mr. Searle disappears as if into a London fog.

Martha is spending the morning with her mother on the beach while Edward walks into town. The sun is out, but it is not bright enough to give Martha what she calls a "sea headache" and what her mother refers to as "a touch of the sun." Martha does not like it when the sun's rays glance off the water and fill the air around her with sharp little flashes. This morning is a propitious time for what she has in mind. Martha has a question for her mother and will ask it when she is quite ready. This will be, Martha decides, when the children she is watching catch their third crab.

There are five children, all from one family, each one two inches taller than the next, except for the baby, for whom, Martha decides, you would really have to think in terms of length, not height. Each child is dressed in blue and white leggings; as the legs get longer there are more stripes curving their way up. It is difficult to tell with the child one step up from the baby whether it is a boy or a girl; its tiny body looks like a child's drawing: legs, a middle covered with a tunic, and a mop of blond curls. This child will not catch a crab unless the nurse helps. Martha is uncomfortably aware that, although she can tell that the three older children are a boy and two girls, she cannot even guess how old they are. She has not had much experience with children.

Each child has a net with a bright handle. The nets look quite new; perhaps they were bought at Smart's, Littlehampton's biggest shop. The handles flash red and blue in the sun. Only the oldest girl is actually using her net; the others squat in the tidal pools and feel with their hands, squealing when they come in contact with something hard. The nurse looks wary; she literally has her hands full with the baby, who reaches over her arm toward his – or is it her? – sister's net.

"That young woman needs to take more care," says Martha's mother. "She'll have the baby headfirst in the sand."

There is a particularly loud squeal from one of the children, and Martha realizes the first crab has been caught. It is hanging from the hand of the one obviously male child. The nurse gently puts the baby down and runs over; the other children gather round, all except the eldest, who has just caught a crab in her net. Expertly, the little girl turns the net over her bucket. Martha does not see the crab in the bucket, but the girl's confident expression makes Martha willing to count it.

The boy is crying now, but he still seems to resent the nurse pulling on his crab. "Ow!" he screams, "you're making it worse!"

The nurse continues to pull, but the crab resists. Behind her back the baby crawls toward the tidal pool.

"My goodness," says Martha's mother, "that baby will drown." Neither Martha nor her mother moves. The three middle children have grouped themselves around the screaming boy and the nurse, as if posing for a seaside painting, a study in nautical colors. It is hard to imagine disturbing the picture, or even moving toward it.

The older girl has finished with her crab and has seen the danger. She carefully puts down the net and splashes across the pool toward the baby. She lifts the baby with a movement that suggests both tenderness and scorn. When the girl hands the baby to the nurse, Martha catches a glimpse of her face and sees that there is only scorn left on it. Martha watches her talking to the nurse – a tiny matron in stripes – as composed and derisive as if she were older, even, than Martha. The girl returns to her net.

"What a lovely good girl," says Martha's mother. "She reminds me of the way Eliza was when Jessy was a baby, always looking after her."

Before Martha's mother has finished speaking, the picture has recomposed itself, the colors scattered. The crab has been disengaged from the boy's arm by his little sister, who squeals in her turn. The nurse settles the baby once more in her arms and moves away from the older children. The oldest girl takes up once again the work of crabbing. All too soon she has caught one – the third one – and it is time for Martha to speak.

"Mama," says Martha, according to her plan of last night, "do you remember when I was so faint I could not go to church last Sunday?"

It is obvious that Mama now feels it is her duty to watch the nurse. "She's quite a big girl," says Mama.

Martha is momentarily confused, then realizes that her mother is no longer talking about the oldest child but about the nurse. Mama would not say "big" after she had said "lovely."

Mama turns her face briefly to Martha. "Of course I remember, dear," she says. "I hope you had a lovely rest. I must say the sermon was soporific."

Martha feels a thrill of pride and then the shame that inevitably follows. "Soporific" is the word she herself used two days before for Mr. Gilkes's sermon. Martha tries to make peace with her conscience – how can she think for a moment that she is cleverer than Mama! – by imagining the word as a gift to her mother. Martha reminds herself once again that there are more important things than knowing difficult words.

She thinks of Eliza, resting after the first baby came, in a loose gown that Martha had started, but which she had given to Donagan to finish when the sleeves had not come out quite right. By the time Martha had seen the gown, it was as if it had grown flowers. Donagan was famous for her embroidery. By the time Martha saw them, both Eliza and the baby were quite well, Eliza flushed pink in a big white bed, and the baby – what you could see of her little face – pink, too, against the tiny counterpane, also Donagan's work. In this clean pink and white room full of flowers and the smell of them, Martha, who had heard something about babies coming with blood, looked out of the corner of her eye for some stain, some sign of hurt, and listened with the part of her not attending to Eliza for the echo of a scream. But there was nothing. Perhaps her information (and she blushed to think where she had gotten it) had been wrong; perhaps a baby came and was whole and perfect and rosy and the mother murmured and the baby took little baby's breaths, and no one screamed or cried or bled on the sheets as Martha did once a month when "her visitor" came. She had heard once that having a baby stopped the bleeding. If this were true, it would mean that babies made you more than clean enough.

Martha tries to remember what she had read, almost in the dark, by the case in the library that was usually locked. It had always been a source of great pride to Martha that her father allowed her – with this one exception – to read whatever she wanted in the library. Martha remembers the first time her father had called her "a great reader." It was in Boulogne, and he was talking to a lady who had invited the family out for an evening at the theater. The play was *Cromwell*, by Mérimée, and Martha had read it with very little help from the dictionary. At that moment there had been pride in John Rolls's voice. Mama, however, had changed the subject. Later, John Rolls would use the same words to other guests, but never, Martha thinks, with quite the same pride. As the years went by, reading became what Martha did. It was her parents' way of explaining that Martha rarely went out and that when she did she was awkward. After the family returned to the Hendre, there was finally a place for Martha to read that was not the front parlor, so she no longer had to do it in public. Her father, she thought, returned to being proud.

On the evening in question, the cabinet had been left open, and Martha had crept in before dinner as the winter twilight slowly dimmed gilt titles she did not understand. Even more daunting than the words were the pictures; there was nothing in them that corresponded to what Martha understood to be her body. It took her twenty minutes even to understand which way was up, where the head – which was never pictured – was. Martha felt all the humiliation of a great reader finally confronted with something beyond her capabilities. She blushed with the angry blush she associated with other people's use, in conversation, of Greek. She blushed also, because, as she came to understand, the pictures had no skin on them. Martha had not known until this moment how important skin was to her; she always felt it, under her clothes, as a secret that was hers alone – its heat, its soft firmness, a barrier between herself and other people. Of course, the skin on one's face was public – embarrassingly so for someone who blushed so often and so painfully. Martha could not bear to hear people talk as freely as they often did about her complexion.

After a few minutes with the pictures, Martha had given up trying to match inside to outside; it was too much like the game she and Eliza used to play when they drove up to the Hendre after having done errands in town, trying to match its many windows to what they knew of the rooms. Martha had never told Eliza how frightening she found the game, how horrifying it was not to know, not to remember the way one's own house was laid out.

Martha remembers turning to the words in the thickest book, the one that she thought must contain everything she needed to know. The words were a little easier than the pictures. After a few minutes she was able to understand that "cessation of the menses" meant not getting your monthly visitor. She learned that one's menses – she tried the word on her tongue in what she thought was the Latin way – "ceased" when one was "pregnant." There was only time for one fact, one precious piece of information. It was time for dinner and there were guests. Martha took the fact away with her and thought about it for eleven years.

The fact lived with her until the month before her wedding. It was then that Mama told Martha something different. It was really about when the wedding was to be. Mama asked Martha when she expected her monthly visitor. Then she told Martha that she should ask Edward – no, tell him – that the wedding should be immediately after the expected date. Of course she was not to tell Edward why. Martha was not sure why either, but Mama told her that she would not want her visitor at the very beginning of the honeymoon, that it would be best if her visitor came after an entire month had passed. Then Mama said the most confusing thing of all: that she might not have the visitor at all because of excitement and worry.

Martha thinks about what Mama said and about the book she read. Did "cessation of the menses" – over the years the term came to be more familiar and Martha would think of her visitor, to herself of course, as "my menses" – mean that one had a baby inside one or did it mean that one was anxious? What if one were anxious about having a baby?

Martha's menses are late. They were due to arrive a little after Mama. Is it because Martha worries so much? Martha wishes she could see her body as she saw the drawings in the book. She is sure, now that she is older and cleverer, that she could understand the drawing and where, inside, the baby would be. She wishes there were some way of knowing if there was a baby inside her, the real her. But she is someone who worries, so it is impossible. Other young married girls would, Martha concludes ruefully, have an easier time of it. Other girls wouldn't have to worry about worrying, and so they would know if they were having a baby or not. Girls like Eliza who had a baby every year. Martha might have to wait a long time for the outside of her stomach to swell – her insides are already churning, but that means nothing since it happens all the time. Or she could ask Mama. Martha decided last night that she could not wait.

"Mother," says Martha, hoping that the use of the more formal name will signal something. One of the children screams again. They are continuing to catch crabs despite the fact that, to Martha, the game is over. "Do you think, do you think I might –"

A shadow falls over the sand. It is Edward come with the mail. Mama reaches eagerly for the letters, gloating at their number and their heft. She is a famous correspondent. Martha sees Jessy's writing and an envelope whose handwriting makes her go cold somewhere inside.

As her mother opens the letter from Jessy, she remembers Martha. "Edward dear," she says, "do help Patty back to the hotel. I don't think she's altogether recovered from that faintness of last Sunday."

Edward holds out one hand for Martha's and takes her parasol with the other. He is careful to hold it over her. Automatically, lovingly, she draws him within its pink circle. Husband and wife walk slowly under the moving shadow toward the hotel.

That night, Martha bleeds.

The ship

It is November now, and Martha and Edward are alone together. They have retreated from the wind and the fine sand it brings with it to larger, quieter apartments in the Beach Hotel, away from the sound of the landlady's child at their old lodgings. Martha likes it to be cold, because then even Edward sometimes prefers the indoors. Sometimes she likes to imagine that she and Edward are on a ship beached on the sands of Littlehampton, that Littlehampton is an island, and that they have been shipwrecked. In this fancy the mail is brought by fish with gold and silver backs. Edward and Martha find everything else they need on the ship – tea, of course, but also more exotic foods: oysters in brine and books and strange fruits from wherever the ship has been. She does not tell her mother about her imaginings and does not write about them in her diary. Someday she will tell Edward. In the meantime, she conjures up strange creatures and the food they bring and wonders why Edward is so quiet.

When Martha is not reading, she wonders about Edward and what he can be thinking. Men, she knows, think differently about many things, although when she can get Edward to read with her and talk to her about what they read their thoughts are almost exactly the same. Martha has not known many men except her brothers, and Edward is as different from John and Aleck as they are from her. Part of the difference is that Edward is older, but mostly it is that he had to be a man earlier. John, of course, has all the signs of manhood, especially since Papa died three years ago and he had to take the responsibility for all of the family properties. And he is a father and Edward is not – yet. But Edward has been on his own since he was sixteen, with only William and his sisters to look after him. He has been to war; he has traveled as far as Ceylon. Life is real to Edward in a way that it has never been for John. And Martha has always wanted life to be real, to be important. Now, of course, with Louis Philippe on the horizon, she is facing the terrors that come with the life she has chosen. With God's help, Martha prays, she will be brave.

One thing that her life with her family and her new life with Edward have in common is waiting. First it was her father, who would often come home long after Martha was in bed. On moonlit nights, when they could perhaps expect Papa to come home by horseback, Martha would will him home by lying still as a board angled in her bed so her body was aligned with the moon path. Sometimes he would not come home, and Martha would hear, very late at night, the sound of her mother climbing the stairs, the sound that to this day Martha hears as the sound of giving up. If her father did not come home, it was because Martha had not been still enough. As Martha got older and stayed up later, she could sometimes will her father home through the pages of a book. The best were the French and Italian tales of knights errant, making their way home after their adventures to the women they loved. These stories, with their ability to transport Martha if not always her father, were more powerful than moonlight.

Then, of course, there was the waiting for her brothers. John and Aleck would leave the house and Martha, Eliza, Jessy, and Mama would wait for them to come back and bring everything back to life. Sometimes they were gone for a long time – in London or, in Aleck's case, at university. Exciting times like picnics or plays were saved for their return. When they were gone the house contracted; the family only lit up a few of the rooms. The theater was dark.

In a way there was even more waiting when the boys were only out for the evening. Then every step in the hall, every sound on the gravel could signal their return. Martha came to notice that waiting was even harder for Mama, so she would focus less on herself and more on the tense little figure of Mama, suddenly fragile, as she would ring the bell to tell the servant to hold tea for another ten minutes. After John was married, Mary replaced Martha's sisters. She would wait too, for John.

One had to be grateful, of course, that John was a good son. So much depended on that. He was doing nothing shameful when he was not at home. Mama would never say anything, but one had to wonder whether she worried, as Martha did, that John might gamble his money away or get tipsy. Martha knew the signs of drink: a flushed face, a stumbling gait, and a voice too careful not to slur. When John came home, Martha would quickly glance at his face and listen to his steps and his voice. Sometimes he caught her looking, and she would feel her own face flushing and hear her own voice stammering. John, thank goodness, had never failed the test she risked herself to give. He was always upright, smiling, and filled with little jokes for Mama. While sometimes he would not say very much, what he did say was very clear. As Mama always said, he had a beautiful voice. When he inherited the role of magistrate from

Papa, along with the Hendre, his voice could be heard, sweet and firm, across the room.

It is both better and worse for Martha to wait for Edward. Better, because when Edward comes home there is only Martha, and he talks directly to her. Sometimes he gently lifts the book out of her hands, not as if he doesn't care what she is reading or what she thinks about it, but as if she is more important than the book. She loves it so much when he does that, relieving her of the book and of the weight of words, that now she waits specifically for that moment when his hands close first over the book and then over hers. It is the moment that means that Edward is home. But waiting for Edward is even harder than other kinds of waiting – harder than listening for her brother's gait or even for a letter from Mama – because if he is late, or if he doesn't come straight to her, she becomes ill. Martha is ashamed of how easily she gets ill and especially of how illness turns her into someone who is all a body, all stomach and bowels. It happens so quickly; first her feet disappear, then her hands, and then, finally, her brain; she becomes a round hard ball and there are waves churning inside her like the sea, but burning. Sometimes in her dreams the waves of Littlehampton are hot, and she wakes up sweating into the nightdress that Donagan made exactly like Eliza's when she was married. Martha remembers how thankful she was that the real sea at Littlehampton, when she finally let it touch her through her bathing dress, was as cold as metal.

Martha knows that one of the differences between being married and being on a honeymoon is that there is less waiting on a honeymoon. There will be more waiting later, although Eliza told her once that waiting is easier with babies. Martha is not sure she believes her sister; she does not think now that mama ever felt Martha helped her in her waiting. Now she and Edward are almost always together, and when he is gone she knows where he is and – usually – when he will come back. There is no mysterious world of clubs and shows and streets, no training, no officers: only the town of Littlehampton and, beyond that, Rustington. She understands that Edward needs to walk; sometimes he comes in from the heat or the cold and the sand and the wind, and she can tell he wants to be outside again. Men, she knows, like to be outside; they need, Mama says, to stretch their legs. They cannot be confined. What Martha does not understand, although she prays every day that she will, is Edward's need to be alone. Martha likes to be quiet, but for her being quiet requires two people. If she cannot have Edward, or Mama, or Louisa, she can be quiet with almost anyone – even the landlady at their old lodgings, as long as she does not have that screaming infant with her. But for Edward, she thinks, as her stomach churns, being quiet means being without Martha.

Martha reads her diary

Martha writes in her diary, "Edward is not himself today." The sentence has a familiar shape and feel. Flipping back over the entries from September, she is alarmed to see that Edward was not himself on the 29th. Martha turns back further to find a time when Edward was, indeed, himself: the person who is, or was, Edward himself, as Martha realizes when she arrives at the diary's first page, is missing, except for one lovely day – 30 September. He could, of course, be elsewhere: in the time before the diary or in the moments that live in Martha's memory, but not on the page. Martha thinks back to the first month of the honeymoon, the first month in her life when she could not write. Was Edward himself then? That would also be the month before she thought of herself and Edward as truly one, a month she would like to forget precisely because Edward was one person and she another.

Martha thinks about July, the thirty days without writing. This was the month that Edward seemed, well, happiest. She closes the diary to concentrate on sound: Edward's movements waking her from sleep, the strange sounds of his dressing – first a rustling, then the murmur of trouser legs being drawn up his body, the padding of his stocking feet, the resolution of all those sounds in the definitive clump of his shoes. She remembers also that he sometimes would begin to whistle and then stop himself as if afraid to wake her. Then there would be a sound of his leaving to go down to breakfast, the footsteps in shoes receding down the stairs, and, sometimes, a renewal of the whistling, fainter and fainter until she found herself alone and awake in a silent room suddenly hungry to join her husband. How long had it been since she heard the whistle?

Martha remembers now – she will never forget – what her mother told her before the wedding. "Patty," she had said, "a husband's happiness is in his wife's keeping." In the whistling days, as Martha lay with her eyes closed, she would imagine Edward's happiness as something tangible, something to be held safe in her right hand curled tight under the sheet. Somewhere after the diary began she had forgotten this ritual, had let Edward's happiness drop from her. At this thought, Martha's stomach begins to burn again. "Think, Martha!" she tells herself, trying to stave off her disappearance into pain and churning. She clutches at her diary hoping for time before the words vanish with her brain.

The diary, strangely, tells her nothing. She had thought that she had told her diary everything. Why is there so very little in it? Martha thinks about her mother's diary and how her mother scorns "schoolgirl feelings." Except for a few days where she talks about her love for Edward, there are very few of Martha's real thoughts in the diary. Martha wanted them there but did not write them down. They are gone as if they had never existed.

The oddest part is that there is very little in her diary about Edward. For the second time, Martha forces herself back to the beginning, the beginning that now seems like the ending of it all. "Sat on the beach expecting Mama," she reads, and a surge of something like hate goes through her. Could it be, could it have been, that she, Martha, was so caught up with Mama, so happy in telling her mother of her love that she has caused that love to die of neglect? It is no wonder that Edward seems so unhappy. He cannot know how much she loves him.

Martha's parcel

Edward sometimes thinks of it as a honeymoon of letters. He waits for news from France, instructions from headquarters, but what comes are bulky packets for Martha; most, but not all, are from her mother and sister. She also corresponds with old friends of her childhood: a collection of unmarried girls, mothers of three, gentlemen who have known her since she was a baby and who plan but almost never make visits to Littlehampton, ladies of her mother's age whom Mrs. Rolls has collected around her since her widowhood, and even an old suitor who continues to behave badly. Some of these letters enclose others; these are the ones that tend to start quarrels. And quarrels, he has learned, particularly quarrels by mail, make his wife ill. Edward calls himself the postman; it is he who usually fetches the mail from Rustington to where Martha is waiting – sometimes, it seems, for him and sometimes for the letters in his pockets. She counts her joy by numbers: the thickness of the packets, the quantities of envelopes, or the number of illegible crossings and recrossings. But Edward has learned that his wife's happiness does not always survive the opening. If the letters are not satisfactory, she becomes acutely anxious; usually this takes the form of letter writing, as though what she writes can undo the disagreeableness of the letters she receives. And each fat letter she receives undoes, before it is opened, the unpleasant experience of the last receipt, the last reading, the last frantic writing.

Edward is not a letter writer. During his brief courtship of Martha, he wrote every day, but he thinks of the courtship as a time apart with its own duties and habits. He wonders what will happen if he is called into service and must write from camp or from France; he is not sure he can write enough. Courtship aside, Edward has only two correspondents: his older sister, who writes also for the younger, and his friend George from his days in Ceylon, who never quarrels with him and whose letters are mainly about books now that George has left the army. Edward is not really a reader either, he confesses to himself, but George reads enough for two: memoirs, history, and books on religious matters, although he claims not to believe in God. He also reads novels; he does not scorn novels, although he detests what now passes for wit. George believes that it is one's duty to have opinions, but that one must read everything a man has written before sizing him up.

Sometimes Edward thinks that George and Martha could be good friends; they are both forever reading and scribbling. But he also fears a meeting: Martha would certainly be anxious to like George and to have him like her, but George is unpredictable and he does not usually like women. He cannot risk this for Martha or himself – not yet. Today, as he turns from the post office back south toward the sea and Martha, he carries in one pocket five letters and a small parcel for his wife. In the other, his right, there is a letter from each of his correspondents.

Edward takes his two letters out of his pocket. He knows that he is making Martha wait, and that perhaps he is making her ill, but today he seems to have caught her fever for the mail. His sister's letter is on top, but he reaches first for George's. The single page that greets him as he opens the letter looks like a rendition in miniature of what George usually writes. Even individual characters are smaller. The handwriting is uncharacteristically formal, the loops that usually form his letters having been compressed into something approximating the curves of copper plate. "I hope to have the opportunity of meeting the young lady in person," writes George. "Perhaps she will accept the good wishes of someone who, while still a stranger to her, cannot be uninterested in her happiness." The letter, Edward decides, is really Martha's. He wonders if he will show it to her.

The second letter is vicious. "My dear Edward," writes Letitia, "of course we wish you every happiness. If we have not written before, it is only because we do not quite know how to do so under the circum-stances. It is not that we do not like Martha; indeed she is a person of considerable charm when, as we have done, one takes the time to draw her out. It is not her fault that she cannot in all likelihood give you what you deserve. Of course a woman's age is a difficult subject, especially with someone like Martha who in so many respects seems so *young*, not in looks perhaps but in her dress and demeanor. And I think, as does Ellen, that she did try to deceive you – perhaps not so much by what she said as by what she did not say.

"Let me be frank with you, my dear, dearest brother. It brings us so much grief to think that you might never be a father –"

Edward stops reading and replaces the letter carefully in the envelope. His sisters have taught him to be tidy and the army has given a more masculine turn to their training. Together they have made him the man he is. He must go home now, for Martha will be anxious. "Edward," she will say, "you are not yourself."

Edward, to tell the truth, has not felt like himself for a long time, not since his marriage. But what is he to say to Martha when she asks him why? Everything he can say is unspeakable, nothing that a man, a gentleman, can say to his wife: "I am afraid our marriage is a mistake." This he cannot say. And even if he said it, he could not answer why, not to Martha, and not to himself. "I prefer the company of men," he could say. Or "I want a child and am afraid you are too old to give me one." Both of these statements are true in part, but there are other truths as well: "I am not sure I want a child and I know that you have your heart set on one." "I prefer to be outside." "You ask too much of me." "I am not a happy man." Perhaps he can take her words as a beginning – and even as an ending: "I am not myself."

All these are true reasons for his distance, his low spirits. All of them, according to the code in which he has been brought up, are no reasons at all. One cannot leave one's wife because she is a woman, or because she does as a woman should and depends upon him for her happiness because she wants a child – or even because she cannot have one. One can leave, of course, for short periods – for a walk to fetch the mail or the duration of a war. But one cannot acknowledge that one's marriage is a failure. Edward knows one man, a fellow officer, who is separated from his wife. The only thing he knows about the wife is that no one visits her. Edward tries to imagine Martha in a world without visitors and letters.

Edward does not ask himself if he loves Martha. He does, however, think of her as he saw her before their marriage and remembers that strange mixture of pity and admiration that together they called into love. Pity, because she was so obviously the odd one in the family. So out of place wherever she was. Big-boned and fair in a family of elegant figures and small lively faces, Martha had never been well treated by her mother. Mrs. Rolls is a fine woman; Edward gets on with her as a worldly young man gets on with a woman who is older than he is but still handsome and clever. Martha is not, however, a worldly young man. Even during their courtship, Edward could see that Mrs. Rolls was anxious to get Martha out of the house. Mrs. Rolls had even sanctioned the engagement with that bounder Searles, with whom Martha, poor thing, had fancied herself in love.

What had drawn Edward to Martha was, quite simply, that she was the most feeling person he had ever met. After knowing her for only a few days, he knew what she was feeling at every moment: love, pain, hurt, envy, love again. He had the power to see sometimes that all these feelings could come together in one moment, one exchange with her family, or, even from the beginning, with him. She was unlike any woman he had ever met. A woman like that, he remembers thinking, could teach me what it means to love.

Soon, Edward knows, he will have to talk seriously to his wife. He is behaving like a cad, hiding behind illnesses he seems able to summon up to prevent himself from lying. A headache two days ago, a face-ache, fatigue: Martha greets them all with a medicine chest supplemented by packets from her mother. As he thinks about Martha's doctoring, Edward does the unthinkable. He stops once more and reaches in his other pocket. He takes out the parcel addressed to Martha. As he removes the string and the brown paper, folding it into the tight square upon which his sisters insist, he feels worse about himself than he ever remembers feeling. Inside the parcel is a small bottle filled with brown liquid. For one brief moment, Edward hopes it is poison and thinks he might have the courage to drink it. He is being theatrical. Then he notices the directions in the precise sloping hand of Martha's mother: "One spoonful for four days before the onset of the menses," it says. The sea is within sight; he could toss it there. Instead he puts it in the pocket with his own letters. Although guilt is making him almost physically ill, he comforts himself for opening the parcel with the thought that man and wife are one. Edward pulls his overcoat around him and heads into the wind. It is less than half a mile to the shelter of the Beach Hotel.

Martha greets him at the door to their rooms. She is carrying Michelet's *Chronicles*. Edward's French is not up to reading them. Despite everything he is still able to feel proud that Martha knows so much.

"Edward, you must be chilled through! Has the parcel come from Mama?"

"Only these letters, dear." He counts them out for her.

Briefly, she is pleased. "Five today! I *shall* be busy answering them!"

He notes with relief that today she seems undisturbed by the hand-writing on the envelopes.

"But no parcel, Edward? Are you certain?"

He hears the quick beginning of her alarm. "Do you not trust your postman?"

Martha is always comforted by the small jokes that have collected between them. She does not think of them as "wit." Edward is happy to see her alarm give way, for now, to playfulness.

"He is the handsomest, dearest postman ever to dirty his coat and shoes in the sand! Do let me take his coat and brush it for him!"

The postman clutches his coat. He feels the weight of the bottle in his left pocket. Edward has anticipated something like this scene. Martha likes him to be clean, likes to remove every trace of the outdoors. For the first time since their marriage he will brush her hands away. He will walk the short distance across the parlour to the bedroom, and he will take off the coat there. Although it is a simple plan, it will shock Martha. Edward finds he cannot carry it out.

"Leave the coat, Patty," he says. "I am cold."

Martha has never heard these words before. "Edward, my darling, you must tell me. You must tell me what is the matter."

"I am cold – that is all. I have been out in the wind."

"The cold must have entered your chest! If only I had asked Mama for that poultice. Edward, it is my fault – I should have written to her at once."

"It is only a cold."

"But Edward, I have never seen you this way. It must be something else. My darling, what is it? I am your wife –"

"But this is not something a man should say to his wife. You must let me alone till I am ready –"

"Edward, oh Edward, is it as bad as all that? You cannot keep it from me. I will imagine the worst. I will imagine everything horrible. I will not sleep – how can I sleep or read or live until you tell me –"

"I cannot have you making yourself ill."

"I am ill, very ill indeed."

"Then, Martha, you must sit still and listen."

"Look at me, Edward, I am sitting down. I am doing as you say. I will be quiet, I will."

Edward reviews the explanations he can offer. He tries to give himself time.

"I am not myself."

Although Martha has used these words, although the words are hers and she has just read them in her handwriting, they mean nothing to her. "Tell me. Tell me now what you mean."

Edward reviews the possibilities again. He cannot say any of the sentences he has framed on his walk. As he turns to Martha, he realizes she is still clutching the letters. He remembers one that came two months ago, the letter that agitated Martha so.

"I am ashamed to tell you." He still is not sure what he will say.

"Ashamed!"

"It is Mr. Searle," he says, glad that the name comes to him so quickly.

A light breaks on Martha's round, loving face. "What can you mean?" she asks, but he can see that she looks different. She is no longer really afraid. Martha understands jealousy and will experience it as love.

"I cannot rid myself of the fancy that you care for him," says Edward.

Martha has her arms around him. She knows that this fancy can be cured.

Leaving Martha: the epilogue

In my introduction I promised that Martha would have the last word, but I find that I cannot give it to her. Even if I ended here, of course, it would not "really" be Martha who is speaking. And perhaps it would not really be Martha if I ended with a quotation from her diary, the real and tangible one with the brown cover and the evidences of age upon it. If I had ended without the fiction and with the annotated diary I would, perhaps, be ending not with Martha but with the readers of it, and the readers of this book, each of whom would carry with them beyond December of 1840 and beyond the covers of *Victorian Honeymoons* a different version of Martha and her secrets.

It is difficult, having exposed Martha and Edward first to the apparatus of scholarship – the notes, the brackets, the italics – and then to the exigencies of fiction – character, voice, and, perhaps most distasteful to Martha, narrative irony – not to come back to some version of the idea of privacy so central to the history of the honeymoon. I am reminded of one of my few attempts to teach real-life honeymoons during my first semester at Rice, when I assigned the Ruskin chapter in Rose's *Parallel Lives* to students in a Victorian culture course. A handful of these students – and these generally the most ambitious, the ones who always asked for extra reading – had started the chapter and then refused to read on. When I asked them why, they told me that reading about intimate details of the wedding night felt like a violation of privacy. When I suggested that the Ruskins were, regrettably, long dead and thus perhaps immune from the effects of being read and talked about, they argued that this made no difference: "It's not as if they are *fictional*," one of them said, in the tone that students sometimes take when explaining the obvious to a teacher who, in the idiom of teaching evaluations, has "stretched things too far." For many people, including these students, the undeniable lived reality of Effie and John, Martha and Edward, confers on them, as it were, a right to privacy as slippery and yet as urgent as that sought by proponents of reproductive and sexual choice in the US Constitution. For my students this right inheres in being – or in having been – real. To be long dead is only proof of life and of the epistemological status of not being, in my student's words, "fictional." The project of turning real people into fiction is, then, a violation not only of generic but of personal boundaries. I do not know whether my students would have agreed to read my fictional account of Martha and Edward.

Honeymoons, like other events defined by silence, invite speculation. This is a term, finally, I prefer to "fiction," because it includes so many of the efforts I have made in this book, and so many that I have invited readers to make. I hope that the speculative ending of this book in some way thematizes the paradoxical nature of privacy as it is embodied – and indeed enshrined – in the honeymoon. As we have seen, despite its characteristic isolation, the honeymoon was, by the middle of the century, an institution that, like the institution of marriage that gave it meaning, enabled by a paradoxical relation between public and private. At once a time of withdrawal and monogamy, on the one hand, and of the production and consumption of spectacle, on the other, Victorian honeymoons complicate notions of modesty, visibility, aloneness, and publicity. Reading and writing about honeymoons, as my students so clearly understood, foregrounds the idea of privacy and its possible violations. For those students who told me they felt like "voyeurs" of the Ruskin marriage a scholarly relation to the honeymoon is, if not impossible, at least deeply morally suspect. For them, perhaps, the sense with which I began that "nothing happened" on the Victorian honeymoon might be the ethical place to end. Nothing might, in other words, be enough. I have obviously chosen another path, another relation to the "nothings" that so often begin and end our discussions of Victorian sexuality. If I have had often to speculate on the content of that nothing; if at times my sources have had nothing – or very little – to say; if "what happened" was not, perhaps, what our own investments in the period or in individuals who lived in that period would dictate; if I have had to redefine nothing by wrenching it out of the protections of the private sphere, I am nonetheless convinced that something, that *some things* happened and that they are worth thinking, writing, and speculating about.

Case study

Name	Place/Date	Family	Length	Occ.	Pregnancy	Chapter(s)
Abbatt, Jonathan Mary Dilworth	27/6/55 Lake District	D	U	M/B	Prob	
Abbatt, William Mary Lucas,	1853 Leamington (Warwickshire)	U	U	M/B	U	1
Arnold, Matthew Frances Lucy ("Flu") Wightman	10/6/51; 1/9/51 Alderstoke; Paris, Rhone, Grenoble	N	1M	P/I	Yes	1, 2
Bagehot, Walter Eliza Wilson	21/4/58 Devonshire	N	U	P/I	U	2
Baldwin, Alfred Louisa Macdonald	9/8/66 Liverpool, Scotland	N	1M	M/B	No	
Berkeley, James Cavan (Col.) Maud Tomlinson	21/1/92 Isle of Wight	N	2W	Mi	No	2
Birchall, Dearman Emily Jowitt	22/1/73 France, Switzerland, Rome, Vienna	N	2M+	M/B	No	2
Boycott, William Charlotte Hotzapfel	27/8/31 Isle of Wight	D	2W	M/B	U	1, 2
Brookfield, William Henry Jane Octavia Elton	18/11/41 Weston–super– Mare (Somerset)	U	1M	C	No	
Buchanan- Wollaston, Stanley Caroline Harper	19/12/77 Paris	N	U	M/B	CT	1
Burne-Jones, Edward Georgiana Macdonald	9/6/60 Chester (aborted)	N	1W	P/I	No	1

Campbell-Bannerman, Henry Charlotte Bruce	13/9/60 Switzerland, Rhone Valley, Rome	N	2M+	POL	No	1
Cavendish, Lord Frederick Lucy Lyttelton	7/6/64 Continent; Chiswick House (near London)	N	1M	POL	No	1, 2
Cobden, Richard Catherine Anne Williams	14/5/40 Isle of Wight, Switzerland	N	2M+	POL	Yes	1, 2, 3
Coleridge, Henry Nelson Sara Coleridge	3/9/29 Lake District	S	1M	P/I	No	
Creighton, Mandell Louise von Glehn	8/1/72 Paris	N	1W	C	CT	1, 2
Dilworth, David Emma Goodall	19/4/55 Leamington (Warwickshire)	U	1W	C	CT	1
Disraeli, Benjamin Mary Anne Wyndham Lewis	27/8/39 Tunbridge Wells, Baden Baden, Paris	N	2M+	POL	No	1
Drew, Harry Mary Gladstone	2/2/86 Berkhamstead in Hertfordshire	N	U	C	CT	1
Ellerman, William Louisa Larpent	3/12/56 Paris	N	2M+	U	Yes	
Fuller, John Stratton Juliana Taylor	23/10/66 Torquay (Devonshire)	N	1M	L	U	1, 2
Galton, Francis Louisa Butler	1/8/53 Switzerland, Italy, Rome	N	2M+	P/I	No	
Gaskell, William Elizabeth (Cleghorn) Stevenson	30/8/32 Wales	N	1M	C	Poss	1
Gladstone, John Margaret King	July 1869 Perthshire (Scotland); West Country (2)	D	1M	C	No	1, 2
Glover, George Ellen Kelsall	May 1853 Scotland	U	1M	U	CT	1
Gosse, Edmund Ellen ("Nellie") Epps	13/8/75 West Country	N	1M	P/I	No	

Halsey, William Stirling Sophie Wilson ("Sophy")	3/8/59 Dumbleton	N	2W	CLE	Prob	1
Harper, Hugo Mollie (Mary) Harness	19/12/50 Lynton (Devon)	N	U	P/I	CT	1
Hardy, Thomas Emma Gifford	17/9/74 Brighton, Rouen, Paris	N	2W	P/I	No	1
Holt, David Sarah Perrin	6/8/53 Lake District	N	U	CLE	No	1
Hughes, Arthur Molly Thomas	July 1897 Salisbury	N	1W−	P/I	CT	1
Jackson, James Elizabeth Labrey	3/30/54 Lake District	U	2W	M/B	CT	1
James, Acland Clarissa Larpent	20/1/53 France, Italy	D	2M+	C	No	1
Kingsley, Charles Frances Eliza "Fanny" Grenfell	10/1/44 Cheddar (Devon)	N	1M	P/I	Yes	2, 3
Lyttelton, Lord Alfred Laura Tennant	21/5/85 Melchet House, Salisbury (borrowed)	N	2M+	POL	Yes	1
MacDonald, Ramsey Margaret Gladstone	23/11/96 Exeter (Devon)	N	1W	POL	No	1, 3
Macready, Edward Martha Rolls	1/8/40 Littlehampton (W. Sussex)	D	2M+	Mi	No	P, 1, 2, 3, 5
Meinertzhagen, Daniel Georgina "Georgie" Potter	1873 Paris, Black Forest	N	U	P/I	No	
Meredith, George Mary Ellen Peacock Nicholls	9/8/49 Rhineland	N	2M+	P/I	Poss	1
Messel, Leonard Maud Sambourne	28/4/98 Paris, Northern Italy	N	1M	M/B	No	P, 3
Monkswell, Lord (Robert Collier) Mary Hardcastle	21/8/73 Puttenham House (Surrey), Paris, Rome	N	2M+	POL	No	1
Morris, William Jane Burden	26/4/59 France, Paris, Basel	N	1M	P/I	No	

Nicholls, Arthur Charlotte Brontë	29/6/54 Wales, Ireland	S	1M	C	No	1
Patmore, Coventry Emily Andrews	11/9/47 Hastings	N	U	P/I	CT	1
Poynter, Edward Agnes Macdonald	9/8/66 Oxford, Lynmouth (Devon)	N	1M	P/I	No	
Roberts, Ernest May Harper	3/8/86 Romania, Switzerland	S	1M	C	No	1
Rossetti, Dante Elizabeth Gabriel "Lizzie" Siddal	23/5/60 Paris	N	1M	P/I	No	
Ruskin, John Effie Gray	10/4/48 Blair Atholl (Scotland)	N	2W	P/I	No	P, 1, 2, 3
Sambourne, Linley Marion Herapath	20/10/74 Continent, Rome	N	U	P/I	Prob	
Stephen, Leslie Harriet Marian "Minny" Thackeray	19/6/67 Alps	N	1M	P/I	Prob N	1, 2, 3
Symonds, J. A. Catherine North	10/11/64 Brighton	N	1M	P/I	Yes	2, 3
Talbot, Edward Lavinia Lyttleton	29/6/70 Ingestre (Staffordshire); Continent	D	1M	C	U	1, 2
Talbot, John Meriel Lyttelton	19/7/60 Ingestre (Staffordshire); Continent	D	1M	L	Prob	1, 2
Tennyson, Alfred Emily Sellwood	13/6/50 Lynton (Devon)	N	2M+	P/I	Yes	1
Thackeray, William Isabella Shawe	20/8/36 Versailles (from Paris)	S	1W	P/I	CT	1, 2
Thorndike, Arthur Agnes Bowers	15/9/81 Folkestone (Kent)	N	1M	C	No	1, 2
Thornycroft, Hamo Agatha Cox	8/1884 Lynton, (Devon)	N	U	P/I	No	
Trollope, Anthony Rose Heseltine	11/6/44 Lake District	S	1M	P/I	No	1

Wemyss, Francis Eliza Dickinson	23/1/38 Malabar Point, India (from Bombay)	N	1W−	Mi	No	P, 1, 2, 3
Wilde, Oscar Constance Lloyd	29/5/84 Paris	N	2M+	P/I	Yes	
Williams, Arthur Dyson Rosalind "Rosie" Potter	1888 Unknown	N	U	P/I	No	

FAMILY	LENGTH	CLASS/OCCUPATION	PREGNANCY
D Couple divides time between being alone and being with family	U = Unknown	M/B Merchant/business	Yes
S Couple stays with family all or most of the honeymoon	2M+ = more than two months	P/I Professional/intellectual	No
N Couple honeymoons without family	1M = 1–2 months	C Clergyman	Prob – Probably
U Unknown	2W = 2 weeks–1 month	Mi Military	Poss – Possible
	1W = 1–2 weeks	POL Politician	Prob N – Probably not
	1W − = less than a week	CLE Clerk	U – Unknown
		L Landowner U Unknown	CT – Can't tell

Archival sources

Campbell-Bannerman Papers, British Library

Richard Cobden Letters 1833–1865, Department of Special Collections, Charles E. Young Research Library, UCLA

Colchester-Wemyss Family Papers, Gloucestershire Record Office, Gloucester

Juliana Taylor Fuller Diaries, Wigan Record Office, Leigh

Galton Collection, University College Library, London

Charlotte Hotzapfel Diaries, Wigan Record Office

Clarissa de Hochepied Larpent James diary, Papers of John James Larpent, Baron de Hochepied, 1814–1876, Huntington Library

Papers of the King and Thomson Families 1833–1914, Public Record Office, London

Correspondence of Margaret Ethel MacDonald 1870–1911, Public Record Office, London

S. M. Miers diary, Wigan Record Office, Leigh

Rolls Family Papers, Gwent Record Office, Cwmbran, Wales

Maud Sambourne Messel letters, Royal Borough of Kensington and Chelsea, Sambourne Family Archive

Linley Sambourne letters, Royal Borough of Kensington and Chelsea, Sambourne Family Archive

Marie Stopes Papers, Wellcome Library for the History and Understanding of Medicine, ML [Married Love]-Gen[eral], London

Index

CAMBRIDGE STUDIES IN NINETEENTH-CENTURY
LITERATURE AND CULTURE

General Editor
Gillian Beer,
University of Cambridge